NEW JERSEY

OFF THE BEATEN PATH®

OFF THE BEATEN PATH® SERIES

TENTH EDITION

NEW JERSEY

OFF THE BEATEN PATH®

DISCOVER YOUR FUN

KAY SCHELLER & BILL SCHELLER

Globe
Pequot

Essex, Connecticut

All the information in this guidebook is subject to change. We recommend that you call ahead to obtain current information before traveling.

Globe Pequot

An imprint of Globe Pequot, the trade division of
The Rowman & Littlefield Publishing Group, Inc.
4501 Forbes Blvd., Ste. 200
Lanham, MD 20706
www.rowman.com

Distributed by NATIONAL BOOK NETWORK

British Library Cataloguing in Publication Information available

LCCN: 2023002497

978-1-4930-7050-3 (paper)
978-1-4930-7051-0 (electronic)

♾™ The paper used in this publication meets the minimum requirements of American National Standard for Information Sciences—Permanence of Paper for Printed Library Materials, ANSI/NISO Z39.48-1992.

To Alice and William G. Scheller, two New Jerseyans
who helped immensely in researching and revising this book

Contents

About the Authors

Bill Scheller was born in Paterson, New Jersey, where several generations of his family worked in the local locomotive, silk, and aircraft industries. He attended Paterson schools and both St. Peter's Preparatory School and St. Peter's College in Jersey City.

Mr. Scheller is the author of more than 20 books, including *New York Off the Beaten Path*, *Country Walks Near New York*, and *The Hudson River Valley*. His articles have appeared in the *Washington Post Magazine, the Christian Science Monitor, Islands*, and *National Geographic Traveler*, and he is senior editor of the online quarterly cultural journal *Natural Traveler*. Along with his friend and occasional collaborator, the late New York photographer Chris Maynard, Mr. Scheller was profiled in a *New Yorker* "Talk of the Town" piece for having canoed the length of New Jersey's Passaic River and for circumnavigating (also by canoe) Manhattan Island.

Kay Scheller is a coauthor of *New York Off the Beaten Path* and a contributor to National Geographic's *Crossing America* and the *Insight Guides* to Boston, New England, and New York State. Ms. Scheller was a coauthor of the New England volume in National Geographic Society's Driving Guides to America series.

The Schellers are the authors of *The Best Drives in Maine, New Hampshire, and Vermont*, published under their own Jasper Heights Press imprint. They live in central Vermont.

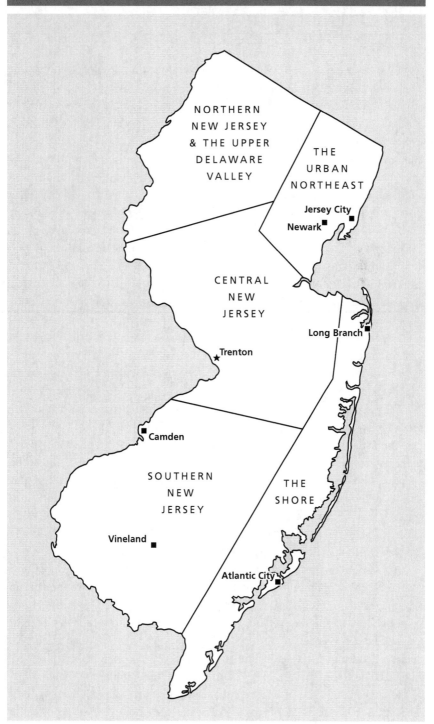

NORTHERN
NEW JERSEY
& THE UPPER
DELAWARE
VALLEY

THE
URBAN
NORTHEAST

Jersey City ■
Newark ■

CENTRAL
NEW
JERSEY

Long Branch ■

★ Trenton

■ Camden

SOUTHERN
NEW
JERSEY

THE
SHORE

Vineland ■

Atlantic City ■

Introduction

This tenth edition marks 34 years of *New Jersey Off the Beaten Path*. What's new? We've discovered museums filled with antique bicycles and snowmobiles, a gallery of African art, excursions in antique railroad cars and hot-air balloons, a rock 'n' roll tour of the Jersey Shore, and an ice-cream parlor with a singing waitstaff. And what's to eat? How about Portuguese food in Newark, Ethiopian in New Brunswick, and Korean in Palisades Park? As in our nine previous outings, we've found that the Garden State is full of surprises while remaining true to its past, and that it can still revel in its stereotypes while standing the conventional wisdom on its head. That old Jersey joke might ask, "What exit?"—but that ramp off the turnpike or the parkway is just as likely to lead to a colonial village or a wildlife preserve as to an all-night diner or a factory outlet.

With a population of some 8.9 million, a healthy economy based on both service and manufacturing industries, and a steady influx of immigrants from all parts of the world, the Garden State often seems to be a place where change is the only constant. But much of New Jersey defies rapid transformation. People throughout the Middle Atlantic states can still enjoy what remains one of the most beautiful beaches in the world, the 120-mile stretch of white sand that extends from Sandy Hook to Cape May, where the ocean is bracing but (at least by July) never forbiddingly frigid, where good Italian restaurants are as thick as they are in Naples, and where you can turn your back on the machines that ate your quarters in Atlantic City and enjoy gorgeous expanses of federally protected salt marsh.

The Pine Barrens, the heart of which has also been protected from development, are still splendidly desolate almost to the point of eeriness, and the exurban lanes of southwest Jersey, around Greenwich, are in much the same league as the byways of up-country New England, even if the terrain is a bit flatter. If you want more rugged country, there are always the Kittatinny Mountains that stand sentinel above the Delaware Water Gap, away up north near the New York and Pennsylvania borders.

For such a small state, New Jersey has a tremendously varied topography. The black basalt cliffs called the Palisades tower formidably above the Hudson River at the state's northeastern gateway and slope westward toward the great marshy basin of the Hackensack Meadows. More than 280 species of birds have been observed in the Meadows, hundreds of acres of which have been preserved despite the encroachment of condos, office parks, and a football stadium. The Great Swamp, near Chatham and Summit in the north-central part of the state, is the site of an even more impressive preservation effort. Here more than 6,000 acres of primeval freshwater wetlands were set aside under federal protection after citizens rallied, more than 50 years ago, to keep out a projected jetport.

Nor has New Jersey any apologies to make when it comes to historical associations. This was an old and well-settled place by the time of the American Revolution; during the century and a half that went before, Dutch and English settlers in the north and Swedes in the south had been hewing farms and homes out of the land of the Lenni-Lenape Indians. Men smelted iron in the Pine Barrens and the Ramapo Mountains in the middle of the 18th century, and the Revolution was barely over when Alexander Hamilton stood at the Great Falls of the Passaic and decided that here would be built America's first planned industrial city.

All too often we tend to limit our geographical notions of the War of Independence to the early battlefields of Massachusetts and the political arenas of Philadelphia, but more of that eight-year struggle took place in New Jersey than anywhere else, and the state well earned its title "Cockpit of the Revolution."

You Know You're from New Jersey If:

- You don't think of citrus when people mention "The Oranges." *
- A good, quick breakfast is a hard roll with butter.
- You remember that the "Two Guys" were from Harrison. **
- You know what a "jug handle" is. ***
- You don't go "to the shore," you go "down the Shore." And when you're there, you're not "at the shore"—you're "down the Shore."
- Even your school cafeteria made good Italian subs.
- You've gotten on the wrong highway trying to get out of the mall.
- You've had a Boardwalk cheese steak and vinegar fries.
- You've never pumped your own gas. ****

For You Non-New Jerseyans:

* Orange, East Orange, South Orange, West Orange—all are towns near Newark. There is no North Orange.

** Two Guys from Harrison, a now-defunct discount store chain—"Two Guys" for short.

*** An exit ramp shaped like one.

**** Self-service pumps are illegal in New Jersey.

Here the Continental army waited out winters as devastating to morale as the one at Valley Forge; here George Washington accomplished what has been called the greatest strategic retreat in military history; and here, at Christmastime in 1776, the American commander-in-chief won the Battle of Trenton after his legendary crossing of the Delaware.

New Jersey's role in the Industrial Revolution was no less impressive. Basic resource-extraction enterprises, such as the mines at Ringwood and Batsto, soon began to be eclipsed by manufacturing, with Paterson rising to become the nation's preeminent weaver of silk and its second most important builder of locomotives (after Philadelphia). Railroads have figured prominently in New Jersey ever since John Stevens demonstrated America's first working steam locomotive on his Hoboken estate in 1824. The state became vital to rail enterprises such as the Pennsylvania and Erie Railroads and the Delaware, Lackawanna & Western, which operated electric passenger trains perfected by the Wizard of Menlo Park (New Jersey), Thomas Edison. And the Wright Aeronautical division of Curtiss-Wright Corporation, based in Paterson, built the engines for Charles Lindbergh's *Spirit of St. Louis* as well as those used in American bombers during World War II. Today the petroleum, petrochemical, and pharmaceutical industries are among the state's largest employers.

The purpose of this book is to distill New Jersey's wonderful diversity— geographic, ethnic, historical, and industrial—into the description of selected sites in the five major areas of the state. These places haven't been chosen because they're the major New Jersey attractions; the premise of the Off the Beaten Path series is the discovery of places many guidebooks overlook. You'll find some familiar spots, but our hope is that most of the territory covered in these pages will be as new as the perceptions it may inspire. If, while following this guide, you drive along the turnpike, eat in a diner on Route 9, and listen to Sinatra or Springsteen, that's all right. Just remember, there's a lot more to New Jersey than those stereotypical experiences suggest.

Please be sure to call ahead when making travel arrangements, as prices and hours and dates of operation change. To help with planning, we have used a scale for the prices of restaurants and accommodations. Entrées (without

They Just Can't Leave

At last count New Jersey had some 578,000 state and municipal employees. Where do they go when they retire? They stay right here, spending their pension checks in the Garden State. Far more of the state's pensioners live in New Jersey than in Florida.

The Poetry of New Jersey Names

When it comes to being celebrated in song, New Jersey has been shortchanged. There's no Jersey equivalent of "Moonlight in Vermont," and New Jerseyans have to be envious when they hear Gladys Knight sing "Midnight Train to Georgia" or the Bee Gees harmonize on "Massachusetts." There is, of course, John Pizzarelli Jr.'s whimsical "I Like Jersey Best"—but our favorite, if little-known, paean to New Jersey is the late folk legend Dave van Ronk's "The Garden State Stomp." "Stomp" consists of nothing but a litany of New Jersey town names—Allamuchy, Piscataway, Parsippany, Egg Harbor—a long, mellifluous celebration of Indian, Anglo, and Dutch nomenclature that only a map of Jersey could have inspired.

beverage) are classified as inexpensive, less than $20; moderate, $21 to $29; and expensive, $30 and up. For motels, bed-and-breakfasts, and hotels, prices are per night: inexpensive, less than $100; moderate, $101 to $180; and expensive, $181 and up.

We hope you enjoy exploring New Jersey as much as we have—and that the next ten editions of *New Jersey Off the Beaten Path* find the Pine Barrens just as desolate, the surf at Ship Bottom every bit as invigorating, and the state's restaurants offering cuisines we haven't even heard of yet, much less sampled. For us, that would define progress.

New Jersey Information

TRAVEL/TOURISM INFORMATION

New Jersey Division of Travel and Tourism
PO Box 460, Trenton 08625
(800) VISITNJ or (609) 599-6540
www.visitnj.org

New Jersey B&B Innkeepers Association
Preferred Inns of New Jersey
PO Box 108, Spring Lake 07762
(866) 449-3535 or (732) 449-3535

New Jersey Campground Owners & Outdoor Lodging Association
PO Box 808, Marmora 08223
(609) 545-0145
www.campnj.com

AREA CODES

All local calls require callers to dial the area code plus the 7-digit number for calls within the area codes.

AVERAGE TEMPERATURES

32.1 degrees Fahrenheit December–February

51.6 degrees Fahrenheit March–May

74.4 degrees Fahrenheit June–August

57.1 degrees Fahrenheit September–November

TRANSPORTATION

Major Airports

Atlantic City International Airport, (609) 645-7895, www.sjta.com

Newark Liberty International Airport, (973) 961-6000, www.newarkairport.com

Philadelphia International Airport (for destinations in southern New Jersey), (215) 937-6937, www.phl.org

Trains

Amtrak, (800) USA-RAIL, www.amtrak.com

New Jersey Transit Passenger Rail System, (973) 275-5555, www.njtransit.com

MAJOR NEWSPAPERS

Jersey Journal (Jersey City)

Star-Ledger (Newark)

New Jersey Herald (Passaic County)

Bergen Record (Bergen County)

Philadelphia Inquirer (Philadelphia, Pennsylvania—read widely in southern New Jersey)

POPULATION

9,288,994 (2020 census)

SOME SELECTED WEBSITES ABOUT NEW JERSEY

General information/events/travel publications: www.state.nj.us

New Jersey Audubon Society: www.njaudubon.org

Up-to-the-minute traffic reports/alerts: www.511nj.org/home

New Jersey Road Map: www.milebymile.com

The Urban Northeast

New Jersey's heavily urbanized northeastern corner often serves the popular imagination as a metaphor for the entire state. It might just as well represent all the United States—not because the entire country is as densely populated as New Jersey, but because, at its best, it is as richly textured and heterogeneous as New Jersey's contribution to the New York metropolitan area. One of the most striking aspects of this compact region is its racial and ethnic diversity; remember that Ellis Island is only a few hundred yards from Jersey City. People come here, people stay, people pass through on their way to somewhere else. (Union City, once a Swiss preserve, is now largely a Cuban community.) Within this chapter we'll visit the home of an Italian labor organizer, farmhouses that belonged to the earliest Dutch settlers, and a rich display of African art and artifacts.

Dense population, with the complicated patchwork of cities, suburbs, and industrial districts that it engenders, seldom gets good press, and there's no denying that it has spawned its share of problems. But an often-overlooked virtue of the Jersey metropolis is its variety, the quickness with which one environment gives way to another. When so many towns and

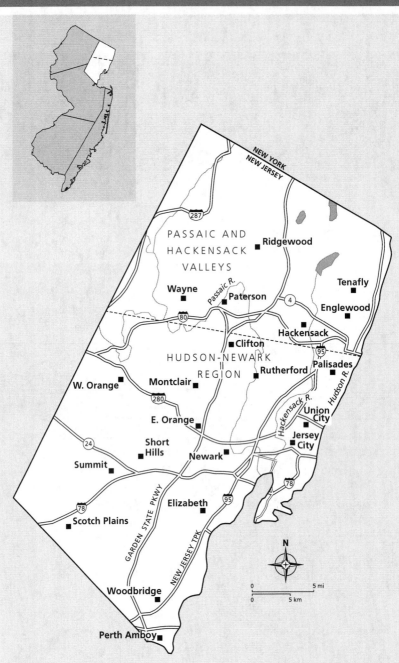

PASSAIC AND
HACKENSACK
VALLEYS

Ridgewood

Wayne

Passaic R.

Paterson

Tenafly

Englewood

Hackensack

Clifton

HUDSON-NEWARK
REGION

Rutherford

Palisades

W. Orange

Montclair

Hackensack R.

Hudson R.

Union
City

E. Orange

Jersey
City

Short
Hills

Newark

Summit

Scotch Plains

Elizabeth

GARDEN STATE PKWY

NEW JERSEY TPK.

Woodbridge

Perth Amboy

NEW YORK
NEW JERSEY

N

0   5 mi
0   5 km

cities are this close together, even locals usually have to admit that there is plenty they haven't seen (or maybe even heard of) right within their county limits. Distances don't shrink under these circumstances—they expand: People in eastern Wyoming probably know more about western Wyoming than the folks in Hoboken know about Hackensack.

Note: The orientation in this chapter is roughly north to south.

Passaic and Hackensack Valleys

The ***Palisades*** are the dark, beetling cliffs that begin near the border of Hudson and Bergen Counties and continue northward into New York State. The Palisades are more than just the foreground for the Jersey sunsets that sell terraced Manhattan apartments; they are a window into deep geological time and the focus of one of the region's earliest and most successful preservation movements. They're also a great place to take a hike.

By the mid-19th century extensive quarrying operations were set up, and before long the southerly reaches of the cliffs were all but obliterated. Fortunately, early preservation activists persuaded the states of New York and New Jersey to purchase the Palisades, along with the land at their base and summit. Quarrying stopped in 1900, and by 1909 ***Palisades Interstate Park*** had been dedicated.

THE URBAN NORTHEAST'S TOP PICKS

Palisades	Presby Memorial Iris Gardens
Waterford Gardens	Aviation Hall of Fame and Museum of New Jersey
Hiram Blauvelt Art Museum	
The African Art Museum of the SMA Fathers	Afro-American Historical Society Museum
Great Falls/S.U.M. National Historic Landmark District	South Mountain Reservation
Lambert Castle	Turtle Back Zoo
American Labor Museum	Watchung Reservation
Van Riper–Hopper Museum	First Presbyterian Church
Dey Mansion	Eagle Rock Reservation
The Montclair Art Museum	Branch Brook Park

The best way to enjoy the Palisades today is to hike along either the **Long Path**, which runs along the crest of the cliffs and offers lovely views of the Hudson and the New York shore, or the **Shore Path**, which follows the riverbank at the base of the towering rocks. To begin the latter route, which is marked with white blazes and extends 10 miles northward into New York State, park at the Englewood Boat Basin, just north of the New Jersey approach to the George Washington Bridge. A good access point for the Long Path is 5 miles north (via Route 9W) at the turnoff for the Alpine Boat Basin. At Alpine, both trails are connected by a steep switchback path. Whatever you do, stick to marked paths such as this one when ascending or descending in the Palisades. Much of the rock is loose and makes for extremely dangerous climbing.

Waterford Gardens in Saddle River is likely to be different from any garden center you've ever seen. Its exclusive focus is water plants—day- and night-blooming tropical water lilies, lotuses, floating plants, and aquatic border plants—as well as ornamental fish.

The company's displays of its living wares are beautifully arranged along the banks of the Saddle River, in an array of ponds and pools that are more suggestive of a pristine bayou than the vicinity of exit 163 on the Garden State Parkway. Best of all, you don't have to be shopping for water lilies to visit the gardens. They're open to casual visitors—although we suspect that many of those visitors won't be so casual once they start thinking about the possibilities of water gardening, and that lily ponds will start appearing in more and more suburban backyards.

Waterford Gardens, 74 E. Allendale Rd., (201) 327-0721, www.waterford-gardens.com, is open Mon through Sat from 9 a.m. to 5 p.m. year-round; it's also open Sun from 9 a.m. to 4 p.m. from mid April through the end of July. Admission is free.

The Making of the Palisades

The grand, dark cliffs called the Palisades, which dominate the New Jersey side of the Hudson River from the George Washington Bridge to the New York State border and beyond, had their origin 190 million years ago, when molten rock forced its way upward into fissures in layers of sandstone and shale. The molten material cooled beneath the surface, hardening into a rock called diabase, before being exposed by erosion. The columnar, prism-like structure of the cliffs is a result of the contraction and vertical splintering that took place as the rock solidified. That structure also gave the formation its name: To early settlers, the cliffs resembled a palisade, a military enclosure made of sharpened stakes driven into the ground.

The **Saddle River Inn**, housed in a rustic yet elegant 150-year-old barn for more than a quarter of a century, is consistently voted one of the state's best restaurants. It seats just 70 diners and offers artfully prepared cuisine and excellent service. French/continental specialties prepared by Swiss-born chef Jamie Knott and his talented staff might include appetizers (ranging in price from $16 to $26) such as Wagyu steak tartare, kale Caesar salad, or Hudson Valley foie gras. Entrée prices range from $32 to $64 and include veal chop parmigiana, wild-caught Dover sole, filet mignon with béarnaise and chestnut butter, and house-made cavatelli Bolognese. A service of Ossetra caviar is also available. Guests are invited to bring their own wine.

The Saddle River Inn, 2 Barnstable Ct., (201) 825-4016, www.saddleriverinn .com, is open for dinner Tues through Sat; call for lunch hours. Reservations are highly recommended.

Our friend, ardent gardener and writer Betsy Hays, told us about the **Celery Farm Natural Area** in Allendale. Technically not a garden, and no longer a working celery farm, this 107-acre wildlife sanctuary is ablaze with wildflowers and home to a multitude of critters, including warblers, mink, and bullfrogs. Owned by the Borough of Allendale, it's located on the Franklin Turnpike (Route 507), just north of the intersection with E. Allendale Avenue. Admission is free. Open daily from dawn to dusk; (201) 818-4400; www.fykenature.org.

Bergen County's only 18th/19th-century house, the **Hermitage**, is a National Historic Landmark. The original structure, built circa 1740 as a two-story brownstone, was owned by British officer James Marcus Prevost and his wife. Their visitors included George Washington and Aaron Burr, who married Mrs. Prevost here after the British officer died.

In 1807, the Hermitage was purchased by Dr. Elijah Rosencrantz for his bride, Cornelia Suffern. The family of the doctor—who became one of the area's leading industrialists—occupied the home for the next 160 years. In 1847 one of his sons, Elijah Jr., hired architect William Ranlett to renovate the Hermitage. Ranlett razed most of the existing structure, added a wing, and remodeled the home into the romantic Gothic Revival mansion that stands here today.

The home's last owner, Mary Elizabeth Rosencrantz, died in poverty in 1970, refusing to sell the Hermitage to developers because she believed her home should be a legacy to the public. She bequeathed it to the State of New Jersey upon her death. Today the landmark, due to the hard work of the Friends of the Hermitage, is a fine interpretive museum of America's late Victorian era.

The Hermitage, 335 N. Franklin Turnpike, Ho-Ho-Kus, (201) 445-8311, www.thehermitage.org, is open for tours Sat and Sun at 1:15, 2:15, and 3:15 p.m. Call ahead to assure times. Admission is $10 for adults and $5 for children 10 and under. Call or check the website for information on special events such as lectures, concerts, car and craft shows, and Revolutionary War reenactments and Civil War encampments held throughout the year. Park grounds are open daily 9 a.m. to 5 p.m.

The *James C. Rose Center for Landscape Architectural Research and Design* in Ridgewood was designed and built in the early 1950s by James Rose (1913–1991), the premier figure in American landscape architecture for more than half a century. Tossed out of Harvard for creating "modern" designs, Rose went on to design hundreds of exquisite gardens, write several books, and receive accolades from his clients and peers as well as from the Japanese, who related to his spare, integrated living space and garden designs.

Rose's approach successfully integrated the outdoor and indoor environments and didn't require large pieces of acreage to do so. The Ridgewood home and garden is actually a "tiny village" of three buildings built on an area half the size of a tennis court. Rose's experimental landscape seamlessly fuses the outdoors and indoors and was intended to constantly evolve. Over the nearly 40 years that Rose, his mother, and sister lived on the property, the design changed dramatically. After visiting Japan to participate in the World Design Conference, for instance, Rose was inspired by Buddhism and Eastern design to add a roof garden and *zendo*, a hall for the practice of and training in Zen.

During the last decade of Rose's life, the property fell into disrepair and was almost ruined by fire and flood. Since 1993, under the leadership of Dean Cardasis (James Rose scholar, landscape architect, and associate professor at the University of Massachusetts, Amherst) and a dedicated group of volunteers, the site has been rehabilitated. The center serves students, scholars, and the general public as a catalyst for examining elemental questions about the nature of design.

The Rose Center, 506 E. Ridgewood Ave., (201) 446-6017, www.jamesrose-center.org, is open to the public for self-guided tours from mid-May through early Sept, Tues through Sun from 10 a.m. to 4 p.m., and from early Sept through late Oct, Wed through Sun from noon to 4 p.m. Admission is $10 for adults and $5 for children under 12.

One hundred and twelve kinds of pancakes? You can count them, but we'd recommend not wasting your time when you could be eating them at **Le Café Pancake**, 140 E. Ridgewood Ave., Ridgewood, (201) 444-9090, www.lepancakecafe.com. Not to be missed (or avoided at all costs, depending on your inclination) are buttermilk pancakes with bananas, blueberries, raisins, or nuts. Lunch and dinner entrées include seafood gratin, shrimp in champagne sauce, pork filet with Gorgonzola sauce, and lobster thermidor. The restaurant is open Tues through Sun from 7 a.m. to 5 p.m.

The **Bergen County Zoological Park** is home to an eclectic assortment of birds and animals: alligator, mountain lion, giant anteater, sloth, ocelot, red wolf, capybara, roseate spoonbill, scarlet macaw . . . and lots more. The handsomely kept zoo grounds, traversed by Van Saun Mill Brook, are encircled by a railway that offers a good way to get oriented to the animal exhibits before strolling the grounds; there's also a carousel.

Bergen County Zoological Park, 216 Forest Ave., Paramus, (201) 634-3100, www.co.bergen.nj.us, is open daily from 10 a.m. to 4:30 p.m. (last admission at 4 p.m.). Admission is $8 for adults, $5 for children 3 to 14, and $2 for seniors and the disabled; discount for Bergen County residents. Active military and children under 3 free. Train and carousel rides are $2.

Step into a world where elephants roam the African veldt, Canada geese glide tranquilly across fog-shrouded ponds, and a snow leopard looks down from his lofty perch high in the Himalayas. In 1957 conservationist Hiram Blauvelt donated his private wildlife art and big-game collection to focus awareness on issues facing the natural world and to showcase the artists who are inspired by it. Today the **Hiram Blauvelt Art Museum**, in Mr. Blauvelt's 1893 turreted, shingle-style carriage house, exhibits a large collection of Audubon folios, works by artists such as Carl Rungius and Charles Livingston Bull, and magnificent dioramas. The big-game collection includes a large display of North American mammals.

The Hiram Blauvelt Art Museum, 705 Kinderkamack Rd., Oradell, (201) 261-0012, www.blauveltartmuseum.com, is open Wed through Fri from 10 a.m. to 4 p.m. and Sat and Sun from 2 to 5 p.m.; closed holidays. Admission is by donation.

Hackensack Riverkeeper is an organization dedicated to stewardship of one of northern New Jersey's most important and, sadly, most historically polluted waterways. Its efforts have helped clean and monitor the Hackensack,

AUTHORS' FAVORITE ATTRACTIONS IN THE URBAN NORTHEAST

The African Art Museum of the SMA Fathers	Eagle Rock Reservation
American Labor Museum	Garrett Mountain Reservation
The Hermitage	Patsy's Tavern
Hiram Blauvelt Art Museum	Goehrig's Bakery

TOP ANNUAL EVENTS IN THE URBAN NORTHEAST

Note: Schedules may vary; call ahead.

Cherry Blossom Festival, Belleville/ Newark; Apr; (973) 735-2135; www .newarkhappening.com

Cinco de Mayo Celebration, International Plaza, 38th Street and Palisade Avenue, Union City; May; www .ucnj.com

Newark Black Film Festival, Newark Museum; July; (973) 596-6550; www .newarkmuseumart.org

St. Ann's Italian Festival, Hoboken; July; (201) 659-1114

Jersey City Caribbean-American Carnival, Jersey City; July; (201) 332-5538

Hambletonian Day, Meadowlands Racetrack, East Rutherford; Aug; (201) THE-BIGM; www.playmeadowlands.com

through coordination with local, state, and federal agencies; via environmental education programs that include eco-cruises through the Meadowlands and nature and birding walks; and by offering watercraft rentals and guided trips. The Riverkeeper fleet includes more than 50 kayaks, canoes, and stand-up paddleboards for folks eager to explore the river and its surroundings at their own pace or with a knowledgeable guide. Individual rentals and guided tours and eco-cruises are available on weekends from Earth Day, in late Apr, through the end of Oct. Hackensack Riverkeeper is headquartered at 231 Main St., Hackensack, (201) 968-0808, www.hackensackriverkeeper.org.

Traditionally, many Christian missionaries to Africa regarded the peoples and cultures among whom they worked as inferior to those of the West. Their artifacts were often judged ugly, and objects having any connection with so-called pagan religious practices were frequently collected and burned. At *The African Art Museum of the SMA Fathers*, the Society of African Missions in the United States instead offers a display of art and artifacts that emphasizes the beauty and richness of African cultural expression.

Wandering about the museum, we learn that masks of the Wee people in Liberia, which may at first glimpse seem strange or grotesque, were in fact used as a social control. Each mask represented a specific spirit who wanted to be involved in human affairs. The masks were teachers of the values of tradition and law and the need to preserve those values. Helmet masks of the Baule in the Ivory Coast, which represent horned animals, are used in dances to protect the village, to discipline women, and at funeral ceremonies.

If the Carp Are Jumping, It's Springtime on the Passaic

All too often, North Jersey's Passaic River is portrayed as an example of an urban waterway lost to pollution and streamside blight. But the Passaic does have its pristine stretches. It rises near the Great Swamp and passes through part of that wilderness preserve. Farther downstream the Passaic meanders through an area on the borders of Essex and Passaic Counties called Great Piece Meadow—not a meadow so much as an impenetrable swamp, all the more remarkable for being within a few miles of Route 46 and the giant Willowbrook Mall.

About the only way to get into the heart of Great Piece is by canoe. We've done it in early April and seen one of the true primeval spectacles of northern New Jersey: carp, usually thought of as sedate bottom feeders, jumping like trout during their spring spawning season.

The African Art Museum of the Society of African Missions (SMA), 23 Bliss Ave., Tenafly, (201) 894-8611, www.smafathers.org, is open daily from 8 a.m. to 5 p.m. Donations are welcome.

Even New Jersey trivia lovers might be hard-pressed to name the state's tallest growing tree. It's the moisture-loving tulip tree, which grows up to 200 feet and each May and June sprouts elegant, six-petaled flowers. There are many fine specimens at *Lost Brook Preserve*, a 380-acre sanctuary of ponds, plants, woods, wildflowers, and unique rock formations in the middle of urban Tenafly.

The preserve's diverse habitat is a haven for wildlife, including white-tailed deer, Eastern cottontail rabbits, and water snakes. It's a popular spot for bird-watchers, particularly during fall and spring migrations when it provides a welcome rest stop for a wide variety of bird species. The preserve's newest attraction is the enclosed butterfly habitat in front of the visitor center.

Lost Brook Preserve, Tenafly Nature Center, 313 Hudson Ave., Tenafly, (201) 568-6093, is open daily dawn to dusk. The parking lot closes at 5 p.m. The visitor center is open daily from 9:30 a.m. to 4:30 p.m.; closed holidays. Admission is free.

Flat Rock Brook Nature Center, a 150-acre nature preserve with volcanic bedrock formations, cliffs, ponds, and meadows, is an oasis in the urban north that's home to diverse plant and animal life. The Backyard Habitat for Wildlife exhibits native plants selected to provide food for wildlife and be ornamental. There are 3.2 miles of hiking trails (maps are available), and small kids will love the 800-foot Quarry Boardwalk in front of the center at 443 Van

Nostrand Ave., Englewood, (201) 567-1265, www.flatrockbrook.org. A picnic area and trails are open from sunrise to sunset. The visitor center and greenhouses are open Tues through Thurs from 9 a.m. to 5 p.m. and Sat and Sun from 1 to 5 p.m. Admission is free.

The Passaic Falls, located in the heart of the city that they created—Paterson—are the focus of the **_Great Falls/S.U.M. National Historic Landmark District_**. ("S.U.M." stands for Society for the Establishment of Useful Manufactures, the industrial development organization founded along with Paterson in 1791.) Here the waters of the Passaic River, which has its source nearly 50 miles upstream in the Great Swamp, crash over a 280-foot-wide chasm to continue toward tidewater at Newark Bay.

During the Revolution on July 10, 1778, George Washington and Alexander Hamilton came to stand on the rock ledge opposite the falls and marvel at their fury. To Hamilton, however, the falls were more than a scenic wonder. Once independence was won, he was quick to propose that the waters of the Passaic should be harnessed as a source of power for the nation's first planned industrial city. In 1791 the settlement above and below the cataract was incorporated and named for William Paterson, New Jersey governor and signer of the Declaration of Independence.

Paterson's founders selected French engineer Pierre L'Enfant to design the city's industrial infrastructure. L'Enfant came up with an ingenious system of raceways, but the plan was never completed to his specifications due to its considerable expense. Eventually, Connecticut industrialist Peter Colt finished the job. It was well into the 1820s before Paterson's first significant industry—cotton—gained a foothold, but before long the millraces were supplying waterpower to a host of burgeoning enterprises. The locomotive industry would prosper here throughout the remainder of the 19th century, and the silk industry even longer. By 1900 the "Silk City" would be the fifteenth largest in the United States.

A Real Beat Town

Paterson's claim to literary celebrity is nearly always linked with William Carlos Williams's epic poem of the same name. But the Silk City also figures in the defining work of the Beat Generation, Jack Kerouac's *On the Road.* Early in the novel Kerouac's autobiographical hero, Sal Paradise, refers to "Paterson, New Jersey, where I was living with my aunt." Soon afterward, Sal makes Paterson his point of departure for his first trip to the West Coast. Kerouac knew the city through his friend, Paterson native Allen Ginsberg. The poet appears in *On the Road* as "Carlo Marx."

You Know It's Easter in Paterson When . . .

Throughout the cities and suburbs of northern New Jersey, the days right before Easter bring the delicious aroma of Easter Pie. Perhaps not as well known as baskets and dyed eggs but beloved by the descendants of the Italian immigrants who populated this part of the Garden State, Easter Pie (*pizza piena*, or "full pie," in the language of the old country) is an over-the-top celebration of the end of Lent. It keeps in the fridge for at least a week and serves equally well, hot or cold, as breakfast, lunch, and dinner. Here's our family recipe, courtesy of Bill's late mom, Alice Marchitti Scheller. It makes six pies, so you can give them to friends and family as Easter presents.

Crust:
2 teaspoons salt
Black pepper (optional)
7 cups flour
1½ cups butter, chilled and cut in pieces
¾ cup lard
8 egg yolks plus enough ice water to equal 2 cups

Filling:
1 pound soppressata (coarse, cured Italian salami-like sausage), skin removed, diced
1 pound prosciutto, diced
1½ pounds mozzarella, sliced or diced
1½ pounds fresh ricotta (sold in Italian markets as "basket cheese"), sliced
6 hard-boiled eggs, sliced
1 dozen eggs
½ gallon milk
Freshly ground black pepper
1 egg yolk mixed with 2 tablespoons water, for brushing

To make the crust, sift salt and pepper (if using) into the flour, and work in the butter and lard with your fingers. Add the egg-water mixture, stirring until it forms a ball. The dough should be soft, but not sticky. A little more flour may be added if necessary. Refrigerate for several hours or overnight.

Roll out half of the dough and line six 9-inch pie or cake pans (they should be 2 to 3 inches deep), leaving a little overhang. Set oven at 350 degrees.

Fill pastry-lined pans half full with soppressata, prosciutto, mozzarella, ricotta, and sliced eggs. Beat eggs with milk, adding black pepper to taste. Pour this mixture over ingredients in pans, filling to within ½ inch of top.

Roll out remaining dough and cover each pan, sealing edges tightly. Make several slashes in top for steam to escape. (If you have dough left over, you can use it to decorate the tops. Mom used to put crosses on for Easter, with a Star-of-David variation for her Jewish daughter-in-law and grandson.)

Brush with egg-water wash and bake for 40 minutes or until crust is lightly browned. Allow to cool slightly before cutting, so the filling can set. If you use a deeper pan, increase baking time to 1 hour.

Who's on Cianci Street?

One of Paterson's favorite sons, comedian Lou Costello, is commemorated with a life-size bronze statue in a little park named for him at the intersection of Cianci and Ellison Streets, in a tiny remnant of what was once the city's largest Italian neighborhood. Lou wears his trademark derby, and he shoulders a baseball bat—a reminder of his and Bud Abbott's most famous routine, "Who's on First?"

So far, we haven't heard of any plans to erect a Bud Abbott statue in Asbury Park, hometown of Lou's straight man.

The Great Falls Historic District is primarily concerned with the legacy of Paterson's industrial heyday. Sites within the district include the falls themselves and several of the more important mills that once dominated the area: the **Rogers Locomotive Erecting Shop** (now housing the Paterson Museum, described below); the wheelhouse of the **Ivanhoe Paper Mill**; the home of John Ryle, who first introduced silk manufacturing to Paterson; the **Benjamin Thompsen House** (circa 1835); the **Phoenix Mill Complex**; the two remaining stories of the 1836 mill in which Samuel Colt built his first regular production revolvers; and the impressive Beaux Arts **City Hall**.

Guided group tours start at the **Great Falls Historic District Cultural Center**, 65 McBride Ave., (973) 279-9587, www.patersonnj.gov. The center is open year-round Mon through Fri from 9 a.m. to 5 p.m. and Sat and Sun from 12:30 to 4:30 p.m.

The **Paterson Museum**'s collections of photographs and artifacts document the textile and locomotive-building industries, as well as Paterson's short-lived involvement in Samuel Colt's firearms enterprise. Perhaps the most famous of the museum's holdings, however, are the two earliest experimental submarines, built in 1878 and 1881 by John P. Holland, father of the modern submarine. The museum's interests also range to the natural and social history of the North Jersey area, and one of the state's finest mineral exhibits includes a fluorescent display in a simulated mine. Finally, two most fitting exhibits stand in the courtyard outside the Paterson Museum building: Alco-Cooke locomotives, built just across Market Street from the Rogers plant. Number 299 was built in 1906 to help in the construction of the Panama Canal.

The Paterson Museum, 2 Market St., (973) 321-1260, www.patersonmuseum.com, is open Mon through Sat from 9:30 a.m. to 4:30 p.m. Admission is $2 for adults.

Patsy's Tavern is the kind of place that harks back to a time when many of Paterson's neighborhoods had a strong ethnic identity. There aren't many

Italians still living in the Riverside area now, but Patsy's—established in 1931 and still in the same family hands—has hung on. It's a place where the old guard still gathers in the bar for wine, where you practically walk through the kitchen to get to the dining room and its classic southern Italian menu . . . and where the pizza has been cited again and again as the best in the state. Patsy's Tavern, 72 7th Ave., (973) 742-9596, www.patsystavern.com, is open for lunch Thurs and Fri from 11 a.m. to 1 p.m. and dinner Tues through Sat from 4:30 to 9 p.m. Entrées range from $14 to $22; large pizzas are $14.75 to $25.75. Cash only.

In its industrial glory days at the turn of the 20th century, Paterson supported a comfortable capitalist class. None of the silk barons lived so lavishly as Catholina Lambert, a man whose home, appropriately enough, has come to be called **Lambert Castle**. Today the home of the Passaic County Historical Society, this great sandstone pile still stands in lordly isolation on the brow of Garret Mountain, looking down over the mills and the city that made its builder rich.

Lambert built his Garret Mountain castle, which he called Belle Vista, in 1892; four years later he built the 70-foot tower that still stands behind the house. Belle Vista became more than a home for Lambert and his family; it was also a magnificent art museum. Lambert died at the castle in 1923, at nearly 90 years of age. His house and grounds were acquired by the Passaic County Park Commission in 1928, and the building was opened as a museum six years later.

The castle and its museum are closed for renovations until 2024, but the building serves as an excellent starting point for an exploration of the 568-acre **Garret Mountain Reservation**, jewel of the county's park system, and there's

When Beer Flowed through Fire Hoses

Mention Prohibition beer barons and most people think of Chicago. But Paterson, a city that supported five major breweries back before the Volstead Act became law, had its own underworld brewmaster. He was Waxey Gordon, a onetime pickpocket and mob enforcer who set up shop in the city's old Sprattler & Mennel Brewery on Marshall Street. In order to avoid the suspicion that would have been aroused by a constant stream of trucks loading at the brewery, Waxey and his boys ran high-pressure fire hoses through the city sewers to distribution points around town.

The operation was even dramatized in an episode of TV's *The Untouchables*. But it was an income tax evasion rap, and not a raid on his brewery, that finally brought Waxey down. He was released from prison in 1940, and died at Alcatraz in 1952 while awaiting trial for heroin distribution.

a spectacular view of New York City from the mountain's 500-foot elevation. That doesn't sound like much, and "mountain" may be stretching things a bit, but the land is flat between here and the Hudson, and you'll be looking across much of Passaic and Bergen Counties. A walk through the reservation grounds should include a circuit around picturesque Barbour Pond, a popular fishing spot.

The Lambert Castle Museum, Valley Road, Paterson, (973) 247-0085, www .lambertcastle.org, is open in July and Aug, Wed through Fri from 1 to 4 p.m. and Sat and Sun from noon to 4 p.m.; call for off-season hours. Admission is $5 for adults, $4 for seniors, and $3 for ages 5 to 17. The grounds are open daily dawn to dusk.

Visitors who would like to tour the reservation by horse can head over to the **Garret Mountain Equestrian Center**, which offers guided trail rides with both English and western saddles. For information call (973) 279-2974 or visit www.eliteequinegroup.com.

More than 70 nationalities live within Paterson's 8³⁄₁₀ square miles, and adventurous diners can sample foods of the world without leaving city limits. In a few blocks, you can sample *acili ezme* (hot and spicy chopped vegetables) at **Alaturka Turkish Cuisine**, 838 Main St., (973) 523-6060; nachos, quesadillas, and other classic Mexican dishes at **Hacienda**, 102 McLean Blvd., (973) 345-1255, www.haciendanj.com; authentic Peruvian fare at **La Tia Delia Restaurant**, 28 Market St., (973) 523-4550; and home-style Italian cooking at **E&V Restaurant**, 320 Chamberlain Ave., (973) 942-4664, www.evrestaurant .com. There are also Lebanese bakeries, falafel stands, sub shops, and even homemade ice cream at **Guernsey Crest** at 134 19th Ave. You might leave Paterson broke, but you won't leave hungry.

The other side of Paterson's industrial past is told in a far less imposing structure than Lambert Castle, located in the nearby town of Haledon. This is the 1908 Victorian home of Italian immigrants and mill workers Pietro and Mario Botto. Designated a National Historic Landmark, the Botto House is home to the **American Labor Museum**.

The Bottos were silk workers carrying on a trade learned in the "old country," Italy. It was a tough life. Workers suffered with low wages, long hours, poor lighting, and harsh production demands. In 1913, when one of Paterson's companies tried to introduce the four-loom weaving system, workers realized that at least half of them would be put out of work. Spontaneously, they walked off their jobs and onto picket lines. One by one the mills were closed by the strikes and 25,000 people were out of work.

During the 1913 Paterson silk strike, Pietro Botto opened his doors to leaders of the Industrial Workers of the World (the IWW, or "Wobblies"), such

Home-Fries Memories

Growing up in Paterson in the 1950s, I lived just a few blocks from a factory that turned out one of New Jersey's most famous products—diners. Standing on E. 27th Street and watching a gleaming, freshly minted stainless-steel eatery roll out of the Silk City Diner Company's plant was every bit as exciting as watching a new battleship slide down the ways. After all, I had a proprietary interest in Silk City diners: My grandfather, John Marchitti, owned one. For two decades his Hiway Diner, on Route 4 in nearby Fairlawn, was a beacon to truckers, salesmen, families, and travelers of all sorts. I learned how to make home fries at the Hiway and how to craft the perfect Taylor ham and egg sandwich. A world that could use more of John Marchitti's counter-side jokes hasn't heard them for more than 50 years now, and I'm told that the Hiway Diner is someplace out in Pennsylvania. If any readers know just where, let me know and I'll be off quicker than it takes to fire up a griddle.

—Bill Scheller

as William "Big Bill" Haywood and Elizabeth Gurley Flynn. For as long as the strike lasted, thousands of Paterson mill workers would stand outside the house while Haywood and the others stirred them with oratory from its balcony. The American Labor Museum's collections of photographs, union memorabilia, tools, and household artifacts document not only the silk strike itself, but also the way of life of a generation of working-class immigrants.

The American Labor Museum/Botto House National Landmark, 83 Norwood St., Haledon, (973) 595-7953, www.labormuseum.net, is open Wed through Sat from 1 to 4 p.m. or by appointment; call to confirm before visiting. There is a suggested donation of $5 per person. Come at least 45 minutes before closing time.

The *Van Riper–Hopper Museum* in Wayne is a fine example of New Jersey Dutch Colonial architecture. The one-and-a-half-story building, built in 1786 by Uriah Van Riper, has five lower rooms and four upstairs bedrooms in the main section of the house. The three rooms in the frame section are the former slave quarters. Typical of the New Jersey Dutch style, the house faces south, and the majority of windows are in the front to receive full benefit of sunlight. As was the custom with Dutch houses of the time, all additions were made to the side of the house rather than the rear.

There are six fireplaces throughout the house. During the year the fire in the huge basement fireplace, which contains a Dutch oven, was never allowed to die out for fear it would bring bad luck. Only on New Year's Day was the fireplace cleaned out, and then a new fire was promptly built.

A Bad Year for Paterson

On February 8, 1902, fire broke out in the streetcar barns near Paterson's Market Street. By the time the blaze was extinguished, the Silk City had lost nearly 500 buildings, including the heart of the business district. The city's Beaux Arts City Hall, then only eight years old, was heavily damaged—it survives today, but with extensive renovation.

Patersonians were barely beginning to tally the damages when, on March 2, the Passaic River roiled over its banks and carried away many of the mills, homes, and bridges that had not been lost in the fire.

The walls in the Van Riper–Hopper House are 20 inches thick and made of local fieldstone. The floors are wide pine planks. Open ceilings are supported by heavy hand-hewn beams. A mortar of clay, straw, and hair holds the stone walls in place, and the plaster of the inside walls is an inch thick.

The homestead was saved from destruction in 1964 after the Passaic Valley Water Commission planned the Point View Reservoir, which now provides a waterfowl sanctuary and attracts devoted bird-watchers (who still reminisce about the rare sighting of a Hudsonian godwit). Flower and herb gardens are maintained by Wayne garden clubs.

The Van Riper–Hopper Museum, at 533 Berdan Ave. and adjacent to the Point View Reservoir, (973) 706-6640, is part of a complex that includes the 1706 **Van Duyne House**, moved here in 1974, and the **Archaeological Laboratory**, which contains thousands of artifacts excavated from local sites. Tours are by appointment.

You may love some of the sculptures on the campus of **William Paterson University** . . . You may love them all . . . Or you may hate them all. But as long as you have some feeling about them, they've served their purpose. They've all been chosen as part of the school's Sculpture on Campus program, initiated to create an environment in which sculpture—whose development has generally been perceived as provocative and controversial—can be discovered, discussed, and, if necessary, challenged. Among them: Albert E. Henselmann's *Untitled*, Lyman Kipp's *Yoakum Jack*, Michel Gerard's *Mary Ellen Kramer Memorial Sculpture*, and Tova Beck-Friedman's *Magna Dea*.

The university's **Ben Shahn Center for the Visual Arts** houses several galleries for exhibits in a wide variety of media, and it also houses the college's African and Oceanic art collections. Call the center at (973) 720-2654 for a schedule. The William Paterson University of New Jersey is at 300 Pompton

Rd. in Wayne, (877)720-2000, www.wpunj.edu. The Shahn Center is open Tues through Fri from 11 a.m. to 5 p.m. Admission is free.

There is a house in Wayne where George Washington not only slept but spent part of 1780 planning strategy as the Revolution drew toward its decisive final year. This is the **Dey Mansion**, a graceful brick Georgian home, built about 1740 for Bergen County militia commander Colonel Theunis Dey. A visit here is as instructive of how a comfortable country family lived in America in the latter half of the 18th century as it is of the circumstances in which the commander-in-chief conducted his councils of war and lived out his days far from his own Virginia home. Period furnishings, weapons, prints, and documents all help to tell the tale.

The Dey (pronounced "die") Mansion, 199 Totowa Rd., (973) 706-6640, is open Wed through Fri from 1 to 4 p.m. and Sat and Sun from 10 a.m. to noon and 1 to 4 p.m. The last tour begins at 3:30 p.m. Admission is $1; children under 10 are free.

Albert Payson Terhune's estate, Sunnybank, is gone now; it was torn down in 1969. But **Terhune Sunnybank Memorial Park** in Pompton Lakes—on the lake's western shore—serves as a memorial for the man who immortalized his collie, Lad, in such books as *Lad, A Dog* and *Lad of Sunnybrook*. And Lad himself is remembered, buried beneath a small marble marker that reads "Lad, Thoroughbred in Body and Soul, 1902–1918."

whoneeds niagara?

Paterson's Great Falls of the Passaic River is one of the largest waterfalls east of the Mississippi.

A visit to the **Yogi Berra Museum & Learning Center** "ain't over till it's over." You'll learn not only about the record-setting career of Yogi Berra, catcher for the Yankees during their glory years in the 1950s and later manager of both the Yankees and the Mets, but also about New Jersey's many connections to America's national pastime.

The Yogi Berra Museum & Learning Center, on the campus of Montclair State University, 8 Yogi Berra Dr., Little Falls, (973) 655-2378, www.yogiberra museum.org, is open Wed through Sun from noon to 5 p.m.; closed major holidays. Admission is $10 for adults and $5 for seniors and those under 18. Veterans and Montclair State students free.

The area's ethnic diversity is also evident at **Corrado's Family Affair**, at 1578 Main Ave. in Clifton, (973) 340-0628, www.corradosmarket.com. This huge, warehouse-style grocery store is jam-packed with foods from every nation: prosciuttos and mozzarellas, chayotes and tomatillos, kosher knishes,

Afghani flatbread—and on, and on, and on. There's also a branch at 201 Berdan Ave. in Wayne, (973) 646-2199.

Four-course taster menus ($115), with portions larger than appetizers but smaller than entrées, are specialties at the highly regarded **Café Matisse**. Diners can choose from such treats as sushi tuna with chipotle white bean hummus, spicy goat cheese basil fritter and long-stem speck-wrapped artichoke, and pan-seared venison medallion with roasted foie gras. All menus include dessert. Café Matisse, 167 Park Ave., Rutherford, (201) 935-2995, www.cafematisse.com, is open for dinner Tues through Sun. The BYOB restaurant, with a lovely outdoor patio for alfresco dining, is conveniently located behind a wine shop.

Hudson/Newark Region

When American art began to claim serious critical attention in the early 1900s, a farsighted New Jersey collector and the remarkable institution he inspired were in the forefront of efforts to make works by American painters accessible to the public. The collector was William T. Evans, who in 1909 offered the town of Montclair 26 paintings on the condition that a museum be built to house them. The building request was met, and today the Evans collection forms the nucleus of **The Montclair Art Museum**. Opened in 1914, this was the first art museum in New Jersey to be open to the public, and it remains one of the few institutions of its kind to limit its concentration entirely to American art—including an excellent collection of Native American art and artifacts.

Montclair was the home of the great landscape painter George Inness, and many of his most familiar works depict the Montclair environs. Most appropriately there are 12 Inness canvases in the museum's collection of more than a thousand paintings, watercolors, and other works. Also represented are such American luminaries as John Singleton Copley, Winslow Homer, Reginald Marsh, John Singer Sargent, Childe Hassam, Robert Henri, William Morris Hunt, and James McNeill Whistler. In addition, the museum houses a 14,000-volume research library.

The Montclair Art Museum, 3 S. Mountain Ave., (973) 746-5555, www.montclairartmuseum.org, is open Fri and Sat from 10 a.m. to 6 p.m. and Sun from 11 a.m. to 5 p.m. Admission is $15 for adults, $12 for students and senior citizens, and free for children under 12. Parking is free.

In 1796, Israel Crane, at the age of 22, constructed a turnpike that opened New Jersey's heartland to early trade; he also built a Federal-style mansion that was to become home to seven generations of his family. Today the 10-room **Israel Crane House** has been restored to look as it did between 1796 and

1840, and it houses a superb collection of 18th- and 19th-century furniture, paintings, and decorative arts. Uniformed docents are on hand to provide a glimpse into life during that period. The house, part of a complex maintained by the Montclair Historical Society, also includes the 1818 Nathaniel Crane House and the 1894 Clark House.

The Montclair Historical Society, Montclair, (973) 744-1796, www.montclairhistory.org, opens its properties for tours on Sunday afternoons (except holidays) from Apr through Oct. Admission to the Crane houses and Clark House is $8 for adults and $5 for children 10 and under.

The 408-acre **Eagle Rock Reservation** at Prospect and Eagle Rock Avenues in West Orange, on the crest of the Watchung Range's First Mountain, provides a magnificent view of the Manhattan skyline. An open-air "casino" (shelter) built there in 1911 has been transformed into the **Highlawn Pavilion** restaurant, (973) 731-3463, www.highlawn.com, and offers New American cuisine (dinner nightly except Mon and Tues, with entrées ranging from $32 to $46), along with incomparable views.

If you happen to be in or around Montclair between the middle of May and early June, don't leave without visiting the National Historic Trust Site **Presby Memorial Iris Gardens** in Mountainside Park. These gardens are the legacy of Montclair citizen Frank H. Presby, a breeder of irises and a founder of the American Iris Society.

Having begun with a modest planting that included several of Presby's own iris hybrids, the gardens have grown to include six species with more than 4,000 varieties of irises, including some that date from the 1500s. If you wish to refresh your memory of spring's iris pageant, return to Presby Gardens in September and October, when the *remontant* (reblooming) irises come into bloom.

Presby Memorial Iris Gardens is at 474 Upper Mountain Ave., Upper Montclair, (973) 783-5974, www.essexcountyparks.org. The grounds are open in season from dawn to dusk. Call for information on times to see the iris displays. There is a suggested donation of $10 per person.

The **Van Vleck House and Gardens** are the legacy of a Montclair family who cultivated their 12-acre property for generations and bequeathed their Italianate villa and its surroundings to the Montclair Foundation in 1993. Maples, cedars, dogwood, ginkgo, and many other tree species shade walkways, and hundreds of perennials flower with the season—but the stars of the show here are the dozens of varieties of rhododendrons and azaleas that blaze in color each spring. The Van Vleck Gardens, 21 Van Vleck St., Montclair, (973) 744-4752, www.montclairfoundation.org, is open dawn to dusk, every day of the year. Admission is free.

If you've ever thought about what it would be like to be an air traffic controller (but lack the tolerance for stress and superhuman doses of responsibility that go with it), head over to the *Aviation Hall of Fame and Museum of New Jersey* in Teterboro. Teterboro Airport, one of the nation's busiest facilities that serves private and commuter aircraft, needed a new control tower a while back. Instead of tearing down the old one, though, authorities incorporated it into the Aviation Hall of Fame. Now, after looking over the Arthur Godfrey collection of aviation artifacts and watching films of historic events in New Jersey aviation history, visitors can head upstairs and witness takeoffs and landings from the same perch controllers used for years. There's even an audio hookup, broadcasting the directions that controllers in the new tower are giving to incoming pilots. (The Arthur Godfrey connection with Teterboro, by the way, is both famous and infamous. One day the radio and television personality buzzed the tower in a fit of temper, and later he recalled the event in a song called "Teterboro Tower.")

The Education Center adjacent to the control tower has a facsimile control tower; aircraft, helicopter, and rocket exhibits; and hands-on airplanes to "fly." New Jersey–built piston, jet, and rocket engines and a military aviation display dominate the Great Hall. There's a Hall of Fame, where exhibits present aviatrixes such as Amelia Earhart and Kathryn Sullivan (the first woman to walk in space) and astronaut Buzz Aldrin, a native New Jerseyan.

The Aviation Hall of Fame and Museum of New Jersey, 400 Fred Wehran Dr. (Route 46), (201) 288-6344, www.njahof.org, is open by reservation Wed through Sat from 10:30 a.m. to 3:30 p.m. Admission is $12 for adults and $10 for senior citizens and children 3 to 12.

Teterboro sits on the fringes of a vast tract of land that was for centuries an uninhabited and virtually uninhabitable wilderness, even after populous cities and suburbs sprang up all around it. Variously called the *Hackensack Meadows*, the Secaucus Meadows, or simply the Meadowlands or Meadows, the marshy basin that surrounds the estuarial reaches of the Hackensack and Passaic Rivers constitutes a remarkable ecosystem that is, unfortunately, famous chiefly for the ways in which it has been abused over the past hundred years. Construction of any magnitude was stymied because the Meadows' foundation consists of up to 200 feet of unconsolidated muck. Within recent memory, railroads and their attendant structures were the only substantial fabricated works in the Hackensack Meadows.

In spite of this construction problem, people did find some uses for the Meadows, and the uses they found were responsible for the dubious reputation the area once carried. Sixty years ago, when you were driving on the turnpike through the Meadows on a hot summer day, you would roll up your windows (this was before auto air-conditioning) when you got near Secaucus because of the stench of the pig farms that occupied the edges of the Meadows. And if it wasn't the pigs, it was the garbage—communities in North Jersey long ago took to using the Meadows as a giant solid-waste landfill. Finally, as if pigs and garbage weren't enough, there were all the jokes about missing mobsters who were spending eternity beneath the marsh grasses.

In the early 1970s, everything started to change. Construction engineers figured out how to build on the Meadows' soil, and the Meadowlands were zoned, divided, and conquered. Fortunately the planners who undertook the development of the Meadows found room for the preservation of one of the

> ## didyou
> ## know . . . ?
>
> It is believed that Snake Hill in the Hackensack Meadows is the eroded stump of an ancient volcano.

more undisturbed tracts as the multiple-use **Richard DeKorte State Park**. It includes hiking and nature-observation trails as well as a mini wilderness wildlife-management area. For all the depredations of the past, the Meadows are still a fine place for birding.

The park also offers another viewing opportunity. Monday and Wednesday evenings (weather permitting) are public viewing nights at the **William D. McDowell Observatory**, at the park's **Meadowlands Commission Center for Environmental and Scientific Education**. Programs are free but limited to 25 people on a first-come, first-served basis. The park and observatory are at 2 DeKorte Park Plaza in Lyndhurst, (201) 460-1700.

For a historical perspective on the Meadowlands and environs, visit the **Meadowlands Museum** in Rutherford. This small institution, which is housed in a Dutch Colonial farmhouse, maintains files of historical photographs and documents that are available to researchers if not currently on display. In addition to the first-floor exhibits, which change three or four times a year, the museum also features reconstructions of colonial and turn-of-the-20th-century kitchens on its lower level as well as exhibits of antique toys and dolls and New Jersey minerals on the second floor.

The Meadowlands Museum, 91 Crane Ave., Rutherford, (201) 935-1175, www.meadowlandsmuseum.com, is open Sat from 10 a.m. to 4 p.m. Call before you go, as the museum is closed to the public when it hosts children's groups. Donations are most welcome.

Segovia, one of the state's first Spanish restaurants, is known for its small tables, noisy crowds, reasonable prices, and large portions. The menu is extensive and offers tapas, traditional Spanish seafood dishes such as pan-fried baby sardines and whole fresh squid cooked in garlic and white wine, and Iberian ham, as well as an assortment of Italian dishes ($15 to $75). Segovia is at 150 Moonachie Rd., Moonachie, (201) 641-4266, www.segoviarestaurant.com. Open for lunch and dinner daily.

Head east now to the bluffs above the Hudson River at Weehawken. Known to motorists as the town on the New Jersey side of the Lincoln Tunnel and to aficionados of Edward Hopper's paintings as the setting for his *East Wind over Weehawken*, this is where the career of Alexander Hamilton, the brilliant American statesman, Federalist Papers writer, and first US secretary of the treasury, was cut short in a duel with vice president Aaron Burr. Burr, who felt that his recent candidacy for the governorship of New York had failed largely because of the vociferous criticism of his old enemy Hamilton, made the formal demand for satisfaction; the two men met at what was then a secluded spot on the Jersey side of the Hudson on the morning of July 11, 1804. Pistols were the weapons of choice. Hamilton's shot missed; Burr's did not. The author of many of the Federalist Papers died a day later, while Burr, his political career finished, left the area and began his descent into the shadows of American history.

newjersey fastfacts

New Jersey . . .

- is only four times larger than Rhode Island.

- has the highest population density in the country.

The actual **Hamilton-Burr Duel Site**, which is marked today by a small park and a modest tablet, is on John F. Kennedy Boulevard East (also called by its old name, Hudson Boulevard East). Nearby is **Veterans' Memorial Park**, where there is a more impressive monument and bronze bust of Hamilton. Historical considerations aside, this is a particularly scenic spot at dusk on a late fall or winter afternoon, when lights twinkle on across the river in Manhattan.

If you've always wanted to visit the Ginza but haven't had a chance, plan a stop at **Mitsuwa Marketplace**, a large, bustling mall whose vendors specialize in Japanese goods. The centerpiece here is a giant market filled with exotic produce, fresh fish and noodles, and imported packaged goods. Go there hungry; the food concessions are a bit more eclectic than the shops, offering everything from sushi to kung pao chicken to Korean hot pot. The mall, at 595 River Rd. in Edgewater, (201) 941-9113, www.mitsuwa.com, is open Sun through Thurs from 9:30 a.m. to 8:00 p.m. and Fri and Sat from 9:30 a.m. to 9:00 p.m.

In 1915 Pope Benedict XV issued a plea for world peace, and the Reverend Joseph N. Grieff, pastor of Holy Family Church in Union Hill (now Union City),

Let Jersey Entertain You

Sure, New Jersey has produced literary figures (Allen Ginsberg, William Carlos Williams, Philip Roth), Supreme Court justices (William Brennan, Antonin Scalia, Samuel Alito), and even a moon walker (no, not Michael Jackson—Apollo 11 astronaut Edwin "Buzz" Aldrin). But the state really shines in its roster of big names in the entertainment world. A partial list:

Count Basie	Nathan Lane
Jon Bon Jovi	Queen Latifah
Danny DeVito	Jerry Lewis
Michael Douglas	Joe Pesci
Kirsten Dunst	Frank Sinatra
Vera Farmiga	Bruce Springsteen
Connie Francis	John Travolta
Ed Harris	Frankie Valli
Whitney Houston	Sarah Vaughan
The Jonas Brothers—Kevin, Joe, and Nick	And let's not forget three guys who played Jersey characters on *The Sopranos*: Joe Pantoliano (Ralph Cifaretto), Vincent Curatola (Johnny Sack) . . . and Tony himself, James Gandolfini.
Ernie Kovacs	

responded. He envisioned a production of an "Americanized" Passion play, modeled on the one presented every 10 years since 1680 in Oberammergau, Bavaria. Thus began Union City's annual—and the country's oldest—Passion play. In 1931 the **Park Performing Arts Center** was built specifically for the Passion play, which is now performed here each Easter season. The 1,400-seat Moorish-style opera house also hosts other cultural events throughout the year.

The play tells the story of the last days of Jesus as he preached, journeyed to Jerusalem, presided at the Last Supper, and was crucified. The play received an overhaul in 1985, when Father Kevin Ashe rewrote the script to alter the anti-Semitic reputation Passion plays had earned over the years. "The Park Theater's Passion play is an art form that teaches a lesson to Christians," Father Ashe states. "In times of social unrest, the play teaches us that we all come from the same roots. Christ himself was Jewish." The center is at 560 32nd St., Union City; call (201) 430-5067 or go to www.parktheatrenj.org for a schedule of events.

Union City has a large Hispanic population, so it's no surprise that some of New Jersey's best Latin restaurants and grocery stores are here. Mexican tortillas, Chilean empanadas (crusty turnovers), Colombian *batidos* (a drink of whipped milk, fruit, and sugar)—the 3½-mile route along Bergenline Avenue running toward West New York is a Latin fresser's dream come true.

There's a good reason Union City has sometimes been called "Cuba's Northernmost Province"—starting in the mid-1960s, Cuban émigrés flocked to the Hudson County community and enlivened its cultural, social, and business environment. According to local tradition, though, the first Cubans to settle in Union City arrived back in 1948. They were Lyda and Manuel Rodriguez, a recently married couple who had planned to live in New York City but were attracted by job opportunities on the New Jersey side of the Hudson River. News of Manuel Rodriguez's success as an entrepreneur reached Cuba, prompting Union City's attractiveness as an immigrant haven. Today, new Americans from throughout Central and South America, as well as Mexico, contribute to a population that is over three-quarters Hispanic.

The 20,000-square-foot grocery store **Mi Bandera**, 518 32nd St. (off Bergenline Avenue), (201) 348-2828, is a great place to stock up on provisions from countries including Uruguay, El Salvador, and Chile, as well as hard-to-find imported beers. An icy brew would be perfect to wash down a veal and lamb gyro or lamb shish kebab at **Beyti Kebab**, a BYOB Turkish restaurant at 4105 Park Ave., (201) 865-6281, www.beytikebabnj.com. On Saturday nights there's usually live music and a belly dancer. The restaurant is open daily from 11 a.m. to 9 p.m.

The Hoboken piers immortalized in Elia Kazan's 1954 movie *On the Waterfront* were once among the busiest on the East Coast. From the mid-19th century until the beginning of World War I, two ocean liner companies, Hamburg-American and North Germany Lloyd, owned docks here and landed so many German immigrants that the city earned the nickname "Little Bremen." (By the mid-1850s, almost one-quarter of the city's population of 7,000 was German.) World War I's American Expeditionary Forces sailed from Hoboken to Europe. During the war, almost 3,500 workers were employed here, working on the new steel ships that required more skilled labor.

Since World War I, the piers have been home to several companies, including Bethlehem Steel (1938–1980), but by the 1970s the rising popularity of containerization and the lack of space on the Hoboken docks were the death knell for the steel company and its employees. The company sold the shipyard to the Braswell Corporation in 1982, but after a few years it also closed its doors. A lingerie manufacturer purchased the site with plans to convert it to luxury housing, and a wrecking crew had actually demolished a corner of the 1890

Hoboken Terminal

Thousands of workers take commuter trains in and out of Hoboken every day, but how many stop to take a look at the station? Built in 1907 for the Delaware, Lackawanna & Western Railroad, Hoboken Terminal was one of the great transportation temples of the age. Much of the exterior—especially on the Hudson River facade where the DL&W ferries used to dock—is copper, its surface aged to a mellow green. Inside, the 90-by-100-foot main waiting room is lavishly decorated in limestone and bronze. The restored ferry concourse once contained a restaurant with river-facing balcony, a sumptuous barbershop, and even an emergency hospital.

Machine Shop—the oldest building on the waterfront—before it was stopped by members of the community.

Today the Machine Shop is home to the ***Hoboken Historical Museum***, 1301 Hudson St., (201) 656-2240, www.hobokenmuseum.org, which hosts exhibits, lectures, and walking tours of piers left largely intact. Call for a schedule of tours. The museum is open Tues, Wed, and Thurs from 2 to 7 p.m., Fri from 1 to 5 p.m., and Sat and Sun from noon to 5 pm. Admission is $5. Museum guests receive three hours of free parking at Littleman Parking–Independence Garage, 12th Street and Shipyard Lane. Have your ticket validated at the museum.

Out beneath the 607-foot train sheds, prosaic New Jersey Transit commuter cars now depart on short suburban runs—a far cry from the glory days, when crack overnight trains like the Phoebe Snow sallied out of Hoboken on their way to the cities of the Midwest. Frank Sinatra is immortalized on a "hall of fame" of photographs at ***Leo's Grandevous Restaurant***, just a few blocks from the onetime home of the "Chairman of the Board" (his birthplace, at 415 Monroe St., has been torn down; his boyhood home at 841 Garden St. is still standing). While you're there, you can chow down on some fine, moderately priced Italian dishes, including saltimboca and spinach ravioli, or have a drink at the bar, where you can order from an extensive list of personal-size pizzas and perhaps listen to a local spin a tale about Frank. The restaurant, at 200 Grand Ave. and 2nd Street, (201) 659-9467, is open for lunch Fri through Sun and dinner nightly. Reservations not available.

Hoboken's ***Elysian Café*** is the city's oldest continuously operated bar and restaurant. Dating to 1895—and having survived Prohibition by selling ice cream instead of alcoholic libations—it has the look of a place that time forgot, but that its owners always remembered to keep in tip-top shape: The ornate ceiling alone is worth the price of a beer at the long, mirror-polished wooden bar. But don't just wet your whistle—entrées ($22 to $34) include lobster roll, homemade gnocchi, and skirt steak au poivre. Sidewalk seating is available late spring to early fall. The Elysian Café, 1001 Washington St., (201) 798-5898, www.elysiancafe.com, is open Mon through Fri noon to 11 p.m., Sat 10 a.m. to 11 p.m., and Sun 10 a.m. to 10 p.m.

Many folks believe that tiny, informal, and brightly lit **La Isla** in downtown Hoboken, 104 Washington St., (201) 659-8197, www.aislarestaurant.com, offers the best Cuban fare in the state. Among the favorites: a plate of Chef Omar's stuffed French toast and a cup of Cuban latte to start the day; for lunch or dinner, *media noche* (roasted pork, ham, and Swiss cheese on sweet bread with pickle and garlic *mojo*) or grilled marinated skirt steak with chimichurri sauce. Sunday brunch includes specialties such as La Papa, a stuffed potato cut in half and topped with crispy bacon, fried eggs, melted Swiss cheese, *salsa ranchera*, and field greens. The BYOB restaurant is open Mon through Sat from 7 a.m. to 10 p.m. and Sun from 10 a.m. to 3 p.m. and 5 to 9 p.m. A second La Isla Hoboken location is at 25 12th St., (201) 659-6090.

City Bistro, one of the many upscale restaurants attracted to Hoboken in recent years, serves up fine food and a spectacular view of Manhattan. There are three floors here, including the first-floor sports pub, but, weather permitting, opt for the roof deck, sit back, and enjoy. The food is contemporary American with French and Italian touches, including appetizers such as fried calamari with aioli sauce. Seared diver scallops and grilled sirloin steak are just a couple of the well-prepared entréess. The weekend brunch menu ranges from lemon ricotta pancakes to grilled hanger steak and eggs; dinner might start with crispy calamari and proceed to chicken Milanese and cannoli. City Bistro, at 56-58 14th St., (201) 963-8200, www.citybistrohobokennj.com, is open Mon through Fri from 11:30 a.m. to 10 p.m. and Sat and Sun from 10 a.m. to 10 p.m. The restaurant validates parking for all diners (not bar-only patrons) with checks of $50 or more; parking is at Propark Parking Garage, 1450 Bloomfield Ave.

Jersey City's **Afro-American Historical Society Museum** focuses on New Jersey's African-American people, places, and events, with changing as well as permanent exhibits. Among the latter: a 1930 kitchen reflecting the heart of an urban black home for that time and period; black dolls from the African Diaspora (some dating back more than 125 years); sculptures and paintings; and civil rights artifacts and collections of the 1950s and 1960s. In addition to exhibits, the museum hosts lectures and programs relating to the black experience, and sponsors a Kwanzaa program each December.

The Afro-American Historical Society Museum, on the second floor of the Greenville Branch of the Jersey City Free Public Library, 1841 John F. Kennedy Blvd., (201) 547-5262, is open by appointment. Call for hours.

Whether or not you're a Jersey chauvinist who thinks the state flag should fly from Liberty's crown, it's nice to know that you can get out to Liberty Island and the **Statue of Liberty** without having to sail from the Battery in Manhattan. **Statue Cruises** operates a ferry that leaves Liberty State Park, off exit 14B of the New Jersey Turnpike, and stops at Ellis Island State Park and the Statue of Liberty. The ferry operates daily, but hours vary with the season. Fare prices vary from $24 for round-trip ferry service and admission to the statue and Ellis Island to $74 for the ferry and the guided Ellis Island "Hard Hat" tour. There is also a parking fee. The best time to go is in the morning, before the crowds arrive; visitors who depart in late afternoon will only be able to visit Liberty Island or Ellis Island. To avoid waiting in line for tickets, and to assure you can travel on the day you wish, book in advance at the ferry's website, www.statuecruises.com. If you wish to visit the crown, try to book at least a few months in advance. For general information check the National Park Service website, www.nps.gov/stli, or call (212) 363-3200.

The carhops are gone now, but little else at the **White Mana** has changed since 1939 (it originally opened at the World's Fair). Dedicated patrons continue to pack the tiny, classic diner for the house specialty, a grilled burger with onions on a soft bun and a side of crispy fries and/or onion rings. Some people love this place; others say the burgers are better at White Castle. But for local color, it can't be beat. The diner is at 470 Tonnele Ave. in Jersey City, (201) 963-1441. **Note:** There is a White Manna Hamburgers at 358 River St. in Hackensack that is not affiliated with White Mana in Jersey City, but it garners rave reviews for its burgers.

Ready for dessert? **Goehrig's Bakery** has been buttering up customers since 1934. Specialties include rum and cheese cakes, ricotta raisin tarts, bread pudding (made with their own challah and raisin bread), chocolate dipper strawberries, and incredibly delicious Italian butter cookies. The bakery is at

katynmemorial

At Exchange Place, the busy centerpiece of Jersey City's revived business district along the Hudson River waterfront, stands one of the most stark and unsettling statues to ever commemorate a historic event. It is a standing soldier, his face frozen at the moment of death, impaled on a bayonet. The statue memorializes the execution of 11,000 Polish army officers by Soviet troops in the Katyn Forest during the spring of 1940. It serves as a reminder that Jersey City's considerable Polish population refuses to forget the betrayal, devastation, and slaughter that was its fate during World War II.

475 Central Ave. in Jersey City, (201) 659-4513, and is open Mon through Sat from 7 a.m. to 7 p.m. and Sun from 7 a.m. to 5 p.m.

Newark, New Jersey's largest city, has two major troves of regional historical materials, the Newark Museum and the lesser-known *New Jersey Historical Society*. This society is the repository of what has been called "an unparalleled collection of New Jerseyana," and the sheer bulk and diversity of its holdings support the claim. Here is a library of 80,000 volumes, open to the public for reference use, and a collection of 2,000 maps, 22,000 prints, and 1 million manuscripts, including the original New Jersey charter of 1664. The society owns 300 portrait and landscape paintings and thousands of drawings, as well as furnishings, silver, glass, and porcelain of New Jersey manufacture.

The New Jersey Historical Society, 52 Park Place, (973) 596-8500, www.jerseyhistory.org, is open Tues through Sat from 10 a.m. to 5 p.m. The library is open Tues through Sat from noon to 5 p.m. Admission to the museum is $3; to the library, $5. Appointments are necessary for the library.

heavystuff

Jersey City boasts two of the "world's biggest" of their kind: the largest concrete monument, a 365-ton fountain erected in 1911 at the main entrance to Lincoln Park, and the 2,200-pound Colgate Clock, whose 50-foot face overlooks the Hudson River on Hudson Street.

The magnificent *Cathedral Basilica of the Sacred Heart* is a church of superlatives: It's the fifth largest in the country, has the second-largest rose window in the United States (37 feet in diameter), and is considered by many to be the purest example of classical French Gothic architecture in the Western Hemisphere. It also has the state's largest church organ, a Schantz, and free half-hour concerts begin at noon on Wednesday (followed by an optional guided tour of the basilica). The church hosts a superb concert series; the schedule is on its website, www.newark-basilica.org. There is a suggested donation of $15. The cathedral is open to visitors Mon through Fri from 9 a.m. to 5 p.m. and Sat from 9 a.m. to 4 p.m. Guided tours are given on the first Sunday of the month, following noon Mass. The National Historic Site is at 89 Ridge St., Newark, (973) 484-4600; the music office phone number is (973) 484-2400.

It's rumored that pals Joe Pesci and Robert De Niro stop in at *Dicky Dee's Pizza* at 380 Bloomfield Ave. in Newark whenever they get a craving for one of Jersey's finest pies. We're not sure what kind they order, but we can heartily endorse the special, as well as the great antipasto and the house special—deep-fried hot dogs. The sandwiches, on circular loaves of bread, are also great. The restaurant is open for lunch and dinner; (973) 483-9396.

The city's 24-acre **Branch Brook Park** is lovely at any time of the year but magnificent in April when 2,700 Japanese cherry trees—the largest collection of Japanese flowering trees in the country—come into bloom. The park is open from dawn to dusk daily. Each

summer the park hosts "Under the Stars," a free entertainment series featuring music, movies, and dancing. For more information call (973) 268-3500 or visit www.essexcountyparks.org.

In nearby Bloomfield, you can visit the place—and maybe sit in the booth—where the last scene of *The Sopranos* was filmed. While you're wondering what happened next, have a cheeseburger deluxe (with fries, $8) and wash it down with an ice-cream soda at **Holsten's Brookdale Confectionery**, an old-fashioned ice-cream parlor that also makes candy. Save room for Holsten's special: four scoops of ice cream topped with fruit salad, hot fudge, whipped cream, and a cherry ($10). The Confectionery, at 1063 Broad St., (973) 338-7091, www.holstens.com, is open Mon through Sat from 11 a.m. to 11:30 p.m. and Sun from noon to 10 p.m.

Before leaving Bloomfield, be sure to take a stroll through the lovely **Town Green Historic District**, whose large town green is lined with more than 200 handsome homes of diverse architecture, including Federal, Italianate, and Queen Anne. Contact the Historical Society of Bloomfield, 90 Broad St., Bloomfield 07003, (973) 743-8844, www .bloomfieldhistorical.org, for a map of the walking tour.

The 2,047-acre **South Mountain Reservation** is the most spectacular parkland in the greater Newark area. Covering parts of Millburn, Maplewood, and West Orange, South Mountain is maintained as a balanced mix of forest, meadows, bridle and bicycle paths, and secluded hiking trails. From Washington Rock on the Crest Drive along the reservation's eastern border, there are magnificent views of the skylines of Newark and New York; on the Lenape

Trail deep in the interior, it's possible to forget that there is any urbanization or even human settlement for miles.

Near the northern end of the South Mountain Reservation, on 16 acres, sits **Turtle Back Zoo**. Northern New Jersey's largest zoo houses 500 animals of 200 different species, with an emphasis on animals originally found in New Jersey. Exhibits include a marine animal touch tank, a butterfly tent, Big Cat Country, and a sea turtle recovery center. There are flight cages for the golden and bald eagles, and the gray wolves and black bears are presented in a naturalistic setting. More exotic animals include penguins, llamas, mouflon sheep, addaxes, and squirrel monkeys.

itstartedin
newark

Although the state has plenty of open spaces, it isn't unusual for people to associate New Jersey with pavement. But there's a historical as well as a visual reason for the connection: The first application of asphalt for street paving in the United States was in Newark, in 1870.

Admission includes the Turtle Back Railroad train ride through the scenic reservation (the train runs from Apr through Nov, weather permitting), as well as access to picnic areas. There are also pony rides, a carousel, and a playground. The Turtle Back Zoo is at 560 Northfield Ave., West Orange, (973) 731-5800. In Apr and May, the zoo is open daily from 10 a.m. to 4 p.m. Admission is $17 for adults and $14 for children ages 2 to 12 and senior citizens.

Nearby Union County has also set aside some fine parklands. The best place to head for a day's ramble hereabouts is the roughly 2,000-acre **Watchung Reservation**, located between Summit and Scotch Plains. Although there are cultivated rhododendron plantings within the reservation, most of the land within its borders has been left as much as possible in its natural state. As at South Mountain, there are extensive hiking and bridle trails; for the hardy, a 10-mile loop called the Sierra Club Trail makes a circuit of the reservation, just within the boundaries.

Near the New Providence Road entrance to the Watchung Reservation is the **Trailside Nature and Science Center**, a well-run facility recommended to anyone who visits the park with children. State-of-the-art exhibits focus on local animals, fossils, Lenni-Lenape Native Americans, minerals, plants, and pond ecology. The center is open daily except Mon from 10 a.m. to 4 p.m. and is located at 452 New Providence Rd., Mountainside, (908) 789-3670, www.ucnj.org. Admission is free.

At the **Stage House Restaurant & Tavern**, a brick structure dating to 1737, chef Eric Hambrecht creates entrées such as bacon-wrapped bourbon-glazed pork chop ($24.95), goat cheese ravioli ($19.95), and crab-stuffed Atlantic flounder ($24.95). Steaks, pizza, and house-made pasta round out the menu. The restaurant, at 366 Park Ave., Scotch Plains, (908) 322-4224, www.stagehousetavern.com, is open for lunch and dinner daily.

You don't have to visit Vermont to show the kids where the syrup they're putting on their waffles comes from. Each February environmental scientists at the 16-acre *Cora Hartshorn Arboretum and Bird Sanctuary* tap the arboretum's sugar maples and boil up batches of delicious maple syrup. The process requires cold nights and warm days, so call ahead to find out when the sap is running. The 16½ acres of wooded grounds at the arboretum encompass 3 miles of trails. An exhibit of stuffed and live animals is housed in the Stone House (closed Sun). Dogs are not permitted. The arboretum is at 324 Forest Dr., Short Hills, (973) 376-3587, www.hartshornarboretum.org. Trails and grounds are open year-round during daylight hours. Naturalist-guided walks can be arranged, upon availability, for a fee.

feltville

An unexpected find amid the leafy glades of Summit's Watchung Reservation is the cluster of old wooden buildings that constitute the remains of the deserted village of Feltville. Feltville was the creation of New York businessman David Felt, who chose this site for a model paper manufacturing and printing operation, complete with workers' housing. The place boomed from 1845 until about 1860, and has been a ghost town since 1880. Since then, Watchung Reservation, a county park, has come to enclose the old industrial site.

History of an abrupt and dramatic variety was made on the steps of Elizabeth's *First Presbyterian Church* (founded in 1664) by its minister, the Reverend James Caldwell, during the Revolutionary War Battle of Springfield. As the battle raged over the fields, Continental troops ran out of the wadding that was used between powder and ball in the muzzle-loading muskets of the

In This Case, with a Paddle

My most unusual excursion through my home state of New Jersey took place in the spring of 1985, when five friends and I traveled the entire length of the Passaic River by canoe. Starting at the river's source near the Great Swamp, we made the 75-mile trip over the course of three days. Our longest portage was around the Great Falls of the Passaic in Paterson. Our strangest overnight stay was when we pitched tents on the riverbank in downtown Summit. And the successful conclusion came at Newark, when we paddled our three canoes under the Pulaski Skyway and entered Newark Bay.

—Bill Scheller

day. Caldwell, an ardent separatist and chaplain of one of the New Jersey regiments, dashed into the church and emerged with as many copies as he could carry of the then-standard Watts hymnbook. Tossing them to the soldiers at the foot of the church steps, the minister called out, "Give 'em Watts, boys. Put Watts into them." Many a Continental musket ball was seated atop a wadded page of hymns that day.

Caldwell was minister of the First Presbyterian Church of Elizabeth from 1762 to 1781, when he was shot and killed. He preached with loaded pistols in the pulpit and kept a lookout in the belfry to warn of an approach of the British, who came on forays from Staten Island. The church building of Elizabeth was burned by the British and rebuilt in 1785–87. The church burned again in an accidental fire in 1946, but the outer walls are the original 1787 structure. The inside was restored to its colonial style and is an authentic representation of Georgian architecture. The adjacent graveyard represents an unbroken continuum of history that dates back to the late 17th century.

The church, at 42 Broad St., (908) 353-1518, houses a museum and will be opened for visitors by appointment. The grounds and cemetery are open daily during daylight hours.

Far different, and more ancient, associations are suggested by a visit to Beth Israel Memorial Park, a Jewish cemetery in Woodbridge. Here are the **Bible Gardens of Israel**, conceived as a means of bringing the physical environment of the Holy Land to life in the New World. The vehicle used for this ambitious enterprise was horticulture; here are hundreds of the plants mentioned in the Bible, from olive, fig, and pomegranate trees to myrtle, oleander, and bay. The trees, shrubs, and flowering plants are arranged in four main gardens: the Garden of the Promised Land, the Garden of Moses, the Garden

He Got the Benz

The stonecutters at Rock of Ages in Barre, Vermont, are used to unusual requests: They've carved granite headstones shaped like a soccer ball, an easy chair, and even a soldier's wife appearing in a puff of cigarette smoke. But the request to carve a full-size 1982 Mercedes-Benz was definitely among the more unusual.

It's a memorial for Ray Tse Jr., a Chinese boy who died at the age of 15, before he could receive his driver's license. Commissioned by his brother, the 36-ton monument took three Rock of Ages workers a year and a half to complete.

Ray's Mercedes is in the Asian section (the northern end) of the Rosedale and Rosehill Cemetery, 335 E. Linden Ave., Linden. The cemetery is open from 9 a.m. to 6 p.m.

of Jerusalem (Garden of Peace), and the Garden of the Kings. Each individual specimen is identified by its Hebrew, English, and Linnean names.

In order to bring an added note of authenticity and significance to the biblical plantings, the garden's designers have incorporated boulders from Mount Canaan, Elath, and the River Jordan; stones from Aijalon, Galilee, and Mount Zion; and numerous other physical reminders of the land where the Scriptures were written. Artworks of marble, bronze, and wrought iron are tastefully integrated into the gardens. The gardens, on Route 1 (near the Garden State Parkway), Woodbridge, (732) 634-2100, are open daily during daylight hours. Admission is free.

Places to Stay in the Urban Northeast

Grand Summit Hotel
570 Springfield Ave. East,
Summit
(908) 273-3000
www.grandsummit.com
Expensive

Hilton Hasbrouck Heights/Meadowlands
650 Terrace Ave.,
Hasbrouck Heights
(800) HILTONS or (201) 288-6100
www.hilton.com
Moderate–expensive

Hilton Woodcliff Lake
200 Tice Blvd., Woodcliff Lake
(800) HILTONS or (201) 391-3600
www.hilton.com
Expensive

Marriott Courtyard Jersey City
540 Washington Blvd.,
Jersey City
(201) 626-6600
www.marriott.com
Expensive

The Pillars of Plainfield B&B Inn
922 Central Ave., Plainfield
(908) 753-0922 or (888) PILLARS
www.pillars2.com
Moderate–expensive

Robert Treat Hotel
50 Park Place, Newark
(973) 622-1000 or (800)780-7234
www.rthotel.com
Moderate–expensive

Sheraton Lincoln Harbor Hotel
500 Harbor Blvd.,
Weehawken
(201) 617-5600
https://sheraton.marriott.com
Expensive

Places to Eat in the Urban Northeast

Amarone's
63 Cedar Lane, Teaneck
(201) 833-1897
A vast traditional Italian menu, from clams oreganata, to penne with artichoke heats and olives, to pork osso buco. Extensive wine list features five—of course—Amarones. Lunch and dinner Mon through Fri noon to 9:30 p.m.; dinner Sat 5 to 9:30 p.m. and Sun 3 to 9 p.m. Inexpensive–expensive.

The Cuban
333 Washington St.,
Hoboken
(201) 795-9899
Authentic Cuban cuisine, with favorites such as ropa vieja, churrasco (grilled skirt steak with chimichurri and yuca fries), and paella.

Cuban brunch weekends. Open Mon through Thurs 3 to 10 p.m., Fri 3 to 11 p.m., Sat noon to 11 p.m., Sun noon to 10 p.m. Moderate.

Da Pepo
54 Fairfield St., Montclair
(973) 655-8825
Traditional southern Italian cuisine in a chef-owned, 19-seat trattoria includes spaghettoni carbonara made with guanciale, orrechietta with sausage and broccoli rabe, and an assortment of panini. Lunch Mon through Sat noon to 3:30 p.m.; dinner Mon through Sat 5 to 8:30 p.m. Inexpensive–moderate.

Dino & Harry's
163 14th St., Hoboken
(201) 659-6202
Terrific steaks and chops in a traditional steak house atmosphere. Dinner nightly. Expensive.

El Artesano
4101 Bergenline Ave., Union City
(201) 867-7341
An unpretentious little spot with a long red counter as well as table seating, and some of the area's finest traditional Cuban fare, including pan-fried shredded beef and grilled red snapper filet. Breakfast, lunch, and dinner daily. Inexpensive–moderate.

Highlawn Pavilion
1 Crest Dr. (Eagle Rock Reservation), West Orange
(973) 731-3463
American cuisine with a European flair is the specialty at this restaurant housed in a 1909 Florentine-style building overlooking Manhattan. Many dishes are prepared on the French rotisserie or in the wood-burning Italian brick oven. Jackets required in dining room. Pizza and focaccia are on the menu in the piano bar. Lunch and dinner Tues through Sun. Expensive.

Ho-Ho-Kus Inn
1 East Franklin Turnpike, Ho-Ho-Kus
(201) 445-4115
Built in 1796 and turned into a tavern a century later. Traditional menu features modern touches such as crab spring rolls, lobster pappardelle, and braised short ribs with mission figs. Lunch and dinner Wed through Sat 11:30 a.m. to 10 p.m., Sun 11 a.m. to 9 p.m. Moderate–expensive.

Kitchen Step
500 Jersey Ave., Jersey City
(201) 721-6115
A neighborhood bistro featuring New American cuisine, including hanger steak, baked buttermilk chicken, and ricotta gnocchi. Small plates available. Indoor or outdoor patio dining. Open for dinner Tues through Sun;

Sat and Sun brunch. Moderate–expensive.

Liberty Prime Steakhouse
111 Montgomery St., Jersey City
(201) 333-3633
With the panache of a New York steak house that crossed the river to Jersey City's Gold Coast, Liberty serves up prime cuts including dry-aged porterhouse, double rib, and tomahawk steaks. There's a raw bar and starters such as crab cake and steak tartare. Lunch and dinner Sun through Thurs noon to 10 p.m., Fri and Sat noon to 11 p.m. Expensive.

Mina's on the Mountain
140 Rifle Camp Rd., Woodland Park
(973) 279-7400
A picturesque spot on the shoulder of Garrett Mountain is the setting for fine northern Italian cuisine. Outdoor seating; live entertainment Wed and Sat evenings. Dinner nightly. Moderate.

Raymond's
28 Church St., Montclair
(973) 744-9263
A classic American menu with a touch of the international includes everything from turkey meat loaf and fish-and-chips to quinoa-crusted salmon and rigatoni Bolognese. Breakfast and lunch Mon through Fri, dinner nightly; Sat and Sun brunch. Inexpensive–moderate.

Saddle River Inn
2 Barnstable Ct., Saddle River
(201) 825-4016
One of northern New Jersey's most elegant suburban eateries specializes in dry-aged steaks, including a spectacular Wagyu tomahawk; also chops, duck, and wild-caught seafood. Dinner Tues through Sat 5 to 9:30 p.m. Expensive.

Sagres Bar and Grill
44-50 Prospect St., Newark
(973) 589-4070
Traditional Portuguese fare such as shrimp in garlic sauce and *carne de porco a Alentejana* (brazed pork cubes with clams), grilled steak, and seafood. Dinner nightly. Live music begins at 9 p.m. Mon through Thurs. Outdoor seating. Moderate.

Samba Montclair
7 Park St., Montclair
(973) 744-6764
A homey Brazilian atmosphere sets the tone for a menu crafted around Brazil's traditional cuisine, including *feijoada*, a hearty pork and black bean stew. Lunch Mon through Fri, dinner nightly; Sat and Sun brunch. Moderate–expensive.

So Moon Nan Jip
238 Broad Ave., Palisades Park
(201) 944-3998
Do-it-yourself cooking is elevated to an art at this authentic Korean barbecue. Waiters deliver pans of charcoal to the table and customers grill their selections. The tiny bowls filled with condiments range from the cooling to the excruciatingly hot. Try the seafood pancake. Dinner nightly. Moderate.

Other Attractions in the Urban Northeast

Boxwood Hall State Historic Site
1073 E. Jersey St., Elizabeth
(908) 282-7617

Dr. William Robinson Plantation
593 Madison Hill Rd., Clark
(732) 340-1571

East Brunswick Museum
16 Maple St., East Brunswick
(732) 257-1508

Edison National Historical Park
211 Main St., West Orange
(973) 736-0550

SELECTED REGIONAL INFORMATION CENTERS, CHAMBERS OF COMMERCE & VISITOR CENTERS IN THE URBAN NORTHEAST

Gateway Tourism Council
PO Box 2011
Bayonne 07002
(201) 436-6009 or (877) 428-3930

North Jersey Chamber of Commerce
27 Horseneck Rd.
Fairfield 07004
(973) 470-9300

Hudson County Chamber of Commerce
185 Hudson St.
Jersey City 07306
(201) 386-0699
www.hudsonchamber.org

Passaic County Cultural & Heritage Council
1 College Blvd.
Paterson 07505
(973) 684-5444

Fort Lee Historic Park
Hudson Terrace, Fort Lee
(201) 461-1776

**Grover Cleveland
Birthplace**
207 Bloomfield Ave.,
Caldwell
(973) 226-0001

**Historic New Bridge
Landing Park**
1201 Main St., River Edge
(201) 343-9492

Liberty Science Center
Liberty State Park, 222
Jersey City Blvd., Jersey
City
(201) 200-1000

**Long Pond Ironworks
State Park**
West Milford
(973) 962-7031

Newark Museum
49 Washington St., Newark
(973) 596-6550

**Thomas A. Edison
Memorial Tower and
Museum**
Christie Street and Route
27, Edison
(732) 549-3299

Northern New Jersey & the Upper Delaware Valley

Not too long ago it was fair to state simply that the northwestern corner of New Jersey offered a marked contrast to the heavily urbanized communities to the east. Here were dairy farms, upland pastures, dense forests, and tucked-away lakes; between one small town and another, there was only a strip of two-lane blacktop and maybe an old-fashioned roadhouse with a pair of antlers over the bar.

Now things have gotten a little more complicated, and this part of New Jersey contrasts as sharply with itself as it does with any other portion of the state. The past 30 years have seen a substantial amount of suburbanization in Sussex and northern Warren Counties, and it's no longer unusual for someone to live out past Lake Hopatcong or up near Sparta and commute to a job in New York City. Dairy farmers have sold out by the score (the actual number of farms is up in Sussex, but acreage is down—the result of smaller specialty operations that replaced dairying), and developers have moved in, building houses and shopping centers where milk cows once grazed.

But development tends to cluster along the major highways of northwestern New Jersey, and it still isn't hard to find a back road that will take you into a landscape more typical

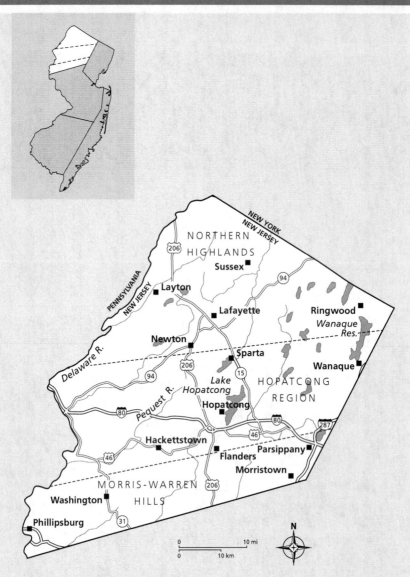

NEW YORK
NEW JERSEY

NORTHERN
HIGHLANDS

206

Sussex

94

Layton

Lafayette

PENNSYLVANIA
NEW JERSEY

Ringwood

Wanaque
Res.

Newton

Delaware R.

Sparta

206

15

Wanaque

94

Lake
Hopatcong

HOPATCONG
REGION

Pequest R.

Hopatcong

80

80

287

46

Hackettstown

46

Flanders

Parsippany

Morristown

MORRIS-WARREN

206

HILLS

Washington

Phillipsburg

31

0   10 mi
0   10 km

N

of the rural stretches of neighboring New York State and Pennsylvania. There are still lovely country vistas along the Delaware River, from Phillipsburg north to High Point, and the most beautiful part of the upper Delaware Valley has wisely been preserved as the Delaware Water Gap National Recreation Area— a wonderful place for hiking (the Appalachian Trail parallels the river on the Jersey side) and canoeing. So don't write off Sussex and environs just yet—it's a safe bet that there will still be plenty of open spaces to enjoy hereabouts for quite some time to come.

   Note: This region is divided into three sections: the Northern Highlands, the Hopatcong Region, and the Morris-Warren Hills.

Northern Highlands

Hard upon the Delaware River, just north of the point where I-80 crosses into Pennsylvania, is a community devoted entirely to the perpetuation and teaching of fine craft. The ***Peters Valley School of Craft*** is a cluster of 22 buildings, 13 of which are on the National Historic Register, but its importance to artisans throughout America far outweighs its size. One of only three dozen such communities in the country, Peters Valley offers up to 150 intensive courses—with live-in accommodations—in blacksmithing, ceramics, fiber (basketry, paper and book arts, and surface design), fine metals, photography, weaving, and woodworking. Courses range from two to five days, with basic to advanced instruction in eight professional craft studios.

NORTHERN NEW JERSEY & THE UPPER DELAWARE VALLEY'S TOP PICKS

Peters Valley School of Craft	Four Sisters Winery at Matarazzo Farms
Paulinskill Valley Trail	Well-Sweep Herb Farm
Franklin Mineral Museum, Inc.	Fosterfields Living Historical Farm
Stokes State Forest	Frelinghuysen Arboretum
Space Farms Zoo and Museum	Historic Speedwell
Ringwood Manor	Stickley Museum at Craftsman Farms
Skylands Botanical Garden	Lakota Wolf Preserve
Pyramid Mountain Natural Historic Area	

You don't have to be interested in actually learning a craft to come to **Peters Valley Craft Store and Gallery**—simple appreciation will do. Every Sat and Sun from late May through mid-Sept, the studios are open between 2 and 5 p.m. so that visitors can watch resident craftspeople work and ask them questions. Evening slide lectures/presentations are held throughout the summer by workshop faculty and are open to the public free of charge. In addition, Peters Valley is well stocked with the work of more than 300 American craftspeople, including the residents, and features changing displays and exhibits. Their annual Craft Fair, held the last weekend in Sept at the Sussex County Fairgrounds in Augusta, hosts more than 185 juried exhibitors, live music, food, and craft demonstrations.

Peters Valley School of Craft is on Route 615, south of Layton (mailing address: 19 Kuhn Rd., Layton 07851), (973) 948-5200, www.petersvalley.org. The store and gallery are open daily from 10 a.m. to 5 p.m., with extended hours in Nov and Dec. Tuesday afternoons at 1 p.m. during the workshop season, there's a lively auction of crafts made by students and instructors.

"We feed the deer and people, too" is the motto of the folks at the **Walpack Inn**. They've been doing both since 1949. The deer come to within 20 feet of the restaurant to feed, and because the restaurant is a giant greenhouse (hundreds of plants are suspended from the ceiling), there are plenty of windows from which to watch the animals and enjoy views of the Kittatinny Ridge. The Friday night prime rib ($34 per person), served with a salad from the restaurant's huge salad bar and homemade brown bread, is a house specialty, and on Friday from 4 to 6 p.m., oysters on the half shell are $1.50 each.

Even Some New Jerseyans Don't Know That . . .

- New Jersey is the only state in which every county is classified as a metropolitan area.

- New Jersey has more racehorses than Kentucky.

- New Jersey has the most densely concentrated system of highways and railroads in the United States.

- Northern New Jersey has seven major shopping malls in a 25-square-mile area, the densest concentration of malls in the world.

- Union, New Jersey, boasts the world's tallest water tower.

The Walpack Inn, on Route 615, Walpack Center, (973) 948-3890, www .walpackinn.com, is open all year, Fri and Sat from 4 to 9 p.m. and Sun from 2 to 7 p.m. There's live piano music on Sat and Sun evenings.

When one of Canadian Joseph-Armand Bombardier's children died when he couldn't be transported through a blizzard to a hospital after an attack of peritonitis, he intensified his earlier efforts to develop vehicles that could travel on snow. In 1936 he sold his first Ski-Doo, and thus was born the snowmobile industry. Dan Klemm is a great fan of snowmobiles. In fact, he has the world's largest collection of snowmobiles and related memorabilia, and his museum exhibits more than 300 of his antique and vintage sleds, which span more than 90 years of the industry's history. The **Snowmobile Barn Museum**, housed in two 6,000-square-foot barns, is on his farm, and visitors with kids will be delighted to discover that they're invited to visit the barnyard and feed some of the animals. The museum, at 928 Cedar Ridge Rd. in Fredon, is open by appointment. Call (973) 383-1708 between 8:30 a.m. and 4 p.m. for information.

Enjoy a leisurely stroll through the 23,000-square-foot **Lafayette Mill Antiques Center**, an 1850s gristmill that houses the wares of more than 55 dealers. Just off Route 15 at 12 Morris Farm Rd. in Lafayette, (973) 383-0065, www.millantiques.com, the center is open Thurs through Sun from 10 a.m. to 5 p.m. The Millside Cafe at the center serves breakfast and lunch.

At **Abbey Glen Pet Memorial Park**, 187 Route 94 South, Lafayette, (800) 972-3118, Saint Francis of Assisi, patron saint of animals, watches over the "Hillside Burial" area. A special section of the 14-acre park is reserved for seeing-eye and therapy dogs, police canines and horses, and other animals that have dedicated their lives to public service. In the "Country Burial" area, pets' names are inscribed on a Gift of Love Plaque. The park is an inspiration to all animal lovers.

As the 26-mile **Paulinskill Valley Trail**, paralleling the Paulinskill River, winds through farm fields, rolling hills, woods, and swamps, it passes by nearly one-quarter of New Jersey's plant species and offers spectacular views of the rural northwestern countryside. Once the bed for the New York, Susquehanna & Western Railroad, this rail-trail passes by several old railroad-era buildings and still has whistle posts, mileage markers, and other railway relics. At milepost 89 (you're 89 miles from Jersey City), there's a great view of the Hainesburg Viaduct, considered the eighth wonder of the world when it was completed in 1911. The trail endpoints are Brugler Road near Columbia and Sparta Junction. For information contact the Park Superintendent, Kittatinny Valley State Park, PO Box 621, Andover 07821; (973) 786-6445.

It seems only fitting that getting to the state's last remaining glacial lake should require some effort. But knowing your effort is not going to go unrewarded counts for a lot. The 41-acre, spring-fed **Sunfish Pond**, a designated National Natural Landmark, lies in a chestnut-oak forest high in the Kittatinny Mountains. It's a popular spot for hikers as well as migratory waterfowl and raptors.

Several steep and rocky paths lead to Sunfish Pond (called "Hidden Lake" by Native Americans). The trailhead for one of the most popular, the Appalachian Trail, begins at a parking lot just off I-80 (exit at the rest area/parking area for Dunnfield Creek). The 3¾-mile hike to the top passes through a hemlock forest and Dunnfield Creek Natural Area and then climbs to the pond.

For information on Sunfish Pond Natural Area, contact Worthington State Forest, HC 62, Box 2, Columbia 07832; (908) 841-9575; www.stateparks.com/worthington.html.

Hiking the Trail

Seventy miles of the Appalachian Trail, which stretches from Maine to Georgia, run through New Jersey. On the north the trail enters the state at Greenwood Lake, then follows the New York–New Jersey border west along the Kittatinny Ridge and continues to the Delaware Water Gap. Three-sided shelters and campsites are located at 8- to 12-mile intervals, at High Point State Park, Stokes State Forest, and Wawayanda State Park. Backpackers will find campsites at Worthington State Forest. Camping is allowed at the Delaware Water Gap National Recreation Area. For information contact them at 1978 River Rd., Bushkill, PA 18324; (570) 426-2452; www.nps.gov/dewa.

We Called Him Uncle Guy

Probably no one in the Upper Greenwood Lake area, near the border of Passaic and Sussex Counties, remembers a remarkably ingenious storekeeper named Guy Futrell. Arkansas-born, a onetime cowboy, and a chief petty officer in the US Navy during World War I, Futrell came to Upper Greenwood Lake in the 1920s and built the first gas station in that then-wild region. His station, and the store he ran with his wife, Josephine, had Upper Greenwood Lake's first electric lights, run off a generator he built himself out of an old Model T. There was little Guy Futrell couldn't do, using his hands and his wits. In later life, he decided he'd like to make a violin. He read everything he could on the subject, then took a month just to fashion the necessary tools. Three months after that, he had two violins judged tonally near-perfect by a New York appraiser—a man who found it hard to believe that Futrell couldn't read a note of music.

—William Guy Scheller Jr.

New Jersey's last operating zinc mine is now a National Historic Site. **Sterling Hill Mining Museum** has more than 30 acres of exhibits, displays, and historical buildings. Those persons not suffering from claustrophobia will enjoy the underground mine tour, which winds through ⅓ mile of tunnel and passes by a spectacular mineral fluorescence display.

The mine is at 30 Plant St., Ogdensburg, (973) 209-7212, www.sterling-hillminingmuseum.org. The gift shop is open daily from 10 a.m. to 3 p.m. The tour (guided only) schedule varies by the season; call or check the website for details. Tour admission is $14 for adults, $13 for seniors, and $11 for children 4 to 12 (not recommended for children under 6). The Mine Run Dump collection area is open to visitors from 10 a.m. to 3 p.m. on days when the museum is open for tours. Rock collecting on the Mine Run Dump is recommended for those 18 and over. Sluicing is recommended for children, but is not an option in winter. Bring a jacket or sweater and good walking shoes. Call ahead to make sure the mine is open, and check the website for special events.

There's a lot more than zinc in the North Jersey hills. The Franklin-Ogdensburg area of eastern Sussex County has yielded a greater number of species and varieties of minerals than any other location in the world—at last count, more than 340 species and 360 varieties. The Franklin minerals—the discovery of which was largely associated with nearly three centuries of zinc-mining operations that ended in 1954—are on exhibit at the **Franklin Mineral Museum**. Franklin's rich mineral deposits are the result of a complex series of geological events that date back a billion years and were never duplicated elsewhere; hence the occurrence in local ore deposits not only of such an incredible diversity of minerals but of 30 types discovered nowhere else on Earth. For the layperson, perhaps the most interesting facet of the museum's display is the collection of fluorescent minerals—the world's largest—exhibited under ultraviolet light, which brings out their color and luminosity.

The mineral museum also includes a replica of the interior of a zinc mine, realistic to the last detail because it is made up of actual equipment used in the operations of the New Jersey Zinc Company in the days of active mining in the area. Under conditions such as those replicated here, miners discovered many of the rare and beautiful specimens on exhibit in the museum. Visitors can collect mineral specimens on the mine waste pile, adjacent to the museum, and test them for fluorescence. The Welsh Mall exhibits more than 5,000 mineral specimens from around the world. Other exhibits include American Indian relics and fossils.

The Franklin Mineral Museum, 32 Evans St. (off Route 23), Franklin, (973) 827-3481, www.franklinmineralmuseum.org, is open Apr through Nov, Wed through Fri 11 a.m. to 4 p.m., Sat 10 a.m. to 5 p.m., and Sun 11 a.m. to 5 p.m. Admission to the museum is $15 for adults, $12 for children ages 3 to 16, and $14 for seniors and veterans. Guided tours are offered hourly (although visitors can view exhibits without a tour guide). The fee for rock collecting only is $12 for adults, $10 for children, and $11 for seniors and veterans. A combination tour and collecting ticket costs $20 for adults, $15 for children, and $18 for seniors and veterans. There is also a fee per pound for specimens collected.

Stokes State Forest, which runs along 12 miles of the Kittatinny Mountain Ridge, offers some excellent hiking opportunities, including a 12½-mile section of the Appalachian Trail. For a particular treat, head over to the southwestern portion and hike to the "teacup" near the bottom of Tillman Ravine. The large pothole carved into rock at the bottom of the falls is a great place to kick back,

They're Probably Telling It Still

How many readers who were Boy Scouts in North Jersey during the 1960s remember the story of the H-Man? Told and retold around the tents and campfires of now-defunct Camp Altaha, on Fairview Lake in Sussex County, this tale was about a guy who lived way out in the woods and had to travel a lot on business. To protect his family from intruders, he had iron bars installed on his windows. One night, he arrived home to find the house in flames, and his family trapped inside. He pressed up against the window bars, screaming, while a big red *H* was seared onto his chest. Of course he went mad, and he ROAMS THESE VERY WOODS . . .

Lights out, boys.

TOP ANNUAL EVENTS IN NORTHERN NEW JERSEY & THE UPPER DELAWARE VALLEY

Note: Schedules may vary; call ahead.

Spring Encampment at Jockey Hollow, Morristown National Historic Park, Morristown; Apr; (973) 539-2016; www.nps.gov/morr

Horses, History, Swords & Archery, High Point Equestrian Center, Montague; June; (973) 293-0033; www .highpointequestriancenter.com

New Jersey Lottery Festival of Ballooning, Solberg Airport, Readington; July; (973) 882-5464; www .balloonfestival.com

Waterloo Canal Heritage Days, Waterloo; July–Oct; (973) 292-2755; www.canalsocietynj.org

Warren County Farmers' Fair, Oxford; Aug; (908) 859-6563; www .warrencountyfarmersfair.org

New Jersey State Fair, Met Life Stadium, East Rutherford; Aug; (201) 355-5911; www.njfair.com

Grand Harvest Wine Festival, Fosterfields, Morristown; Oct; (609) 588-0085; www.newjerseywineevents.com

Fall Wine and Music Festival, Four Sisters Winery, Belvidere; Oct; (908) 475-3671; www.foursisterswinery.com

Ringwood State Park Harvest Fest, Ringwood; Oct; (973) 962-9534; www .njbg.org

soak your weary feet, and listen to the falling waters. The forest is 5 miles north of Branchville on US 206; (973) 948-3820. The park office is open daily from 9 a.m. until 4 p.m. The entrance fee is $10 for New Jersey residents, $20 nonresident on weekends and holidays; free on weekdays; no fee after Labor Day to Memorial Day weekend.

As motoring families began to fan out along the nation's byways in the early years of the automotive age, an institution known as the "roadside attraction" came into existence. These attractions often took the form of small, randomly assembled zoos, many of which could still be found in the rural and suburban back roads of New Jersey as recently as 25 or 30 years ago. The vast majority of the roadside zoos fell victim to either development pressures or concern over the unprofessional way in which they were operated, but, fortunately, the best of the lot in New Jersey has continued to thrive: ***Space Farms Zoo and Museum***, in Sussex, has operated for more than 75 years on a policy of clean surroundings, good care for animals, and public education.

Founded in 1927 by Ralph Space, Space Farms Zoo and Museum has grown under three successive generations of the Space family to comprise a 425-acre integrated operation housing more than 500 animals of over 100 species. The zoo and museum cover 100 acres, and nearly all the remainder is used to grow food for the zoo's hoofed animals and other herbivores. Of the land actually occupied by the zoo, as much as possible is maintained in natural-habitat condition.

Not that New Jersey is the natural habitat of all the creatures at Space Farms Zoo. There are, of course, white-tailed deer, foxes, raccoons, bobcats, black bears (several thousand are believed to roam wild in the state), snakes, and waterfowl indigenous to the area, but the Space collection also includes species such as lion, tiger, llama, yak, elk, jaguar, leopard, monkey, coatimundi, wolf, coyote, and mountain sheep.

An interesting adjunct to the zoo itself is the Space Farms museum complex, which houses an eclectic assortment of more than 50,000 items, including antique cars, motorcycles, dolls, Native American artifacts, and the country's second-largest privately owned collection of antique firearms.

Space Farms Zoo and Museum, Beemerville Road (Route 519), (973) 875-5800, is open daily late Mar through mid-Nov from 9 a.m. to 5 p.m. (last entrance at 4 p.m.). Admission is $22 for people ages 13 to 64, $18 for children ages 3 to 12, and $21 for those 65 and older; free for children under 3.

If present-day cities such as Paterson and Hackensack were little more than villages surrounded by farmland in the late 18th century, we can well imagine the circumstances that prevailed in those days in the remote corners of Sussex County—and the hardiness of an individual such as the Reverend Elias Van Bunschooten, who was sent in 1785 by the New Jersey Synod of the Dutch Reformed Church to minister to the area's faithful. The Reverend Van Bunschooten built his Wantage Township Dutch Colonial home in 1787 and lived there until his death in 1815.

The *Elias Van Bunschooten Museum*, now on 6½ acres and overseen by the local chapter of the Daughters of the American Revolution, includes a barn, icehouse, privy, wagon house, and the original home, which contains furnishings and other artifacts characteristic not only of the minister's era but of that of later owners, the Cooper family, throughout the 19th century. Especially interesting is the contrast between the 1787 bedroom furnishings and the far more ponderous articles of 1860, exhibited in an adjacent room. Most important to the modern visitor, though, is the sense of perspective on time and distance that a place like this has to offer: same house, same location; 200 years ago an arduous trek from the Old Dutch towns along the Hudson, today a short scoot up Route 23.

The Elias Van Bunschooten Museum, 1097 Route 23, Sussex, (973) 875-7634, www.vanbunschootenmuseum.com, is open May 15 through Oct 15 or by appointment, second and fourth Sun of the month, from 1 to 4 p.m. Call for admission fees.

High Point State Park occupies more than 14,000 acres that touch the New York State border almost at the northernmost tip of New Jersey and also contains the state's highest peak, 1,803-foot High Point. High Point State Park represents a classic case of collaboration between private and public interests for the preservation of an outstanding natural area. Although the land that the park now occupies was part of a royal grant as far back as 1715, its remoteness ensured that it would remain pristine throughout the following two centuries. The only construction of note was an exclusive resort, the High Point Inn, built in 1888 near the shore of Lake Marcia, which was remodeled into the present structure by the Kuser family of Bernardsville, New Jersey. In 1922 Colonel Anthony Kuser made a gift of some 10,000 acres—the bulk of the modern park—to the State of New Jersey.

A multiuse park, High Point is managed with an eye toward balancing backcountry preservation with the provision of ample recreational facilities. The northernmost part of the park is the 800-acre John D. Kuser Natural Area, much of which is old-growth Atlantic white cedar swamp. Just south of the natural area is the summit of High Point itself, topped with a 240-foot obelisk that affords terrific views of the Delaware Valley, the Catskill and Pocono

When Sussex County Was the Wild Frontier

Swartswood Lake, the lovely centerpiece of a state park just west of Newton, owes its name to an early Sussex County settler who died in what was likely one of New Jersey's last Indian attacks. Captain Anthony Swartwout was a British officer who had served in the French and Indian War, and who in 1756 was living with his family at a homestead near the lake. In that year a party of 13 Indians, wartime enemies of Swartwout, raided his property and killed his wife. The captain shot several of the attackers but was soon captured, whereupon he was carted off and disemboweled by the Indians.

Mountains, and the lakes and forests of the park itself. (The monument, also a gift of the Kuser family, was completed in 1930.) Dryden Kuser Natural Area's white cedar swamp is the highest-elevation swamp of its type in the world; a self-guided tour brochure is available.

There are three public-access lakes within the boundaries of High Point State Park: Twenty-acre Lake Marcia, at 1,600 feet the highest lake in New Jersey, has a supervised bathing beach; Lake Steenykill, west of Marcia, has a boat-launching ramp and two furnished cabins, which may be rented by family groups between May 15 and Oct 15; Sawmill Lake, near the center of the park, also has boat-launch facilities (only electric motors are permitted on the state park's lakes) as well as 50 campsites.

Hiking is one of the prime attractions at High Point State Park. The Maine-to-Georgia Appalachian Trail runs north and south through the length of the park (look for white blazes) and is intersected by a system of nine park trails, varying in length from ½ to 4 miles. Each trail is identified by blazes or markers of a different color, and relative difficulty is noted in a trail guide, available at the park office.

High Point State Park, 1480 Route 23, Sussex, (973) 875-4800, is open daily from 8 a.m. to 4:30 p.m. throughout the year. Park entrance fees of $5 weekdays ($10 non-NJ residents) and $10 ($20 nonresident) weekends and holidays are charged from Memorial Day weekend through Labor Day; there is no entrance fee the rest of the year.

Located in northern New Jersey's scenic Skylands region, **Fox & Bear Lodge** occupies an 1831 mansion with wraparound porches ideal for taking in the views of the Pochuck Valley. Eight handsome guest rooms, all with private bath, have been restored to reflect the home's historic character. Hiking trails, including the Appalachian Trail, are close at hand—which makes Fox & Bear's dog-friendly policy especially attractive. The inn is at 967 McAfee Rd., Glenwood, (917) 267-8184, www.foxandbearlodge.com. Rates are $185 to $225 per night, including full breakfast.

At **Wawayanda State Park** there are 1,300 acres to explore by canoe, on mountain bike, or on foot (20 miles of the Appalachian Trail are within park limits). You can rent a canoe ($14 an hour or $59 a day; call 973-764-1030 for information) for a paddle around 255-acre Wawayanda Lake; throw in a line to fish for trout, bass, pickerel, and perch; or just explore the lake and its islands. Keep an eye out for endangered red-shouldered hawks if you opt for a hike to the top of Wawayanda Mountain for spectacular views of the surrounding mountains. The park, at 885 Warwick Turnpike in Hewitt, (973) 853-4462, is open daily from 8 a.m. to 8 p.m. Park entrance fees of $5 weekdays ($10 non-NJ residents) and $10 ($20 nonresident) weekends and holidays are charged from Memorial Day weekend through Labor Day; there is no entrance fee the rest of the year. During summer lifeguards are on duty at the beach, which is open from 10 a.m. to 6 p.m.

Up along the New York State border, at the northern tip of Passaic County, is a state park rich in historical associations. **Ringwood Manor**, the focal point of **Ringwood State Park**, was established in 1740 and produced munitions for every major armed conflict from the French and Indian War to World War I. The Ringwood iron mines operated intermittently from the 1920s until 1957.

The present structures at Ringwood Manor reflect the period from 1854 to 1936, when the Hewitt family, who operated the mines under the auspices of Cooper Hewitt and Company, used the manor and its 33,000 surrounding acres as their country estate. The manor houses an excellent collection of furnishings, Hudson River School paintings, and prints and lithographs that reflect the tastes of patriarch Abram S. Hewitt and his family. In planning the gardens at the manor, Hewitt was inspired by the classical designs used for the grounds of the Palace of Versailles. Hewitt's son, Erskine, donated Ringwood Manor to the state in 1936. In front of the manor are 26 links of the chain forged to keep the British from ascending the Hudson beyond West Point during the Revolution.

A visit to Ringwood Manor is only part of the attraction of a visit to Ringwood State Park. The house is a fine place from which to head out onto a well-developed system of hiking and cross-country ski trails, some making a short loop on the immediate grounds and others heading northwest for a considerable distance into **Abram S. Hewitt State Forest**. (Detailed trail maps are available at the park office, in the manor.)

One recommended route takes you across the Ringwood River and Sloatsburg Road to Shepherd Lake (1½ miles), a nice place for swimming, fishing, and boating. It then extends another ⁸⁄₁₀ mile to **Skylands Botanical Garden**, also part of Ringwood State Park and formally called the New Jersey Botanical Garden at Skylands.

Skylands was sold in 1922 to Clarence McKenzie Lewis, an investment banker and trustee of the New York Botanical Garden. Determined to make Skylands a botanical showplace, he tore down an existing house and replaced it with a 44-room Tudor mansion (built of native granite), which features interior fixtures and architectural details

. . . andtheworld hasneverbeen thesame

The late Les Paul invented the solid-body electric guitar in Mahwah in 1940.

imported from European châteaus and stately homes, as well as a fireplace piazza and an enormous room used only for arranging cut flowers. He hired the most prominent landscape architects of his day to design the gardens and, for 30 years, collected plants from all over the world and from New Jersey roadsides. The result is one of the finest collections of plants in the state. In March 1984, Governor Thomas Kean designated the 96 acres that surround the manor house as New Jersey's official botanical garden.

Ringwood State Park, 1304 Sloatsburg Rd., off Route 511, Ringwood, (973) 962-7031, is open daily all year from 8 a.m. to 8 p.m. Admission to the grounds is free. An entrance fee of $5 per vehicle ($7 for non-NJ residents) is charged on weekends from Memorial Day weekend to Labor Day to enter the grounds of Ringwood Manor. Tours are offered year-round, Wed through Sun from 10 a.m. to 3 p.m. There is also a $5 vehicle fee on weekends from Memorial Day to Labor Day to enter the grounds of Skylands Manor; the grounds are open daily from 8 a.m. to 8 p.m. Tours ($10 for adults, $7 for seniors 65 and over and children ages 6 to 18) are offered on selected Sundays, Mar through Nov (check the schedule at www.njbg.org).

"In our turbulent world so full of cross-currents, we have found a tiny haven; a place to give a demonstration of how life begins, continues, and, with the wonderful interaction developed eons of years ago, re-creates itself and goes on in peace and beauty." Thus May Weis described the 160-acre parcel of land in Ringwood that she and her husband, Walter, purchased in 1974 for the enjoyment of all. The **Weis Ecology Center** is a wonderful place to stroll or hike, observe nature, and learn about the northern New Jersey Highlands regions.

The New Jersey Audubon Society's Weis Ecology Center, 150 Snake Den Rd., Ringwood, (973) 835-2160, www.highlandsnaturefriends.org, is open daily year-round from 9 a.m. until dusk. Special programs (admission charge) are held on weekends.

Hopatcong Region

The **Whistling Swan Inn**, a 1905 Victorian B&B in Stanhope, is "for those with more refined nesting instincts." Each of the nine rooms and suites is furnished in a theme: Among them are an art deco room, an Oriental antiques room, a White Iron room, and a 1940s Swing room. All the rooms have private baths—one with two claw-foot tubs in it. Rates, from $125 to $289, include a full buffet-style breakfast. The inn is at 110 Main St., Stanhope, (973) 347-6369, www.whistlingswaninn.com.

Waiters and waitresses in Tyrolean costumes serve up German specialties as well as continental fare at the **Black Forest Inn**. Portions tend to be large, the ambience Teutonic, and customers dress up to come to this multiroomed

You Must Be Hooked on a Log—Your Rod's Practically Bent Double

If you're looking to catch a really big fish in New Jersey, you don't have to head for salt water. Muskellunge, the largest and feistiest members of the pike family, have been successfully established in Lake Hopatcong over the past few years, and muskies measuring more than 40 inches with a weight in excess of 20 pounds have been caught in the big lake bordered by Morris and Sussex Counties. Hopatcong muskies must be at least 36 inches long to be legal, but anglers are encouraged to release the fish no matter what their size so that the species will continue to establish its "finhold" in the lake.

roadside inn at 249 Route 206, Stanhope, (973) 347-3344, www.sweetbeezee .com. Sausage dishes abound, of course, or choose from entrées ($24.95 to $38.95) such as weinerschnitzel, beef rouladen, sauerbraten, roast pork shank, or beef stroganoff. House-made desserts include rich German *torten*. The inn is open Wed through Fri 4 to 9 p.m., Sat 1 to 9:30 p.m., and Sun 2 to 8 p.m.

Fresh local ingredients—including produce from their own farm—and an astounding 50-tap selection of draft beers make **Mohawk House** a Sparta favorite. Start at the raw bar, then move on to an impressive array of dry-aged steaks, including tomahawks and porterhouses for two, from the on-premises butcher shop. Entrées range from $36 to $64. Mohawk House is at 1 Mohawk Ln., (973) 729-6464, and is open daily for lunch and dinner from noon to 9 p.m.

The Wooden Duck B&B, right across from Kittatinny Valley State Park, offers privacy, comfortable accommodations, and, in the morning, lots of home-baked goodies. Set on 17 acres of open fields and woodlands, the inn has central air-conditioning, a double hearth fireplace, game room, and swimming pool. Each of the nine rooms and the suite has a queen-size bed, private bath, phone, TV, Wi-Fi, and writing desk. Those wishing ultimate privacy should request a room in the Horseless Carriage House. The inn is at 140 Goodale Rd., Newton, (973) 300-0395, www.woodenduckinn.com. Rates for a standard double range from $144 to $259 and include a full breakfast.

Arctic, tundra, and timber wolves make their home at the **Lakota Wolf Preserve**. Visitors view the wolves from an observation center in the middle of the preserve and learn all about them: the structure of their packs, their eating habits, and how they relate to man. Foxes, bobcats, and lynx also live at the preserve.

The Lakota Wolf Preserve, 89 Mt. Pleasant Rd., Columbia, (877) SEE-WOLF (733-9653), www.lakotawolf.com, is open year-round. The 1½-hour Wolf

Worth Her Weight in Beer

One of the highlights of ScanFest, a celebration of all things Scandinavian held each year on a weekend in early September in Budd Lake's Vasa Park, is a traditional wife-carrying contest. The prize, for the fastest fellow to lug his spouse over the pre-scribed obstacle course, is the lady's weight in beer. We know a guy who once won the event. He was awarded four cases of Carlsberg . . . a Danish brew, of course.

Why Budd Lake? The town near Lake Hopatcong is the home of a sizable population of New Jerseyans of Swedish descent, who along with their Norwegian, Danish, Ice-landic, Finnish, and Icelandic cousins enjoy Scandinavian crafts, entertainers, lectur-ers, and food. For more information log onto www.scanfest.org.

Watch is $15 for adults and $7 for children ages 2 to 11. Two watches are offered daily, and reservations are required. Call ahead or check the website for departure times. No pets are allowed (not even if left in cars) and credit cards are not accepted.

It doesn't taste like butter and it doesn't taste much like milk, but the but-termilk at **Hot Dog Johnny's**, family owned and operated since 1944, is the perfect drink to wash down a couple of dogs and some homemade fries. For the more traditional, there are frosty mugs of birch beer. And it all goes down even better when you're sitting at one of the outdoor tables overlooking the Bequest River. The restaurant, on Route 46 in Buttzville, (908) 453-2882, www.hotdogjohnny.com, is open daily from 9 a.m. to 10 p.m.

Smell fresh-baked doughnuts? The aroma might well be wafting up from **Best's Fruit Farm** to the south. The folks at Best's have been baking dough-nuts and pies and making apple cider for more than 50 years, but the farm is most famous for its fruits and vegetables. The gourmet shop is a wonder-ful place to pick up all the fixin's for a picnic. The farm is on Route 46, just outside downtown Hackettstown, (908) 852-3777. The market/bakery is open year-round Mon through Fri from 9 a.m. to 6 p.m.

If you've ever wondered why New Jersey is called the Garden State, visit **Donaldson Farms Farm Market** and . . . stop wondering. Donaldson's own plantings, and those from neighboring farms, yield a cornucopia of vegetables and fruits throughout the growing season; a handy harvest chart on their web-site (www.donaldsonfarms.net) lets visitors know what's available at its peak of freshness—and when pick-your-own strawberries, raspberries, pumpkins, and apples are ready. Donaldson's hosts an artisan fair and food truck festival each June, featuring the work of local crafters; fall harvest weekends; and a full schedule of kids' programs. Shop here for homemade pies, products made with local ingredients, and a great selection of John Deere toys. The farm is at 358 Allen Rd., Hackettstown, (908) 852-9122, and is open Mon through Sat 9 a.m. to 6 p.m. and Sun 10 a.m. to 5 p.m.

Crossed Keys, built in 1790 as a working farm, is now an elegantly restored inn that is a popular spot for weddings. The inn has five working fireplaces (two in guest bedrooms), a fishing pond/ice-skating rink, a reflecting pool, and three lovingly furnished guest rooms, a suite, and a cottage. Groucho Marx, Mae West, and Charlie Chaplin were known to have kicked back in the Playhouse, now furnished with a pool table and player piano. The rate for a double room with private bath is $150 to $160. The inn's Taproom restaurant is open on weekends. The inn is at 136 Main St., Andover, (973)786-0251, www .crossedkeysinn.com.

During the last ice age, the Wisconsin Glacier passed through northern New Jersey and deposited strange, massive boulders, called "erratics" by geologists. Some historians believe that Tripod Rock on Pyramid Mountain was a sacred place for the Lenni-Lenape people and that two smaller boulders nearby were used as a calendar by early inhabitants. The 243-ton boulder was deposited by the Wisconsin Glacier more than 10,000 years ago.

The 1,000-acre *Pyramid Mountain Natural Historic Area* is an excellent place for hikers and nature lovers. Rugged hills, kettle holes, and streams are home to more than 400 species of plants and wildflowers, 100 species of birds, and 30 species of mammals. Six main hiking trails, each blazed with a different color, traverse the north–south axis of the area. Follow the white trail to Tripod Rock, which perches precariously on three smaller boulders and is one of numerous glacial erratics in the park. Nearby Bear Rock (white/blue trail) is one of the largest in the state.

The Pyramid Mountain Visitor Center, 472 Boonton Ave., Montville, (973) 326-7600, www.morrisparks.net, is open Wed through Sun from 10 a.m. to 4:30 p.m. Trails are open year-round from sunrise to sunset. There are guided hikes most Saturdays and Sundays. To get to Pyramid Mountain Natural Historic Area from I-287, take exit 44A at Main Street in Montville. Turn right on Boonton Avenue (CR 511) and head north 4 miles to the entrance, on the left.

Step back into a bygone age of rail travel with *Delaware River Railroad Excursions*, a great way to enjoy the scenery along the Delaware Valley. On the River & Steam Train, your motive power will be steam locomotive #142, a relative youngster in iron horse terms—it was built in 1989, at a Chinese works that was the world's last builder of steam locos. Other offerings (diesel-powered) along the old right-of-way of the New York, Susquehanna & Western include the Warren County Winery Train, with a stop for tastings at Villa Milagro Vineyards; the Mine Train, featuring gemstone panning at the historic

Snyder Farm; the Corn Maze Train; and, for kids, "A Day Out with Thomas" (the Tank Engine, of course) each August and a Polar Express Train Ride, running between Thanksgiving and Christmas. Adult fares range from $18 to $40, with lower fares for children; 100 Elizabeth St., Phillipsburg, (877) 872-4674, www.877trainride.com.

Grape-stomping parties, Murder Mystery Dinners, a Father's Day pig roast, and harvest weekends with pick-your-own pumpkins and apples are just a few events hosted by *Four Sisters Winery* at Matarazzo Farms. But the big activity here is growing grapes, and since it opened in 1984 the winery has been doing that very well, winning regional, national, and international awards for its red, white, rosé, and fruit wines. Free tours are offered on weekends, and tastings (for a fee) are offered daily. Aunt Sadie's Bakery and Café, open weekends from May through Oct, serves lunch on the deck overlooking the vineyards. Four Sisters Winery is located at 783 CR 519, Belvidere. Call (908) 475-3671 or visit www.foursisterswinery.com for days and hours open, which vary by season.

If you've ever wondered about the origins of those hatchery trout you fish for in spring, a visit to the *Pequest Trout Hatchery and Natural Resource Education Center* should answer all your questions. The Pequest facility, located 9 miles west of Hackettstown, has, since its opening in 1982, produced more than 600,000 brook, brown, and rainbow trout per year for distribution in New Jersey's lakes and streams. It takes 18 months for the hatchery to raise a fish to stocking size, and the job involves careful maintenance of water temperature and aeration, feeding, and disease-prevention measures. The early stages of the operation, in which brood fish spawn and eggs are incubated and hatched, are conducted in closed quarters inaccessible to visitors, but anyone can watch the growing trout through windows in the nursery building and in the mile of outdoor concrete raceways on the Pequest premises.

On the hatchery grounds, the Natural Resource Education Center houses exhibits that explain riverine ecology, with specific emphasis on the life cycle of trout—including a display tank that approximates a cross section of a typical trout stream. Videos and self-guided tours of the hatchery complete the educational experience.

The Pequest Trout Hatchery and Natural Resource Education Center, 605 Pequest Rd., off Route 46 near I-80 (exit 19), Oxford, (908) 637-4125, is open Mon through Fri (excluding holidays) from 10 a.m. to 4 p.m. In addition, there are events and programs scheduled on certain weekends throughout the year. Admission is free.

From ashwagandha to yucca, *Well-Sweep Herb Farm* showcases and sells one of the largest selections of herbs in the country, exhibiting them along with a large collection of perennials in a natural setting. There's also a formal educational display herb garden, as well as medicinal, perennial, English cottage, rock, and vegetable gardens. Among the herbs: 38 types of basil, 85 different lavenders, 104 varieties of thyme, and 72 varieties of scented geranium. The biggest selection—when weather cooperates—is available around May 15, but there's lots to see and buy year-round, and the fields, with flowers drying, are particularly magnificent during July and August.

Well-Sweep Herb Farm, 205 Mt. Bethel Rd., Port Murray, (908) 852-5390, www.wellsweep.com, is open Mon through Sat from 9 a.m. to 5 p.m. year-round and on Sun Apr through Aug from 11 a.m. to 4 p.m.; call or visit the website for Sun hours Nov through Mar.

Morris-Warren Hills

Chester really became a boomtown in 1867, when iron ore was discovered along Main Street. Unfortunately, 25 years later, the ore ran out, and Chester quickly became a ghost town. In the 1950s a local family opened a restaurant at The Crossroads called Larison's Turkey Farm Inn (sadly, now closed), which began to draw tourists back to the area.

As tourists began to return to Chester, residents opened shops along the historic Main Street to attract them. They were attracted, and today downtown Chester (www.chesternj.org) is thriving. Baseball fans may want to pause for a moment at 71 Main St., once home to Billie Dee's Store, which sold newspapers and candy. Billie Dee was also a baseball pitcher and is credited with having invented the curveball when his finger got caught in the covering of a ball. ***Taylor's Ice Cream Parlor***, in the 1876 Centennial Building (18 Main St.), is a great place for a light snack. The ***Publick House***, 111 Main St., (908) 879-6878, www.chesterpublickhouse.com, an 1810 National Historic Landmark, has been beautifully restored. The inn serves lunch and dinner Mon through Sat; offers live entertainment Wed, Thurs, and Fri nights; and is in the process of renovating its guest rooms upstairs. Call to check on their progress.

If you're visiting the area on a Friday, Saturday, or Sunday, be sure to include a stop at ***Alstede Farms***, where family activities include pony rides and hayrides, a petting zoo, and a moon bounce. And don't leave without an ice-cream cone, made with fruit grown right on the farm. In the fall, hop aboard the hay wagon for a ride to the pick-your-own fields and corn maze. Alstede Farms, at 84 Route 513 (Old Route 24) in Chester, (908) 879-7189, www.alstedefarms.com, is open daily year-round.

Before you head toward Morristown, go a mile in the other direction toward Long Valley to visit ***Cooper Gristmill*** on Route 513, one of the few water-powered mills still operating in New Jersey. Built in 1826 on the site of a pre-Revolutionary mill, it was restored in the 1970s by the Morris County Park System, and visitors can watch the massive waterwheel-powered shafts and gears that turn 2,000-pound millstones. The mill is open Apr through Oct; days and hours vary. The last tour starts at 3:30 p.m. There is a small admission fee. For information call (973) 326-7600 or visit www.morrisparks.net.

Heading back east we come to Morristown, perhaps best known to visitors for its National Historic Site that relates to the Continental army's encampments in 1776–77 and 1779–80. The more than two centuries that have passed since Washington and his men camped here have seen the surrounding countryside change from farms to still-growing suburbs, with one important exception. This is *Fosterfields*, a "living historical farm" maintained as an example of what agriculture was like in New Jersey over a century ago.

The 200-acre tract that became Fosterfields had been cultivated for a century or more by 1852, when Paul Revere's grandson, Lieutenant Joseph Warren Revere, bought the land and built his country seat, The Willows, here. There have been only two private owners of Fosterfields since Revere: Charles Foster, who bought the property in 1881, and his daughter, Caroline Rose Foster, who inherited it in 1927 and lived here until her death in 1979 at the age of 102. Near the end of her long life, Miss Foster donated her farm to the Morris County Park Commission, which maintains it, using much the same farming techniques her father employed in the late 1800s. Everything is authentic—tools, plows, and harvesting equipment, and, of course, the horses that turned the wheels of farms and much of civilization itself four generations ago.

A Forgotten Canal

Much of the Delaware and Raritan Canal, which slices across the Garden State at its narrowest part, has been preserved as a park waterway. But the more northerly Morris Canal, which once had its western terminus at Phillipsburg, is gone and largely forgotten.

The Morris Canal reached from Newark Bay to the Delaware River, ascending from sea level to an altitude of 914 feet at Lake Hopatcong and then dropping to 760 feet at the Delaware—all via a system of 23 inclined planes. Completed in 1831 at a cost of nearly $3 million, it could accommodate canal boats weighing up to 25 tons. But like many other waterways dug during America's golden age of canal building, the Morris Canal soon fell prey to competition from the newer and faster railroads. The Lehigh Valley Railroad leased the canal in 1871 and prevailed upon the state to take it over in 1903. Twenty-one years later it was destroyed, by state order.

In addition to following the self-guided trail through the farm or taking one of the guided tours offered on Sun at 2:30 p.m., visitors to Fosterfields are encouraged to participate in a busy schedule of workshops and demonstrations that emphasize old-time agricultural, craft, and home-economics techniques. The Willows, the Gothic Revival mansion on the site, is open for tours Apr through Oct, Thurs through Sun from 1 to 4 p.m. The last tour begins at 3:30 p.m., and there is an additional fee of $1 for the tour.

Fosterfields Living Historical Farm, Route 24 and Kahdena Road, Morris Township, (973) 326-7645, www.morrisparks.net, is open from May through Oct, Thurs through Sat; hours vary. A small admission fee is charged.

Another gem of the Morris County Park System is the 127-acre **Freling-buysen Arboretum**, surrounding the stately Colonial Revival mansion that houses the commission's offices. All the trees in the arboretum are identified by species, and among the numerous trails that crisscross the property is a natural path for the blind, with signs in braille. The Frelinghuysen Arboretum is especially beautiful in springtime, when azaleas, rhododendrons, roses, and spring bulbs bloom in profusion, but cross-country skiers should also keep the trails in mind for fine winter sport.

The Frelinghuysen Arboretum, 353 E. Hanover Ave., near Whippany Road, Morris Township, (973) 326-7601, www.arboretumfriends.org, is open daily from 8 a.m. to dusk; closed Thanksgiving, Christmas, and New Year's Day. Admission is free.

Historic Speedwell recalls the lives and work of a family that played an important part in the transformation of the United States from an agricultural to an industrial nation in the 19th century. Stephen Vail was the owner of the thriving Speedwell Iron Works, a cast-iron foundry powered by the fast-running Whippany River. One of the most important commissions of the Speedwell works in the early 1800s was for the iron machinery used in the SS *Savannah*, the first steamship to cross the Atlantic Ocean.

While attending New York University, Vail's son, Alfred, met Samuel F. B. Morse, who had come to demonstrate a rudimentary apparatus he had devised for sending electromagnetically generated signals over wires. Alfred offered Morse financial backing and helped perfect the device at Speedwell. On January 6, 1838, Alfred sent the first message, "A patient waiter is no loser," on a working model of the improved telegraph. The more famous "first" telegraph message, Morse's own "What hath God wrought," was transmitted to Vail at Baltimore six years later over an improved apparatus featuring a register that recorded the dots and dashes of Morse code on a strip of paper. That machinery, too, was built by Vail at Speedwell.

Today, Speedwell enjoys designation as a National Historic Site. Structures open to visitors at Speedwell include Vail House itself, restored to its 1840s appearance; the 1829 building where the first public demonstration of the telegraph was held on January 11, 1838; and the granary, housing exhibits of antique tools and vehicles. In addition to these original structures, the Speedwell property is the site of three 18th- and early 19th-century houses moved here from Morristown in the 1960s.

Historic Speedwell, 333 Speedwell Ave., Morristown, (973) 285-6550, www .morrisparks.net, is open Apr through Oct, Wed through Fri from 10 a.m. to 5 p.m., Sat from 10 a.m. to 6 p.m., and Sun from noon to 6 p.m. The last tour begins at 3:30 p.m. An admission fee is charged. Tours of the Vail House, factory building, and wheelhouse are also offered.

If you don't mind using your feet to get off the beaten path, Morris County offers some excellent options. The **Farney Highlands Trail Network** in Jefferson and Rockaway Townships encompasses the Four Birds Trail, an isolated, 19$\frac{9}{10}$-mile segment that crosses only one paved road. "Four birds" refers to environments found along the trail: wild turkey in the forests, red-tailed hawk near the cliffs, osprey on the shores of the lake, and, in the marshes, great blue heron. The trail is a great place for migratory bird-watching in the fall. To reach the southern trailhead, take Route 513 north from Route 80 in Rockaway Township and, after 2¾ miles, turn right onto Sunnyside Road. Look for white blazes about 150 feet down on the left. The northern section of the trail is on land owned by the Newark Watershed Conservation and Development Cooperation. Call (973) 334-3131 or visit www.mtnlakes.org for information about a hiking and parking permit. Recreation permits must be obtained in person at 223 Echo Lake Rd., West Milford, (201) 697-2850.

Head over to Morris County's **Mount Hope Historical Park** to see remains of the county's 20th-century iron mines. Pick up a trail guide at the parking lot and then meander along 3 miles of trails that wind past historic sites, including numerous subsidence pits (large holes created by abandoned mine shafts). Keep an eye open for chunks of magnetite iron ore—small, black, somewhat rectangular rocks. To reach the park, take I-80 to exit 35 north toward Mount Hope. After ½ mile, turn left onto Richard Mine Road; then turn right onto Coburn Road after ⁷⁄₁₀ mile. When the name of the road changes to Teabo Road, watch for the parking lot after another ⁷⁄₁₀ mile.

For maps and information on all of Morris County's parks, call (973) 326-7600 weekdays or visit www.morrisparks.net. Maps are available at the Hagarty Education Center at the Frelinghuysen Arboretum.

Gustav Stickley, the foremost American spokesperson for the Arts and Crafts movement, was a proponent of "a fine plainness" in art and the art of

Fort Nonsense

Morristown is rich in relics of the days when New Jersey was the "Cockpit of the Revolution." On the grounds of Morristown National Historical Park are the Ford Mansion, twice Washington's winter headquarters, and the site of the troop encampment at Jockey Hollow. A lesser-known Revolutionary War site on the park's grounds is Fort Nonsense, marked by an earthworks reconstruction on Morristown's Mount Kemble. Why the irreverent name? The fort, constructed in 1777 under George Washington's orders, was never used except for storage of supplies. As the years wore on, locals came to suspect that the commander had built it only to keep his men busy during a long winter bivouac. So they named it Fort Nonsense, in what was perhaps the only instance of that word being connected with the decidedly no-nonsense Father of His Country.

living. He incorporated his philosophy of building in harmony with the environment by using natural materials when he built his log home at *Craftsman Farms* circa 1908–10. As he explained in his magazine, *The Craftsman*, in November 1911: "There are elements of intrinsic beauty in the simplification of a house built on the log cabin idea. First, there is the bare beauty of the logs themselves with their long lines and firm curves. Then there is the open charm felt of the structural features that are not hidden under plaster and ornament, but are clearly revealed, a charm felt in Japanese architecture. . . . The quiet rhythmic monotone of the wall of logs fills one with the rustic peace of a secluded nook in the woods."

Stickley dreamed of establishing a farm school for boys at his "Garden of Eden," but his dream began to fade as the tastes of the American people moved away from the clean, strong lines of Craftsman furniture toward revival of early American and other styles. The dream died in 1915, when he filed for bankruptcy. In spite of these failures, he was a visionary, whose philosophy of art and architecture helped people make the transition from the overwrought interiors of the Victorian era to the modern decorative arts to come.

Twenty-six acres of the 650-acre tract that originally made up Craftsman Farms have been declared a National Historic Landmark. The landmark is owned by the Township of Parsippany–Troy Hills and is operated by the Craftsman Farms Foundation, which is restoring the interior of the house and the gardens as they were in Stickley's time. Many of his original pieces of Mission furniture and comparable period Stickley pieces are on display to show how the house would have looked in his day.

The Stickley Museum is located at 2352 Route 10 West in Morris Plains, (973) 540-0311, www.stickleymuseum.org. As of this writing, the museum is planning to reopen following repairs necessitated by storm damage. During construction, tours are available on a limited basis by appointment only; consult the website for details.

Among the exhibits at ***Imagine That!!!***, a children's discovery museum with 16,000 square feet of hands-on activities, are a science discoveries room, a gravity maze, music and art rooms, and a three-story playscape. Imagine That!!! is at 4 Vreeland Rd. in Florham Park, (973) 966-8000, www.imaginethatmuseum .com. The museum is open daily from 10 a.m. to 5:30 p.m., except major holidays. Admission is $21.99 for children 1 to 10 and $6.99 for children over 10 and adults; infants are free. All children must be accompanied by an adult, and no strollers are permitted.

Places to Stay in Northern New Jersey & the Upper Delaware Valley

The Bernards Inn
27 Mine Brook Rd.,
Bernardsville
(908) 766-0002
www.bernardsinn.com
Expensive

Chestnut Hill on the Delaware B&B
63 Church St., Milford
(908) 995-9761 or (888) 333-2242
www.chestnuthillnj.comw
Moderate–expensive

Inn at Millrace Pond
313 Johnsonburg Rd.,
Hope
(908) 459-4884
www.innatmillracepond .comw
Moderate–expensive

Neighbour House Bed & Breakfast
143 West Mill Rd., Long Valley
(908) 876-3519
www.neighbourhouse.com
Moderate–expensive

Olde Mill Inn
225 Route 202, Basking Ridge
(800) 585-4461 or (908) 221-1100
www.oldemillinn.com
Expensive

Somerset Hills Hotel
200 Liberty Corner Rd.,
Warren
(908) 660-4506
www.somersethillshotelnj .com
Expensive

The Woolverton Inn
6 Woolverton Rd.,
Stockton
(609) 397-0802 or (888) 264-6648
www.woolvertoninn.com
Moderate–expensive

Places to Eat in Northern New Jersey & the Upper Delaware Valley

Arthur's Tavern
700 Speedwell Ave., Morris Plains
(973) 455-9705
Complimentary garlic pickles, hot peppers, pickled tomatoes, and homemade sauerkraut set the tone for a large selection of burgers, sandwiches, and salads; a prime pork chop with marsala mushroom gravy; and the famous bet-you-can't-finish 24-ounce Delmonico steak (for lunchtime fressers, there's a 10-ounce burger), all to be washed down with liter mugs of cold draft beer. Save room for homemade cheesecake.

Lunch and dinner daily. Moderate–expensive.

Churrascaria Paladar
2 US Highway 46, Hackettstown
(908) 813-1700
Beef, pork, and chicken with a Brazilian flair, including sausages and traditional skewered entrées. The "Trio Carioca" brings together steak, grilled chicken, and garlicky shrimp. Open Wed through Fri 4 to 10 p.m., Sat 3 to 10 p.m., and Sun 1 to 8 p.m. Expensive.

Cloves
61 International Dr., Budd Lake
(973) 347-9290
Indian cuisine includes classic vindaloos (from mild to beyond hot), curries, and papadam. Lunch and dinner daily. Inexpensive–moderate.

Dolce
161 Main St., Flemington
(908) 237-1221
Pasta selections include tortellini carbonara, goat cheese gnocchi, and wild mushroom ravioli; chicken and veal are the entrée stars. Dinner Tues through Sun. Bring your own wine. Moderate.

Elias Cole
1176 Route 23, Sussex
(973) 875-3550
A longtime area favorite, featuring homemade soups, baked goods, and daily specials that might include beer-battered seafood, meat loaf, and

prime rib. Bring home a house-made pie. Open Tues through Thurs 8 a.m. to 3 p.m., Fri through Sun 8 a.m. to 7 p.m. Inexpensive.

Good Times
31 Wall St., Oxford
(908) 453-2833
A laid-back atmosphere and a menu with everything from pizza and pasta to escargot and seared salmon with wild mushrooms make this restaurant a popular choice for families. Dinner Tues through Sun. Moderate–expensive.

The Grand Cafe
42 Washington St., Morristown
(973) 540-9444
For more than 30 years, this sophisticated restaurant with its tuxedoed waiters has set the bar for classic French cuisine in the area. Dishes are prepared with a deft touch bordering on the nouvelle, but no calories are spared in the fabulous homemade desserts. Lunch Mon through Fri, dinner Mon through Sat. Outdoor seating. Expensive.

Il Capriccio
633 Route 10 East, Whippany
(973) 884-9175
Piano music, a courtyard with fountains, and candlelight set the mood for a romantic evening of fine Italian dining. The menu is extensive,

with classics such as tortellini with walnuts and Gorgonzola, and buffalo mozzarella with fresh tomato. There's a 400-selection wine list with an astounding variety of Italian selections, and a fine selection of grappas. No hats, T-shirts, or torn jeans. Lunch Mon through Fri, dinner Mon through Sat. Expensive.

Jasper
810 Route 46 West, Parsippany
(973) 334-6088
Classic Chinese dishes include the house special, Peking duck, and steamed striped bass. Lunch and dinner daily. Moderate.

Rattlesnake Ranch Cafe
Foodtown Shopping Center, 559 E. Main St., Denville
(973) 586-3800
Along with Tex-Mex favorites, the eclectic menu includes jambalaya, fried alligator, pork chops balsamico, whole red snapper, and BBQ ribs; the margaritas are enormous. Lunch and dinner daily. Moderate.

Restaurant Latour
Crystal Springs Country Club, 1 Wild Turkey Way, Hamburg
(973) 827-5996
An intimate dining room, spectacular views, and a superb wine list complement the fine contemporary American menu. Menus change

with the seasons and may include appetizers such as oyster strudel and black truffle risotto, and a terrific dry-aged steak and crepinette of pheasant and foie gras. A chef's tasting menu is available. Dress code. Dinner Thurs through Sun. Expensive.

Scalini Fedeli
63 Main St., Chatham
(973) 701-9200
Well-prepared northern Italian food with a French flair served in a romantic room with vaulted ceilings and soft lighting. The menu includes specialties such as boneless veal chop Milanese, pignoli-crusted salmon, and homemade pappardelle in a veal shank and marrow sauce. Lunch Mon through Fri, dinner (prix fixe) Mon through Sat. Expensive.

Other Attractions in Northern New Jersey & the Upper Delaware Valley

Acorn Hall
68 Morris Ave., Morristown
(973) 267-3465

Blue Army of Our Lady of Fatima and the Immaculate Heart of Mary Shrine
674 Mountain View Rd., Washington
(908) 689-1700

Boonton Historic District
210 Main St., Boonton
(973) 402-8840

Bull's Island Recreation Area
2185 Daniel Bray Hwy. (Route 29), Stockton
(609) 397-2949

Cross Estate Gardens
61 Jockey Hollow Rd., Bernardsville
(201) 240-5898

Gallery One Main
1 Main St., High Bridge
(908) 638-3838

The Meadows Foundation
1289 Easton Ave., Somerset
(732) 828-7418

Middlebrook Winter Encampment of Washington's Army
Middlebrook Road, Bridgewater
(908) 722-2124

Millbrook Village
Old Mine Road, Millbrook
(908) 841-9531

SELECTED REGIONAL INFORMATION CENTERS, CHAMBERS OF COMMERCE & VISITOR CENTERS IN NORTHERN NEW JERSEY & THE UPPER DELAWARE VALLEY

Parsippany Area Chamber of Commerce
90 E. Haksey Rd., #322
Parsippany–Troy Hills 07054
(973) 402-6400

Sussex County Chamber of Commerce
120 Hampton House Rd.
Newton 07860
(973) 579-1811

Warren County Regional Chamber of Commerce
445 Marshall St.
Phillipsburg 08865
(908) 835-9200

Rudolf W. van der Goot Rose Garden
156 Mettler's Rd.,
Somerset
(732) 873-2459

Van Campen Inn
Old Mine Road, Walpack
Center
(973) 729-7392

Whippany Railway Museum
1 Railroad Plaza, Route 10,
Whippany
(973) 887-8177

Central New Jersey

The central swath of New Jersey constitutes the narrowest portion of this wasp-waisted state. From the mouth of the Raritan River at South Amboy to the Delaware River at Trenton is barely 35 miles—no wonder this is the crossroads of New Jersey, the place chosen for early New York–to–Philadelphia transportation enterprises such as the Delaware and Raritan Canal and the Camden and Amboy Railroad of the 1830s. More than 50 years before these technological marvels were undertaken, George Washington led his troops westward across Central Jersey in a successful attempt to escape the British threat in New York. Crossing the Delaware near Trenton (a state park commemorates the event today), he struck back at the British and Hessians in one of history's great surprise attacks. In our own day the central corridor of New Jersey is where the famous New Jersey Turnpike makes its dash from the northeastern to the southwestern part of the state.

Central New Jersey, however, is not just a place of comings and goings. Here, at Trenton, is the state capital; here, too, are two of America's finest universities, Rutgers (in New Brunswick) and Princeton. Old industries, like china and glass,

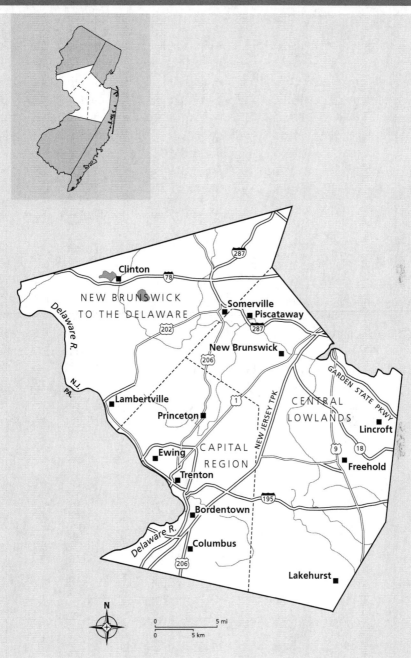

NEW BRUNSWICK
TO THE DELAWARE

CENTRAL
LOWLANDS

CAPITAL
REGION

Clinton

Somerville

Piscataway

New Brunswick

Lambertville

Princeton

Lincroft

Ewing

Trenton

Freehold

Bordentown

Columbus

Lakehurst

Delaware R.

N.J.

PA.

Delaware R.

NEW JERSEY TPK

GARDEN STATE PKWY

287

78

202

206

206

1

9

18

195

N

0   5 mi

0   5 km

and new ones, like electronics and refining, have found Central Jersey a place conducive to growth.

All such boundaries are imprecise, but we might say that central New Jersey begins where the state's northern uplands give way to the gently rolling hills of Somerset County horse country, and it extends south almost to the edges of the Pine Barrens. The western border is, of course, the Delaware River. On the east is the coastal plain, but because the Jersey Shore has such a distinct character of its own, we'll save it for a later chapter.

Note: The orientation in this chapter is east to west, from New Brunswick to the Delaware River; then south, through the Capital Region; and, finally, counterclockwise as we move back north to the Raritan Valley of the Central Lowlands.

New Brunswick to the Delaware

The **Korn Gallery**, in the Dorothy Young Center for the Arts at Drew University, hosts a constantly changing series of exhibits of work by students and members of Drew's art faculty, including senior theses in various media. For up-to-date information on current exhibits, check drew.edu or call (973) 408-3758. The Dorothy Young Center is on the Drew campus on Madison Avenue, Madison, and is open afternoons Wed through Sat.

We're fortunate that many of the everyday objects associated with life in the 17th and 18th centuries weren't discarded, but simply collected dust in attics, cellars, and barns, and if they stayed out of the way of zealous spring

CENTRAL NEW JERSEY'S TOP PICKS

Museum of Early Trades and Crafts	Princeton University Art Museum
Great Swamp	Old Barracks Museum
Red Mill Museum Village	Kuser Farm Mansion
Black River & Western Railroad	Bordentown
Delaware and Raritan Canal State Park	Naval Air Engineering Station
Lambertville	New Jersey Vietnam Veterans' Memorial
Howell Living History Farm	Zimmerli Art Museum
Drumthwacket	Hutcheson Memorial Forest

cleaners, they survived into our own age to be treasured as antiques. The preservation of these artifacts, particularly those associated with the world of work, is the mission of the *Museum of Early Trades and Crafts* in Madison.

The heart of the museum's holdings is the Edgar Law Land collection of 18th- and 19th-century tools and products that pertain to New Jersey homes, farms, trades, and shop crafts. The museum interprets a time when most New Jerseyans lived on farms or in country villages. The collection encompasses both common and unique everyday products of the home, from horn spoons to bobbin-lace pillows, as well as the tools of carpenters, coopers, tinsmiths, masons, cobblers, wheelwrights, bookbinders, and stonecutters plus unusual lens-making tools and early medical equipment.

Exhibits, many of which feature hands-on discovery areas, include a re-created colonial kitchen, shoemaker's shop, one-room schoolhouse, and changing displays. The museum also offers educational programs for people of all ages, including school programs, adult tours, and special programs every Saturday throughout the school year.

The museum, a nonprofit organization founded in 1970, is housed in the former James Library building, which was built in 1900. The building is listed on the National Register of Historic Places as an excellent example of the Richardson Romanesque style. It features stained-glass windows, stenciling, a glass-floor gallery, and an 1899 Seth Thomas tower clock.

The Museum of Early Trades and Crafts, Main Street and Green Village Road, (973) 377-2982, www.metc.org, is open year-round Tues through Sat from 10 a.m. to 4 p.m. and Sun from noon to 5 p.m. Admission is $5 for adults

A New Jersey Lord

The comfortable residential suburb of Stirling, which lies just south of the Great Swamp National Wildlife Refuge, is named after an American-born aristocrat named William Alexander. An American aristocrat? Yes—and not just in the figurative sense of wealth and power, which Alexander also enjoyed. Born in New York, and owner of a magnificent estate in Basking Ridge, New Jersey, Alexander was a direct descendant of the Scottish earls of Stirling.

Despite his noble rank, Lord Stirling was an active and effective participant on the American side in the Revolution. He commanded New Jersey's first body of Continental troops and was soon elevated to the rank of general. He executed a daring strategic retreat at the Battle of Long Island, captured a British supply ship off Sandy Hook, and brilliantly commanded American artillery at the Battle of Monmouth. With Stirling's untimely death at Albany before the war's end, George Washington lost a good friend and a valuable commander—a man Washington always called "my lord."

AUTHORS' FAVORITE ATTRACTIONS IN CENTRAL NEW JERSEY

Princeton University Art Museum	Old Barracks Museum
Great Swamp	Delaware and Raritan Canal State Park
New Jersey State Police Museum and Learning Center	Farm Market at Bobolink Dairy
	Grounds for Sculpture

and $3 for seniors, children, and students. There is a maximum charge of $15 for a single family.

There is one part of New Jersey, just 26 miles west of Times Square, that has changed very little, if at all, since the days when coopers made barrels and wheelwrights wrought wheels. The *Great Swamp* has, in fact, changed hardly at all over the past few thousand years. It isn't going to change in the foreseeable future either, because this more-than-7,400-acre tract of wetland and forest is protected as a national wildlife refuge.

The stories of how the swamp came to be and how it came to be saved are equally interesting. At one time the land occupied by the swamp—and a good deal more of what was to become north-central New Jersey—was covered by a 200-foot-deep lake, fed by meltwater from the receding Wisconsin Glacier of 10,000 years ago. This vast inland sea, called Lake Passaic by modern geologists, did not drain off until the retreating ice had uncovered a gap at Little Falls, through which water could pour downstream to the Atlantic. The bottom of Lake Passaic, however, never dried out completely. Its understructure of dense clay was a poor absorber of water, and wetlands were created along a long swath of North Jersey, extending from the Great Swamp to Fairfield's Great Piece Meadow. Three centuries of development around the fringes of the swamp failed to result in any permanent penetration of its deepest recesses. In the 1950s it was still left to wood ducks and bitterns, to fox, otter, and muskrat.

In 1959, however, the death knell of the swamp was very nearly sounded, in the form of a report from the Port Authority of New York and New Jersey that favored the vast wetland as the site for a proposed jetport. Projects like this had traditionally been viewed as the triumph of civilization over "wasteland," but this time a substantial portion of the citizenry of the surrounding towns did not agree. They banded together to form the Great Swamp Committee and set about raising the necessary funds to buy the threatened land and present it to the US Department of the Interior for use as a refuge. The initial 3,000-acre tract was so dedicated in 1964, and the property in federal hands has since more than doubled. Eighty percent of the swamp is now protected, more than 3,600 acres of it as wilderness, free from motorized traffic and permanent construction.

The **Great Swamp Outdoor Education Center** in Chatham is an excellent place to begin your visit. The center, open daily from 9 a.m. to 4:30 p.m., provides an introduction to the geology and ecology of the area. A wheelchair-accessible boardwalk trail and an observation blind are here as well. The center is at 247 Southern Blvd., (973) 635-6629.

A wildlife observation center, with observation blinds, trails, and restrooms that are wheelchair accessible, borders the management and wilderness sectors of the property. A system of 8½ miles of marked trails extends through the wilderness. Maps are available at the headquarters, as are checklists of the bird, reptile, amphibian, and mammal species, as well as common wildflowers that have been documented here.

The Great Swamp National Wildlife Refuge **Helen C. Fenske Visitor Center** is located at 32 Pleasant Plains Rd., Basking Ridge, (973) 425-9510, www.friendsofgreatswamp.org. The center contains exhibits on the wildlife and natural history of the swamp, and is the starting point for several nature trails. It's open Tues 11 a.m. to 3 p.m., Thurs and Fri 10 a.m. to 4 p.m., Sat 11 a.m. to 3 p.m., and Sun 10 a.m. to 4 p.m.

The Bernards Inn, established in 1907, has long had a reputation for superb dining: *Gourmet* magazine consistently honored it as "one of America's top tables." Served in a beautifully restored, elegant Mission-style building, the cuisine is described as progressive American, with appetizers such as duck confit tacos ($16) and entrées that might include Chilean sea bass with a cassoulet of white bean, escarole, and saucisson sec ($36) or Faroe Island salmon with celeriac and winter greens ($32). An interesting adjunct to the wine list is an offering of tasting flights of dessert wines, sherries, Madeiras, and ports. There are 20 luxuriously appointed guest rooms and suites at the four-star, four-diamond inn; rates start at $264.

The Bernards Inn, 27 Mine Brook Rd. (Route 202), Bernardsville, (908) 766-0002, www.bernardsinn.com, is open for dinner Tues through Sat from 5 to 9 p.m. Jackets are requested.

One of the premier rock gardens in the East has been "growing" since it was first conceived in the late 1930s. The **Leonard J. Buck Garden**, nestled in a 33-acre wooded stream valley, is actually a series of alpine and woodland gardens. Tucked among rock outcroppings are a bewildering variety of rare and exotic rock garden plants, all placed to appear as if they were occurring naturally. Leafy trails connecting the outcroppings are lined with wildflowers. A profusion of heaths and heathers, all varieties of *Calluna* and *Erica*, flourish in a raised peninsula bed at the entrance to the visitor center. On a slope behind the center is the F. Gordon Foster Hardy Fern Collection, which includes Christmas and northern maidenhair ferns, rare fern species such as the tiny rusty woodsia, and painted and autumn ferns from Japan.

Although Buck Garden's peak bloom period occurs in spring, there are splashes of color—or at least a welcome green—almost every week of the year. The garden is maintained by the Somerset County Park Commission, which also oversees the Colonial Park Arboretum and its magnificent Rudolf W. van der Goot Rose Garden, with more than 3,000 roses of over 200 varieties.

The Leonard J. Buck Garden, 11 Layton Rd., Far Hills, is open Mon through Fri from 10 a.m. to 4 p.m., Sat from 10 a.m. to 5 p.m., and Sun from noon to 5 p.m.; call ahead for winter hours. A small donation is requested. For information on the garden or the arboretum, call (908) 722-1200 or visit www.somersetcountyparks.org.

Like Fosterfields in North Jersey and the Museum of Early Trades and Crafts, **Red Mill Museum Village** provides a glimpse into a domestic past that was, historically, just the day before yesterday but seems, in technological terms, as remote as the Middle Ages. Located on the South Branch of the Raritan River just north of I-78, the National Historic Site centers on what was formerly the most important building in these parts: the 1810 Red Mill, in which waterpower at one time ground grain, flaxseed, limestone, graphite, and talc. Today the mill exhibits suggest the rural life of the 19th through early 20th centuries in the Delaware Valley. In many ways things didn't change that much on the farms and in backcountry villages through that long stretch of time.

passwithcare

In 1904, it cost $30,767 to erect the Riegelsville Bridge, which spans the Delaware River between New Jersey and Pennsylvania. The 577-foot-long wire-rope suspension bridge is just 16 feet wide—a tight squeeze for two SUVs passing each other. But even if your letters of transit aren't in order, you can get a fine view without leaving New Jersey.

The "village" that clusters near the Red Mill is a string of period structures, tucked neatly between the river and the 150-foot limestone cliffs that provided much of the mill's work. Here are an old general store/post office, a one-room schoolhouse, a log cabin, a blacksmith shop, and wagon sheds. Unique to this museum are the remains of Mulligan's lime quarry, including office, dynamite shed, lime kilns, and stone crusher.

Each week the natural outdoor amphitheater, created by the cliffs near the mill, is the site for live concerts, Civil War reenactments, and numerous festivals. Halloween, when the mill is transformed into a chamber of horrors, is a ghoulishly great event.

The Red Mill Museum Village's Hunterdon Historical Museum, 56 Main St., Clinton, (908) 735-4101, www.theredmill.org, is open weekends from noon to 6 p.m.; call or check the website for information on resumption of weekday hours. Admission is $12 for adults and $8 for senior citizens and children ages 6 through 12.

The **Hunterdon Art Museum** is housed in a 19th-century stone gristmill that is on the National Register of Historic Places. The museum's permanent collection concentrates on works on paper, and the growing collection emphasizes prints but also includes drawings and paintings. The collection, dating from the 1930s to the present, includes works by both internationally known and regional artists. The museum is at 7 Lower Center St., Clinton, (908) 735-8415, www.hunterdonartmuseum.org. Exhibits and the gift shop are open Thurs through Sun from 11 a.m. to 5 p.m. Admission is $7 for adults and $5 for seniors, military, and students; children under 12 free. Special exhibits and events are posted on the website.

The Ship Inn, an authentic British pub and New Jersey's first brewpub, handcrafts ales in seven-barrel batches using freshly milled whole grain. They also sell a great selection of single-malt whiskies and specialize in cuisine from the British Isles. The inn, at 61 Bridge St., Milford, (908) 995-0188, www.descendantsbrewing.com, is open 5 to 10 p.m. (kitchen to 8:30 p.m.) Mon through Thurs, noon to midnight (kitchen to 9 p.m.) Fri and Sat, and noon to 10 p.m. (kitchen to 8:40 p.m.) Sun.

With the help of their cows, and lots of hard work, Nina and Jonathan White are preserving a 184-acre bit of heaven overlooking the Delaware River. The Whites run the farm, make artisanal cheeses from raw milk produced by their grass-fed herds, bake rustic breads in a wood-fired oven, and, when they have time, offer tours. The **Farm Market at Bobolink Dairy**, 369 Stamets Rd., Milford, (908) 864-7277, is open Mon, Wed, Thurs, and Fri from noon to 6 p.m. and Sat and Sun from 9 a.m. to 5 p.m. Visitors can sign up for tours and get more information at www.cowsoutside.com.

The restaurant at Frenchtown's historic **National Hotel** features a menu that draws heavily on the area's abundant produce—in season, even the pears and spinach in the pear and gorgonzola salad are sourced from local orchards, and soups draw on seasonal flavors. Burgers are crafted from grass-fed beef and served with the famous Jersey tomatoes on house-baked brioche buns; at dinnertime, start with the "Butcher's Board" of soppressata, prosciutto, and capicola, served with a local smoked cheddar, provolone, and fresh mozzarella. Dinner standouts include a grass-fed Wagyu filet with brandy peppercorn sauce ($34) and "Anglo-Indian" boneless short rib stew, gently spiced with Indian flavors and served with basmati rice ($28). The hotel is at 31 Race St., Frenchtown, (908) 996-3200. The restaurant is open Tues through Fri 3 to 10 p.m., Sat noon to 10 p.m., and Sun noon to 8 p.m.

The *Frenchtown Inn*, at 7 Bridge St., Frenchtown, (908) 996-3300, www .frenchtowninn.com, is open for lunch Tues through Sat from noon to 2 p.m.; for dinner Tues through Fri from 5 to 9 p.m., Sat from 5:30 to 9:15 p.m., and Sun from 5 to 8 p.m.; and for Sunday brunch from noon to 3 p.m. The Grill Room is open Tues through Fri from 5 to 9 p.m. and Sun from 3 to 8 p.m.

In Frenchtown, be sure to visit *Decoys & Wildlife Gallery*, which displays carved decoys and wildlife carvings by some of the country's finest artists. It's at 55 Bridge St., (908) 996-6501, www.decoyswildlife.com, and is open daily from 10 a.m. to 6 p.m. or by appointment.

Just down the road from the gallery, chef Roland Huesca cooks up authentic Mexican and Tex-Mex fare at *Cocina del Sol* at 10 Bridge St. It's open for lunch and dinner daily. Be sure to bring your own cerveza (it's BYOB). For information call (908) 996-0900 or visit cocina-del-sol.business.site.

The town of Flemington, with its many factory outlets, specialty shops, and a beautifully preserved historic district, is a popular destination for day-trippers.

TOP ANNUAL EVENTS IN CENTRAL NEW JERSEY

Note: Schedules may vary; call ahead.

New Jersey Home and Garden Show, Edison; Feb; (800) 332-3976; www .visitnj.org/nj/events

Shad Festival, Lambertville; Apr; (609) 397-0055; www.lambertvillechamber .com

Native American Heritage Celebration, Raritan; June; (718) 686-9297; www .visitnj.org/nj/events

Jersey Shore Jazz & Blues Festival, Red Bank; June; (732) 933-1984; www .jsjbf.org

Annual Battle of Monmouth, Manalapan; June; (609) 448-6355; www .friendsofmonmouth.org

Monmouth County Fair, Freehold; July; (732) 842-4000

Middlesex County Fair, East Brunswick; Aug; (732) 257-8858; www .middlesexcountyfair.com

Greek Festival by the Bay, Perth Amboy; Sept; (732) 826-4466

George Washington Crossing the Delaware, Washington Crossing State Park, Titusville; Dec 25; (609) 737-0623; www.washingtoncrossingpark.org

The Martians Landed Here

". . . straddling the Pulaski Skyway . . . evident objective New York City . . . now in sight above the Palisades . . . five great machines . . . wading the Hudson like a man wading a brook."

It was the Martians, and they had landed in New Jersey. The occasion, of course, was Orson Welles's famous radio dramatization of H. G. Wells's *War of the Worlds* on the night before Halloween 1938. Although Welles introduced the story as fiction, his setting of the action in actual New Jersey and New York locations and his use of "live" news bulletins as a narrative device caused listeners who tuned in just a few minutes into the broadcast to believe that alien invaders were really on the march.

For his Martian landing place, Welles chose Grover's Mill, New Jersey, a tiny hamlet in West Windsor Township, near Princeton. Today, a plaque in Grover's Mill's Van Nest Park commemorates the great scare with a depiction of a Martian attack vehicle, Welles at the microphone, and a family gathered around their radio.

But in 1935 the eyes of the world were on the town when Bruno Richard Hauptmann, accused of kidnapping and killing the baby of Charles and Anne Morrow Lindbergh, was put on trial in the **Hunterdon County Courthouse** at the corner of Main and Court Streets. Reporters stayed across the street at the Union Hotel (now a restaurant). At the end of the "Trial of the Century," which lasted six weeks, Hauptmann was found guilty and was executed on April 3, 1936, at Trenton State Prison.

The Borough of Flemington, www.historicflemington.com, hosts numerous events throughout the season, including a summer Music on Main Street concert series; offers a free self-guided walking tour brochure; and provides information on trial reenactments.

At **Northlandz**, the Great American Railway—the world's largest miniature railway—up to a hundred trains scoot along 8 miles of track through a miniaturized landscape of mountains, bridges, and handcrafted cities and villages. At one point a triple-spiral, triple-track trestle bridge provides a route for three trains through desert canyons. The 94-room mansion at the railroad's Doll Museum, complete with indoor swimming pool and ballroom, exhibits more than 200 dolls from around the world. Snacks are served in the Club Car Cafe.

The 16-acre attraction, the culmination of a project begun in 1972 by Bruce Williams Zaccagnino, is at 495 Route 202 in Flemington, (908) 782-4022, www.northlandz.com, and is open Fri, Sat, Sun, and holidays from 10 a.m. to 6 p.m. Admission is $25 for adults, $23 for seniors, $20 for children ages 2 through 11, and free for infants under 2. Rides on the outdoor train are $15.

The steam locomotive is an enduring American icon. It's been more than 75 years since diesels began to outnumber steamers on the nation's railroads, and six decades have passed since the iron horse became extinct in regular United States commercial operation. Still, we can't let go of steam. A guide to rail museums and tourist railroads lists nearly 90 operations that run regularly scheduled or special steam-powered trains. Two of them are right here in New Jersey—one in Allaire State Park (which we'll get to later) and another head-quartered in the small central-western New Jersey town of Ringoes. This is the **Black River & Western Railroad**, which leaves from stations in Flemington (80 Stangl Rd.) and Ringoes (101 John Ringo Rd.).

Trains depart on select Saturdays and Sundays from spring through early fall. The fare for regular 40-minute trips through Hunterdon County is $16 for adults and $10 for children. The railroad offers numerous themed trips throughout the year, including Easter Bunny, Polar Express, corn maze, and Santa Claus trains. For ticket information call (908) 782-6622 or visit www.blackriver-railroad.com. Phone or online reservations are recommended.

In 1933, lyricist Lorenz Hart and composer Richard Rodgers visited **The Stockton Inn**. Inspired by the inn and its environs, they wrote "There's a Small Hotel with a Wishing Well." Rodgers and Hart weren't the only artists inspired by the inn, built as a private residence in 1710. Kurt Wiese, illustrator of the original book *Bambi*, painted murals on the dining-room walls. Bandleader Paul Whiteman kept a regular table at the inn, which came to be known as "Colligan's" for the Colligan family who owned it, and signed off his radio and TV shows by announcing he was going to dinner at "Ma Colligan's." A table favored by Dorothy Parker, Robert Benchley, S. J. Perelman, and friends became known as the Algonquin Roundtable, in honor of their New York City meeting place.

The "Small Hotel with a Wishing Well," which features 11 bedrooms, suites, and studios, including a suite with gas fireplace in the main inn, a loft with fireplace in the 1832 Wagon House, and a suite with a queen-size canopy bed and fireplace in the 1850 Federal House, is as of this writing in the process of changing hands.

Built in 1792, Stockton's elegant stone **Woolverton Inn**, just a mile from the Delaware Canal and River, stands graciously amid 300 acres of rolling hills. Eight of the inn's 13 rooms are in the three-story manor house, and there are six separate cottages. All have private baths and air-conditioning, two have working fireplaces, and three have Jacuzzi tubs. Genuine feather beds are available. The lovely veranda is a wonderful place to rock away idle hours; the elegantly appointed, fireplaced living room a charming spot for tea on a cold winter day.

The Woolverton Inn is at 6 Woolverton Rd., Stockton, (888) 264-6648 or (609) 397-0802, www.woolvertoninn.com. Room rates, which include a three-course breakfast (available in bed upon request), range from $349 to $499. A two-night minimum stay is required on weekends.

You have to go a long way in New Jersey to drive through a covered bridge—to Sergeantsville, in fact. The *Green Sergeant's Bridge* on Route 604 is the only covered bridge on a public road in the state. Built in 1866, it was scheduled to be demolished in the 1950s, but a group of citizens banded together and saved it. The 84-foot-long, wooden, modified queen-post bridge over Wickecheoke Creek is on its original abutments.

Before the great days of railroads, canals were king. A hundred and ninety years ago, when the first toylike locomotives were beginning to chuff and sputter along weak and uneven track, it was considered a tremendous advantage to be able to ship freight along the slow, smooth canals rather than over the treacherous carriage roads of the day—thus the enthusiasm with which New Jerseyans greeted the opening of the Delaware and Raritan Canal in 1834.

From the day it opened, the Delaware and Raritan Canal was one of America's busiest waterways. Along its 44-mile length between Trenton and New Brunswick, coal traveled east from Pennsylvania to New York, finished goods were sent west from the great metropolis, and New Jersey produce was shipped beyond the valleys where it was grown to help boost the agricultural fame of the "garden" state. The canal became so much a part of the fabric of life in New Jersey that even though it last showed a profit in 1892, it remained open to traffic for another 40 years before finally succumbing to the highways and railroads.

A 44-mile canal makes a mighty big white elephant. After the D&R was closed to barge traffic, it was used to channel water for farm irrigation and for industrial and residential use. During this period the canal began to attract recreational users; the old towpaths, along which draft animals at one time pulled the barges, made ideal hiking trails, and fishing and boating were easy along such a long, calm stretch of water, with only 14 locks between Trenton and New Brunswick. Eventually the state legislature responded to what had been a de facto recreational use pattern and created the *Delaware and Raritan Canal State Park*.

Today the 70-mile park, with its wooden bridges, 19th-century bridge-tender house, and hand-built stone arched culverts, is one of the state's most popular spots for canoeing, jogging, hiking, bicycling, fishing, and horseback riding. More than 160 species of birds have been sighted in the park. Small boats are welcome throughout the park, as long as no gasoline engines are involved. Information on privately operated canoe-rental services is available at park headquarters or by mail. Park headquarters can also supply details on the approximately 50 park access points, about half of which offer parking.

The main park office of D&R Canal State Park is at 145 Mapleton Rd. in Princeton; (609) 924-5705. The **Bull's Island Recreation Area and Campground** is at 2185 Daniel Bray Hwy. (Route 29) in Stockton; (609) 397-2949. The web address for both is www.dandrcanal.com. The park is open from sunrise to sunset.

There are big doings in **Lambertville** during the last full weekend in April. Each year the town hosts the Shad Festival—a nationally recognized event that features artists, crafters, and the environment. Through shad-hauling and fish-tagging demonstrations, the festival focuses on the importance of keeping the Delaware River clean. The aroma of cooked shad permeates the town as street vendors serve it up barbecued and fried, and down by the river the boat club and chamber of commerce host grilled shad dinners Sunday afternoon. Tickets for the dinners sell out quickly. For reservations call (609) 397-0055. Their website is www.lambertvillechamber.com.

If your appetite tends toward shopping, you'll be delighted to know that Lambertville is known as "The Antique Capital of New Jersey." Shops such as **Antiques on Union** (32 N. Union St.) and **Bridge Street Antiques** (21 Bridge St.) line the streets in town, and just 1½ miles south of town, the huge **Golden Nugget Antique Flea Market**, 1850 River Rd., (609) 397-0811, www.gnflea .com, attracts throngs of bargain hunters. The market is open Wed, Sat, and Sun from 6 a.m. to 4 p.m.; shops open at 8 a.m.

If you find yourself in Lambertville at breakfast or lunch time, pop into **Liv and Charlie's** for hearty omelets—the "Little Italy" features roasted red pepper, artichoke, fresh basil, and mozzarella—or that Jersey classic, a Taylor

A California Connection

Picturesque little Lambertville, with its upscale bistros, inns, and galleries, has been linked with New Hope, Pennsylvania, ever since Samuel Coryell began running his ferry across the Delaware River in 1732. More than a century later, the little town made a connection with history across a much greater distance. James Marshall, a descendant of Declaration of Independence signer John Hart, was born in Lambertville and lived in the Marshall family's brick house, which still stands at 60 Bridge Street. While supervising the building of Sutter's Mill in northern California in 1848, Marshall discovered the nuggets that set off the fabled gold rush of the following year.

Marshall, by the way, died broke.

ham and egg sandwich on a hard roll or bagel. Later in the day, there's always homemade soup, salads, and a generous selection of sandwiches and paninis. Liv and Charlie's, 5 N. Union St., (609) 397-0009, is open Wed through Sun from 9 a.m. to 2 p.m.

Hamilton's Grill Room at 8 Coryell St., (609) 397-4343, www.hamiltons-grillroom.com, serves contemporary Mediterranean fare prepared on an open grill. A prix fixe ($65) menu is served Wed through Sun both indoors and on an outdoor patio along the Delaware Canal and features grilled meats, seafood, and northern Italian dishes with an accent on seasonal ingredients. No credit cards—cash, check, or Venmo only.

Lambertville Station serves American cuisine in the town's restored Victorian train station. Specialties include crab cakes, jambalaya, and fine aged beef. The restaurant is on Bridge Street at the Delaware River, (609) 397-8300, www.lambertvillestation.com. Lunch and dinner are served daily; an a la carte Sunday brunch is served from 10:30 a.m. to 3:30 p.m. The Station Pub serves lighter fare.

Next door, each of the 45 rooms at *The Inn at Lambertville Station* is uniquely decorated with antiques from throughout the world. It's a perfect spot for those who like the charm of a B&B but the amenities of a small luxury hotel. Rates range from $309 to $414 and include continental breakfast. The inn is at 11 Bridge St., (609) 397-4400, www.lambertvillestation.com.

The AAA four-diamond *Lambertville House*, a National Historic Inn built in 1812, was once a stagecoach stop serving US presidents and dignitaries traveling between Philadelphia and New York. Today the beautifully restored inn, with its imposing facade of quarried stone etched with wrought-iron balustrades, welcomes guests looking for gracious accommodations. The 26 large, elegantly appointed rooms and suites are furnished with antiques and period reproductions; all have jetted tubs, 23 have gas fireplaces, and many have balconies overlooking the courtyard or town. If you prefer to do your people-watching while sipping a martini, settle into one of the cozy chairs at the inn's Left Bank Libations; in warm months the bar's patio offers an even better vantage point. The inn is at 32 Bridge St., Lambertville; (609) 397-0200, www.lambertvillehouse.com. Rates range from $200 to $330 and include a continental-plus breakfast, which you have delivered to your room.

The 130-acre *Howell Living History Farm* has been a working farm for more than 200 years and has been restored to operate like a typical New Jersey family farm circa 1900. A self-guided tour for visitors includes 30 points of interest, including a sheep barn, a chicken house, a wagon house, and an icehouse. There's even a genuine outhouse! Special hands-on programs and seasonal events are offered on Saturday throughout the year. In the fall, a 4-acre corn maze features 2 miles of challenging paths.

Howell Living History Farm, 70 Wooden's Ln., Lambertville, (609) 737-3299, www.howellfarm.org, is open for self-guided tours Feb through Nov, Tues through Fri from 10 a.m. to 4 p.m.; from Apr through Nov, it is also open on Sat from 10 a.m. to 4 p.m. and Sun from noon to 4 p.m. On two Saturdays in July, the farm is closed during the day and instead offers evening hayrides (check their website). Admission is free.

Capital Region

The town of Princeton is forever secondary in the public mind to the great institution that it harbors—Princeton University, New Jersey's entry in the Ivy League—but there is more to Princeton than its university, as a ride down Stockton Street (Route 206) will show. Here are two magnificent mansions that have been the official residence of the governors of New Jersey.

Historic **Morven**, the older of the two mansions, was, for more than 200 years, the home of the Stockton family. Richard Stockton, a signer of the Declaration of Independence, built his original house here in 1701 on land he purchased from Philadelphia's founder, William Penn. The present structure, recently restored, is an agglomeration of additions to that early home, most of them added in the mid-18th century, when the Georgian style predominated.

Morven's garden encompasses a formal, sweeping lawn with beds of heirloom annuals from the 18th and 19th centuries, and a re-creation of an early 20th-century Colonial Revival–style garden. Tours are offered May through Oct.

The mansion, on Stockton Street at Liberty Place, is open year-round to visitors for house tours Wed through Sun from 10 a.m. to 4 p.m. Call for guided tour times. The museum also mounts special exhibitions related to New Jersey's history and prominent citizens. Admission is $10 for adults and $8 for seniors and students; free for active military and children under 7. Strollers are not permitted in the museum. For more information call (609) 924-8144, ext. 103, or visit www.morven.org.

The present executive mansion is **Drumthwacket**, a mile past Morven on Stockton Street. Drumthwacket is a stately Greek Revival structure, with six great central pillars, looking for all the world like an antebellum southern mansion transported to the Delaware Valley. It was built in 1835 by Charles Olden, who later became governor of New Jersey. His building was the original central, columned portion; the wings were added by a later owner in the 1890s.

Drumthwacket is open to the public most Wednesdays for 45-minute tours beginning at noon by advance reservation only. A $5 donation is requested. For information call (973) 204-2860 or visit www.drumthwacket.org.

The permanent collection of the ***Princeton University Art Museum*** ranges from ancient to contemporary art and concentrates geographically on the Mediterranean regions, Western Europe, China, the United States, and Latin America. There is an outstanding collection of Greek and Roman antiquities, including Roman mosaics from Princeton University's excavations in Antioch. The collection of Western European paintings includes outstanding examples from the early Renaissance through the 19th century. Among the greatest strengths are Chinese art, with significant holdings in bronzes, tomb figures, and paintings; and pre-Columbian art, with remarkable examples of the art of the Maya. The museum has important collections of old-master prints and a comprehensive collection of original photographs. Princeton University's John B. Putnam Jr. Memorial Collection of 20th-century sculpture, located throughout the campus, includes works by such modern masters as Henry Moore, Alexander Calder, Pablo Picasso, and Jacques Lipchitz.

The Princeton University Art Museum has been located at McCormick Hall, Nassau Street, but will be closed until late 2024, when it will be housed in a new building designed by noted architect Sir David Adjaye. Call (609) 258-3788 for information or visit artmuseum.princeton.edu.

Behind Palmer Square, near the public library, is ***Princeton Cemetery***, final resting place of notables including Aaron Burr, Grover Cleveland, and Jonathan Edwards. Pick up a map at the superintendent's house near the entrance. The cemetery, at 29 Greenview Ave., is always open. For information call (609) 924-1369.

Stop in at the ***Nassau Inn***'s Yankee Doodle Tap Room for a drink, a bite, or just to see Norman Rockwell's 13-foot-long mural, *Yankee Doodle Dandy*. The inn, which has been accommodating weary travelers since 1756, is at 10 Palmer Sq., Princeton, (609) 921-7500, www.nassauinn.com.

A Brief Presidential Term

Reverend Jonathan Edwards, the famed Congregationalist minister whose fiery sermon "Sinners in the Hands of an Angry God" terrified the faithful when he delivered it from his pulpit in Northampton, Massachusetts, left New England in 1757 to take up the presidency of Princeton University, then known as the College of New Jersey. Just two weeks after arriving at Princeton, however, Edwards died of smallpox, which he contracted after participating in an early experiment with inoculation.

The whole family will enjoy a trip to **Terhune Orchards** at 330 Cold Soil Rd. in Princeton, (609) 924-2310. There are berries, cherries, and apples to pick; fresh-baked goodies to munch on; fresh produce to buy; and lots of old farm equipment for the kids to climb on. Visitors are encouraged to bring along a picnic lunch. The farm store is open Mon through Fri from 9 a.m. to 6 p.m. and weekends from 9 a.m. to 5 p.m. The winery is open weekends from 9 a.m. to 5 p.m. Call for information on special events or check www .terhuneorchards.com.

Trenton, the capital of New Jersey, was in 1776 a tiny village of no more than a hundred houses, important chiefly as the head of navigation on the Delaware River. Since Christmas of that year, however, it has loomed inestimably larger in American history because of George Washington's crossing of the ice-clogged Delaware and defeat of Great Britain's Hessian mercenaries in the Battle of Trenton.

Tradition holds that at the time of the battle, Hessians were quartered in an 18-year-old stone building located near the spot where the New Jersey State House stands today. After having survived many uses and a few dates with the wrecker's ball, this venerable structure survives today as the **Old Barracks Museum**.

The Old Barracks were built in 1758 to house British troops fighting in the French and Indian War. Formerly troops who were waiting out the winter for the next season's campaign had been billeted among New Jersey townspeople and farmers, but popular dissatisfaction with this practice (a resentment against being forced to quarter troops later made it into our Bill of Rights) led to the construction of army housing at five New Jersey locations. Rented out for other purposes by the legislature during the interim between the French and Indian

Elmer Always Leaves Flowers

Yes, Virginia, there was an Elsie the Cow. Her real name was You'll Do Lobelia, and she was a star of the Borden Company's milking exhibit at the 1939 New York World's Fair. "Elsie" had been Borden's cartoon mascot for several years, and when the exhibit opened, so many visitors asked "Which cow is Elsie?" that Y. D. Lobelia— a doe-eyed cutie of a cow—was picked to carry the famous name.

"Elsie" began touring the country, but her career as Borden spokescow was tragically cut short when she suffered fatal injuries in a traffic accident in 1941. She was buried on a farm in Plainsboro, New Jersey, where you can see her gravestone (moved from its original site, which is now part of a housing development) near the Plainsboro Museum on Plainsboro Road.

A Depression-Era Experiment

Located about 20 miles east of Trenton, the town of Roosevelt was founded in 1935 as a community called Jersey Homesteads. Incorporating a women's clothing factory and a 40-acre farm, the settlement would provide a new home for garment workers previously confined to the tenements of New York and Philadelphia. Launched with both government and private funds, the community was to be an experiment in cooperative ownership of factory, farm, and stores, with an equal distribution of profits. New housing was built, and attractive mortgage terms offered.

The Homesteads' manufacturing and agricultural ventures met with little success, however, and within a few years the community was opened to everyone and the cooperative scheme abandoned. Renamed after the death of President Franklin Roosevelt in 1945, the little town evolved into an ordinary suburban community. But many of the severe, international-style homes and public buildings remain, reminders of a certain vision of the future that found appeal during the Depression's darkest days.

and Revolutionary Wars, the barracks were activated again by the British when the rebellion broke out.

When the war was over, the New Jersey legislature sold the barracks to private investors, who began fixing them up for use as civilian housing—one of the earliest instances of a type of "condo conversion" in a former institutional building. Throughout the 19th century, the barracks and officers' quarters served one purpose after another, from tenements to schools to a home for widows. What remained of the complex (a portion was torn down in 1792) was finally purchased for preservation between 1902 and 1914, first by private groups and later by the state. The demolished section was rebuilt, the entire structure restored to its original appearance inside and out, and the Old Barracks Museum came into being.

Today's visitor to the Old Barracks is offered a rare view of what a soldier's life was like 200 years ago. Each of 22 16-by-23-foot rooms, with their fireplaces (one to a room) and single doors, was home to up to 14 men. Life in the nearby officers' quarters was, needless to say, a shade more pleasant. Visitors meet role players in 18th-century dress, who portray Revolutionary War–era soldiers and camp women. In addition there's an orientation exhibit with a video introduction, changing historical exhibits, displays of original firearms, and dioramas of the Battle of Trenton. That battle is reenacted the Saturday after Christmas.

The Old Barracks Museum, 101 Barrack St., Trenton, (609) 396-1776, www.barracks.org, is open Tues through Sat from 10 a.m. to 5 p.m., except major holidays. Tours are given at 10 a.m., noon, and 2 p.m. Reservations are required. Tickets are $10 for adults and $8 for students and seniors; free for active military.

Just minutes from Trenton's State House is a section of town called Chambersburg. Nicknamed **Little Italy**, it's a mecca for lovers of Italian food: Within 1 square mile there are numerous Italian restaurants—Amici Milano, Marsilio's, Rossi's—each with its own ambience and specialties. Perhaps the best way to choose is to wander about and inhale the wonderful aromas.

In September 1921, 120 recruits reported to Sea Girt and began training under the watchful eye of Colonel H. Norman Schwarzkopf, father of General "Stormin' Norman" Schwarzkopf of Gulf War fame. Eighty-one passed the rigorous course and became New Jersey's first state troopers. Their story and many others—including a fascinating, in-depth exhibit on the Lindbergh kidnapping—are told at the **New Jersey State Police Museum and Learning Center**.

Several of the exhibits here are interactive. In the Criminal Investigation area, visitors help a detective search a crime scene for evidence, analyze bullets and fibers under a microscope, and examine fingerprints. Part of the museum is housed in a 1934 log cabin that was originally used as a dormitory and classroom for new recruits. It now houses a transportation exhibit that includes a 1921 Harley-Davidson motorcycle, a 1930 Buick State Police touring car, and a present-day cruiser car in which visitors can sit, activate the light bar, and listen to recordings of actual radio transmissions.

The New Jersey State Police Museum and Learning Center, 1040 River Rd. (Route 175), West Trenton, (609) 882-2000, ext. 6401, www.njspmuseum.org, is open Mon through Fri from 9 a.m. to 3 p.m. Admission is free.

Fred and Theresa Kuser began construction of their magnificent Queen Anne country home in 1888. They spared no expense. In addition to the mansion, a laundry house, barn, coachman's house, chicken house, windmill, shower house, and corncrib were constructed, as well as one of the finest clay

No Doubt It Was a Diner-Saur

New Jersey has two state animals: the horse *and Hadrosaurus foulkii*, a large dinosaur whose remains were found in the town of Haddonfield many years ago. Traces and skeletons of dinosaurs and other fossil animals have been uncovered at Fort Lee, and dinosaur tracks were found in the Triassic rock of the Palisades during construction of the George Washington Bridge. A hadrosaur model is on display at the State Museum in Trenton.

tennis courts in New Jersey. Four years later the family finally sat down to its first dinner at *Kuser Farm Mansion*.

A tour of the mansion includes a visit to the Delft Bedroom, whose fireplace has more than a hundred different delft tiles, and the Kuser Farm Theatre/Dining Room and Projection Room (the family helped finance the Fox Film Corporation, which later became 20th Century Fox). The intricately carved woodwork throughout the mansion was executed by German craftspersons on loan from the Peter Doelger Brewery in New York City. (Mrs. Kuser was the daughter of Mr. Doelger.)

The Kuser Farm Mansion, 2090 Greenwood Ave., Hamilton, (609) 890-3630, is open on Sat and Sun from 11 a.m. to 3 p.m., March through late Oct. Admission is free.

The 35-acre *Grounds for Sculpture*, on the site of the former New Jersey State Fairgrounds, showcases more than 250 works by American and internationally known artists. Permanent pieces by artists such as Magdalena Abakanowicz, Marisol, and Anthony Caro and special exhibitions are displayed in two museums and on the lovely grounds.

There are several dining options at the Grounds for Sculpture. The Gazebo overlooking the lotus pond, a delightful place to enjoy a light lunch, is open from noon to 6 p.m. weather permitting. The Van Gogh Café, with indoor and outdoor seating, is open Wed through Mon from 10 a.m. to 4:30 p.m. for pastries, snacks, and beverages. But for a special outing, *Rat's Restaurant*, "designed to make visitors feel they have stepped into a village reminiscent of French impressionist Claude Monet's beloved town of Giverny" (and named for the beloved character in Kenneth Grahame's book *The Wind in the Willows*), offers an eclectic lunch and dinner menu. Rat's is open Wed through Sun for lunch from 11 a.m. to 3 p.m. and dinner from 5 to 9 p.m. (8 p.m. on Sun). The bar is open Wed through Sun from 11 a.m. till closing. For reservations call (609) 584-7800.

The Grounds for Sculpture, 18 Fairgrounds Rd., Hamilton, (609) 586-0616, www.groundsforsculpture.org, is open year-round, Tues through Sun from 10 a.m. to 6 p.m. (last entry time 5 p.m.), and on Labor Day and Memorial Day. Admission is $20 for adults, $15 for seniors and active military, and $10 for those ages 6 to 17. Reservations must be made in advance, with specified entry time, by calling the number above or visiting the website. Reservations may be made up to two weeks in advance.

Bordentown, on the Delaware River just south of Trenton, is one of the oldest settlements of central New Jersey. The primary thrust of colonization in this part of the state was from the south (along the river) rather than from the New York Harbor area, as it was in the northern counties; consequently,

landho!

It is believed that the first white man to see the New Jersey shore was the Florentine navigator Giovanni da Verrazano, who sailed up the Atlantic coast in 1524.

the ethnic and cultural influences were English rather than Dutch and owed much to the Quaker society of early Philadelphia.

One of the major attractions in this historic town is the *Clara Barton Schoolhouse*, a Bordentown landmark associated with the early career of the woman who was to found the American Red Cross. Barton's later humanitarian accomplishments tend to obscure the fact that she was instrumental in launching the concept of public education in New Jersey. Before she came to Bordentown in 1852, the state's schools were operated primarily by religious institutions; those that were not generally assessed each student a fee that not everyone could afford. The only alternative was the poorly run, state-supported system of "pauper schools," usually conducted in an ill-trained teacher's home. In the year Clara Barton arrived, not one of Bordentown's seven schools occupied a town-owned building.

Barton badgered the Bordentown school committee into reopening the old school building long used by the Quakers and other religious groups and briefly operated as a town school in 1839. In May 1852, she began teaching a class of six students; within a week the school's enrollment was 55. By the following year there were three Bordentown schools, 600 pupils, and eight teachers. The town—and the state—needed no further convincing that a modern system of centralized public education could succeed in New Jersey as it

New Jersey: Diner-Building Capital of the World

Although diners originated in New England—in Providence, Rhode Island, to be exact—they reached the height of their mid-20th-century fame in the Garden State. Great diners were manufactured in New Jersey by companies named Kullman, O'Mahony, Mountain View, Fodero, and Silk City. The last of the state's diner builders was Kullman Industries, which was located in Lebanon, New Jersey, and closed in 2011. Kullman specialized in all sorts of prefabricated modular buildings ranging from banks to schools to prisons—but the firm is best remembered for its diners.

Perhaps the most famous of its surviving creations is the Tick Tock Diner, which has stood along Route 3 in Clifton, New Jersey, since 1948 and has since grown to a brightly lit palazzo of a diner. You can't miss it—when you're driving eastbound on 3, just look for the big clock over the entrance. The Tick Tock motto? "Eat Heavy."

was succeeding in Barton's native New England. Unfortunately Barton wasn't around Bordentown for long to savor her triumph. Sidelined from teaching by the temporary failure of her voice, she was replaced by a new school principal.

Clara Barton's original schoolhouse in Bordentown was acquired by the city in 1920; it has since been restored to its original (at the time of her teaching) appearance. Located on Crosswicks Street near Farnsworth Avenue, it may be visited by arrangement with the Bordentown Historical Society, (609) 298-1740, www.bordentownhistory.org. Visitors can print a self-guided walking tour from the society's website.

Bordentown is also home to the largest facility in the Ocean Spray Cranberries family. Manufacturing began here on an acre of land in 1943; today 32 million cases of cranberry juice are produced each year on 60 acres.

Coal may have long since lost its place as a home heating fuel, but it remains one of the leading contenders in the eternal debate over how to generate the intense heat needed to bake a proper pizza. There's a New York–based school of pizza making that swears by coal, and that's the line followed at **Marcello's**, a Bordentown institution that advertises its take on the Neapolitan staple by the old New Jersey moniker "tomato pies."

Marcello's ovens yield a tremendous variety of pies, ranging from basic San Marzano tomato and mozzarella to versions made with ingredients as varied as roasted peppers and artichokes, baby clams, prosciutto and fig jam, wild mushrooms, and pulled pork ($19 to $26). And for those who believe pizza needs a before and after, the menu offers starters such as calamari oreganata (coal-fired, of course) and eggplant rollatini . . . and for dessert, cannoli shipped in daily from Brooklyn. Marcello's is at 206 Farnsworth Ave., (609) 298-8360, and is open Mon through Thurs 11 a.m. to 10 p.m., Fri and Sat 11 a.m. to 11 p.m., and Sun noon to 9 p.m.

Burlington lies farther south along the river than Bordentown, and is older still. English Quakers arrived here as early as 1677; the settlement was incorporated as a township in 1693 and granted a city charter by King George II in 1734. By the time of the Revolution, Burlington was a center for pottery making and shipbuilding, and it enjoyed the status of a sea-trading port because of its easy river access to the open ocean.

Despite the fact that Burlington was chosen as the place where the New Jersey State Constitution would be written in 1776, the little city harbored a fair number of Tory sympathizers. One of them, a lawyer and mayor of Burlington, was John Lawrence. Lawrence left the United States for Canada at the close of the Revolution, but before he departed, his son James was born at what is now known as the **Lawrence House** on High Street. James Lawrence's politics turned out to be quite a bit different from those of his father, as did his profession. Originally intended by his father to study law, young Lawrence was back in Burlington studying navigation by 1796 and two years later was a midshipman in the US Navy. One year into the War of 1812, he was captain of the USS *Chesapeake*. It was during the *Chesapeake*'s losing engagement with the British ship *Shannon* that Captain Lawrence was mortally wounded, but before he died he uttered five of the most famous words in US naval history: "Don't give up the ship!"

It isn't often that two Americans notable in entirely different fields turn out to have been born in adjacent houses, but this block of High Street in Burlington offers just such a coincidence. In 1798 the **Cooper House**, now the headquarters of the Burlington County Historical Society, was the birthplace of James Cooper (he added the middle name Fenimore as an adult) and his home for 13 months before his parents packed up their large brood and headed for the upstate New York haunts with which the novelist became associated through works such as *The Deerslayer* and *The Last of the Mohicans*. He is remembered today, in the house that bears his name, with a collection of his works and an assortment of associated items. The house also contains a Bonaparte Room, furnished with items once belonging to Napoleon's brother Joseph Bonaparte during his Bordentown sojourn.

The oldest of the three houses that make up the Burlington County Historical Society's High Street Complex is the **Bard-Howe House**, built about 1743. Among the antiques on display at the house is a signed clock built by the accomplished local silversmith and clockmaker Isaac Pearson.

The Lawrence House is at 459 High St., the Cooper House at 457, and the Bard-Howe House at 453. The society's **Corson-Poley Center** exhibits an excellent collection of quilts, tall-case clocks, and samplers, as well as examples of the J. H. Birch Company's jinrikishas (rickshaws). The complex is open Tues through Sat from 10 a.m. to 5 p.m.; admission is $5 per person. For information contact the Burlington County Historical Society, 457 High St., Burlington 08016; (609) 386-4773; www.burlingtoncountyhistoricalsociety.org.

Everything from antiques to vintage clothing to wallpaper is on sale at flea market prices at the **Columbus Farmers' Market**, 2919 Route 206 South; (609) 267-0400; www.columbusfarmersmarket.com. Fresh flowers are for sale along Flower Row, and produce vendors and fishmongers hawk their wares along Produce Row. The indoor market is open Thurs and Sat 8 a.m. to 8 p.m., Fri 10 a.m. to 8 p.m., and Sun 8 a.m. to 5 p.m. The outdoor market is open Thurs, Sat, and Sun 8 a.m. to 3 p.m.

Head on Route 524 to Allentown and **Horse Park of New Jersey at Stone Tavern**, the state's first major horse-show grounds. Activities here continue throughout the year. For a calendar of events, call (609) 259-0170 or visit www.horseparkofnewjersey.wildapricot.org.

Central Lowlands

Webbs' Mill Bog Cedar Swamp in the 27,298-acre Greenwood Wildlife Management Area is one of the few places in the state to hear—and possibly see—the endangered Pine Barrens tree frog, a tiny, bright green frog with lavender stripes. The best time to hear one is in the evening during the months of May and June. A boardwalk and trail run over a bog that's home to the delicate pitcher plant and rare curly grass ferns. The area is also home to the endangered timber rattlesnake: Although meetings are rare, if you do encounter one, just back away quietly. The swamp environment is a fragile one; be sure to stay on the boardwalk and trails.

Webbs' Mill Bog Cedar Swamp is on CR 539 south of Whiting in Manchester Township. For more information contact the New Jersey Division of Fish, Game and Wildlife, Mail Code 501-03, PO Box 420, Trenton 08625; (609) 292-2965.

After observing Germany's successful military use of zeppelins in World War I, the United States established the Lakehurst Naval Air Station and began making its own airships, or dirigibles. The popularity of dirigibles peaked in 1936, after the *Hindenburg* had completed 10 successful commercial round-trips from Europe to Lakehurst, but the romance ended the following year when the dirigible burned while landing at Lakehurst. Lakehurst Naval Air Station is now the ***Naval Air Engineering Station***, and both the memorial

Up in Flames

The town of Lakehurst, long the site of the US Navy's Naval Air Engineering Station, has played a prominent role in the development of lighter-than-air flight. But it wasn't an American airship that figured in Lakehurst's most famous event—it was the German luxury passenger dirigible *Hindenburg*, which used the facility as a landing field in 1936 and 1937. On May 6, 1937, the *Hindenburg* caught fire while approaching her mooring mast. The hydrogen-filled craft was quickly consumed in flames, and 36 people were killed. The disaster marked the end of lighter-than-air transatlantic passenger service, even though airships filled with helium instead of hydrogen would have been impervious to fire and explosion. In the days of the *Hindenburg*, the United States controlled world supplies of helium, which was considered a strategic material and was withheld from the Nazi German regime. In a way, those 36 unlucky airship travelers were among the first victims of the gathering storm of World War II.

plaque for the *Hindenburg* and Historic Hangar No. 1 (the site of the first international airport) are on the center's grounds.

The Navy Lakehurst Historical Society offers a free tour that begins at 10 a.m. Nov through Mar on the 2nd Sat of the month, and Apr through Oct on the 2nd and 4th Sat of the month. Preregistration is required and must be done at least two weeks in advance. The tour includes the Information Center, Historic Hangar No. 1, the Ready Room, the POW-MIA Room, and the crash-site marker. The Naval Air Engineering Station is on Route 547 (north of Route 70). For a schedule and reservations, call (732) 600-8055 or visit www.nlhs.com.

A trip back up the Delaware Valley to Trenton and due east across central New Jersey on I-195 will take you to *The Historic Village at Allaire* in *Allaire State Park*. Allaire Village was a company town, back in the days when the mining and smelting of bog iron was big business in these parts. James P. Allaire, a New York City brass founder, came here in 1822 to exploit this resource by means of an integrated mining, smelting, and forging operation. Within 15 years he had created an entire community around his "Howell Works," with 400 employees, a free school, and even a stagecoach to Red Bank. Allaire's workers lived in substantial brick row houses, among the first examples of company housing in the United States. Some of the products they turned out were kitchenware, stoves, screws, and flatirons.

The iron industry, however, was not destined to become a long-standing New Jersey staple. Once discovered, Pennsylvania anthracite coal became a cheaper fuel than local charcoal for smelting, and eventually large deposits of iron ore from the north-central Midwest made the mining of bog iron obsolete. After 1850 the village of Allaire became a ghost town. The fact that its buildings remain is due partly to the solidity of their brick construction and partly to the wise acquisition of the town and its environment by newspaperman Arthur Brisbane early in the last century. For many years Monmouth County's Boy Scout organization used several of the buildings as headquarters and helped with restoration projects.

In 1941, Brisbane's widow gave the village and much of the surrounding land to the state for use as a park, and restoration efforts continued. Getting an abandoned town back in shape after so long a period of disuse is a big job. Preservation and interpretation of the site continues under the direction of Allaire Village, Inc.

Among the sites to visit at Allaire today are the old carpenter and blacksmith shops, general store, and bakery; workers' houses and foreman's cottage; enameling furnace and casting-house stack; and the picturesque millpond.

Allaire State Park, on Route 524 (off I-195, exit 31B, and off Garden State Parkway, exit 98), (732) 938-2371, is open Apr through Nov, Wed through Fri from 11 a.m. to 4 p.m. and weekends from 11 a.m. to 4:30 p.m. The bakery, general store, and museum are also open in Dec, Fri through Sun from 11 a.m. to 4 p.m. Admission to the village craft shops and historic homes is $5 for ages 4 and up. For museum information call (732) 919-3500 or visit www.allairevil lage.org.

As if a historic village weren't enough to make Allaire unique among New Jersey state parks, this is also the home of the *Pine Creek Railroad*. The trains, which are operated by the New Jersey Museum of Transportation and take passengers through the park along a narrow-gauge track on 15-minute rides, depart every half hour in season from 11:30 a.m. to 3:30 p.m. For the schedule call (732) 938-5524 or check www.njmt.org. Tickets are $6 for persons 3 and older and $2 for children under 3. Nonrefundable tickets are sold online only as of this writing.

Both the Historic Village and the railroad host a busy schedule of special events, which are posted on their websites.

If it has ever gobbled, it's most likely sold at *Hinck's Turkey Farm*, 1414 Atlantic Ave., Manasquan, (732) 223-5622, www.hincksfarm.com, a Jersey Shore tradition since 1928. You can buy a fresh turkey, opt for one oven-ready, or buy one already cooked with all the sides. There's also turkey soup, turkey sandwiches, turkey potpies, turkey croquettes . . . as well as non-turkey options (including barbecued pork ribs with three sides and a rib eye sandwich on a toasted hard roll) and terrific daily specials. Save room for dessert—they're all homemade at Hinck's. The farm is open daily from 9 a.m. to 6 p.m., with special holiday hours. You can get everything "to go" or eat there.

Collingwood Park Auction and Flea Market, with more than 600 indoor and outdoor tables, has been a bargain hunter's paradise since 1957. Vendors sell everything from fresh produce to Tibetan clothing to musical instruments, and there are plenty of food vendors. The market is on Routes 33 and 34 (just ½ mile west of the Collingwood Circle) in Farmingdale, (732) 938-7941, www .collingwoodfleamarket.com. It's open Fri through Sun from 8 a.m. to 5 p.m.

do-si-do

In 1983, the square dance was designated the official American Folk Dance of the State of New Jersey.

Slightly to the northwest of Allaire is a state park dedicated in commemoration not of the long-term production of iron, but the short-term exchange of lead—in the form of musket balls. *Monmouth Battlefield State Park* came into being on June 28, 1978, the 200th anniversary of the Battle of Monmouth. The struggle that took place on that June day in 1778 was the longest of the entire Revolution, and the only one in which both supreme commanders—George Washington and Sir Harry Clinton—were involved against each other.

Among the tales of valor that emerged from the smoke and dust of Monmouth, one of the most enduring is that of Molly Pitcher. While her husband fought with the Continental army as a member of a cannon crew, Molly Pitcher carried water to thirsty soldiers during the heat of battle; when her husband was wounded, she herself took his place with the artillerymen. No one has been able to find exactly where Molly's well was, but just for the sake of heroic tradition, if not accuracy, a reproduction has been set up on Route 522 in the 1,520-acre park. Other park features include a visitor center and a marked footpath through the battlefield.

Another important park attraction is the ***Craig House***, a 1710 farmstead occupied at the time of the battle by the family of John Craig, paymaster for the local patriot militia. Craig fought at the Battle of Monmouth, and his wife, children, and two slaves left their home when it was apparent that the British were approaching the vicinity. The enemy found Mrs. Craig's silver (hidden in the bottom of the well, which is the first place we would look if we were pillaging enemy territory), and used the house to treat their wounded. The place survived the battle intact and has now been restored to its Revolutionary-era appearance. The four-room Craig House, with its massive kitchen hearth and three smaller fireplaces, offers a good look at how 18th-century women lived when they weren't fighting off His Majesty's army or throwing their silver down the well.

Also on the grounds is the 1745 ***Rhea-Applegate House***, whose exterior has been restored. It's the oldest standing two-story Dutch-crafted farmhouse in the state.

Monmouth Battlefield State Park, accessible via Route 9 or Route 33, is at 347 Freehold-Englishtown Rd. in Manalapan, (732) 462-9616, and is open daily during daylight hours. The visitor center is just off Business Route 33 in Manalapan and is open Wed through Sun from 9 a.m. to 3 p.m. There is no admission fee to the park. The Battle of Monmouth is reenacted on the 4th weekend of each June.

The Applegate family has been managing the park's pick-your-own ***Battleview Orchards Country Market and Bakery*** since 1908. From the end of May through Oct, visitors can harvest a succession of fruits, beginning with strawberries, continuing with peaches and nectarines, and culminating with apples and pumpkins. The country store is open daily Wed through Mon from 9 a.m. to 5 p.m. In the fall there are weekend hayrides. For information and picking hours, call (732) 462-0756 or visit http://www.battlevieworchards.com.

You never know what you'll find at the **Monmouth Museum**, founded in 1963 as a "Museum of Ideas." Exhibitions on art, science, nature, culture, and history change constantly. Art and artifacts for the exhibits are borrowed from the nation's leading museums, galleries, and private collections. Kids can participate in a variety of hands-on activities at the Becker Children's Wing, where changing exhibitions complement the curriculum of the local schools.

The Monmouth Museum, 765 Newman Springs Rd., Lincroft, (732) 747-2266, www.monmouthmuseum.org, is open Wed through Sun from 10 a.m. to 4 p.m. Admission is $10 per person; children under 2 are free. Call or check the website for hours for the Becker Children's Wing and Wonder Wing.

There are 366 polished black granite panels arranged in a circle at the **New Jersey Vietnam Veterans' Memorial**—one for each day of the year. Engraved on the dated panels are the names of the 1,555 New Jersey soldiers, marines, sailors, and airmen killed or reported missing in action on each date. At the center of the memorial, under a red oak tree, three large bronze statues represent the more than 80,000 New Jerseyans who served in Southeast Asia.

The 10,000-square-foot **Vietnam Era Museum**, dedicated in 1998, is "devoted solely to gaining an understanding of the violent conflict in Southeast Asia and the surrounding political strife in America." A historic timeline chronicles the events of the era, documenting activities both in Vietnam and in the United States. Eyewitness accounts—letters and other written material—give visitors an idea of the war's emotional toll on those directly involved. Oral histories of those who lived through the Vietnam War era, including a protester and a mother whose son was killed, bring the war even closer to home. There's also a resource center, which houses information on New Jerseyans killed in Vietnam as well as information on all those in the state who served in the armed forces from 1959 to 1975.

The New Jersey Vietnam Veterans' Memorial and Vietnam Era Museum are at 1 Memorial Ln., Holmdel, (800) 648-8387 or (732) 335-0033, www.njvvmf.org. The museum is open Tues through Sat from 10 a.m. to 4 p.m. Admission is $7 for adults, $5 for senior citizens and students, and free for children 10 and under. Veterans and active military personnel are admitted free.

Bruce Springsteen fans will want to walk or drive by two of the homes in Freehold where he lived in his early years. The rock 'n' roll legend lived at 39½ Institute St. from the age of 6 to 13, and at 68 South St. when he was 14. If you find yourself in Long Branch, you may want to drive past 7½ West End Court, the tiny two-bedroom cottage where he wrote his album *Born to Run*. It's privately owned and there's no marker in front.

Until such time as Paterson renames its East Side after Allen Ginsberg or Rutherford comes through with a William Carlos Williams neighborhood,

Matawan will remain the only New Jersey community with a section named after an American poet. The poet is Philip Freneau, known as the "Poet of the American Revolution" because of his biting anti-British satirical verse. Freneau lived on an estate called Mount Pleasant in Middletown Point, as Matawan was then called. After his house burned down in 1818, he spent his last 14 years with relatives near Freehold. Having been out drinking in Freehold village one December night in 1832, the 80-year-old poet got lost while walking home and died of exposure in a bog. He was buried in the family plot on his old estate, in what is now the built-up Freneau section of Matawan. The *Freneau Gravesite*, which may still be visited, is at the end of a short, tree-lined drive on the left side of Route 79, about a mile south of Freneau Center. The grave is marked by a marble shaft, which stands within a small fenced enclosure.

The huge *Jackson Premium Outlets* at 537 Monmouth Rd. in Jackson, (732) 833-0503, includes Gap, Nike, Timberland, and Brooks Brothers. Check their website for individual store hours.

The *Jewish Heritage Museum of Monmouth County* combines a multimedia exhibit, photographs, and artifacts to relate the rich history of the Jewish people in this area. The museum is appropriately housed in the historic Levi Solomon Barn, one of the largest barn structures left in the county and once the home of a descendent of one of the county's earliest Jewish settlers. The museum's centerpiece is its permanent exhibit titled *Three Centuries of Growth and Change: A History of the Jews of Monmouth County*, which chronicles how the community originated with the arrival of a Sephardic Jew who came to peddle his wares.

The Jewish Heritage Museum of Monmouth County, 310 Mounts Corner Dr., Freehold, (732) 252-6990, www.jhmomc.org, is open by appointment only Tues and Thurs from 10 a.m. to 3 p.m. and Sun from 11 a.m. to 3 p.m. It closes Sun at 1 p.m. when 2 p.m. programs are scheduled. A donation of $3 for members and $5 for nonmembers is requested. Check the website for a list of scheduled events and special exhibits.

Ready for some great barbecue? Make a pit stop at *Big Ed's Barbecue*, 305 Route 34, Old Bridge, (732) 583-2626, www.bigedsbbq.com, where one of the big draws on the menu is "all-u-can-eat ribs all of the time." They're served up daily: $18.99 for lunch before 3:30 p.m. Mon through Fri and before 2 p.m. weekends; dinner for $23.99 every day. The restaurant, whose ambience evokes that of a roadhouse deep in South Carolina, also serves up favorites including pulled pork, beef brisket, barbecued chicken, and great fried seafood. Save room for the hot molten lava cake with vanilla ice cream. They're open daily from 11:30 a.m. to 9 p.m.

The Name Game

Rutgers, New Jersey's state university, was chartered in 1766 and ranks as the eighth-oldest institution of higher learning in the British American colonies. But the university, which has its main campus in New Brunswick, wasn't always called Rutgers. It was originally called Queen's College, in honor of George III's consort Queen Charlotte, and was renamed in 1825 after a prosperous local citizen, Colonel Henry Rutgers. Hoping that the colonel would come to the aid of the financially strapped college, the administration effected the name change in his honor before actually receiving a contribution. Rutgers did loosen his purse strings, eventually donating more than $5,000 to the school.

The Jane Voorhees *Zimmerli Art Museum* on the New Brunswick campus of Rutgers University houses the school's collection of more than 35,000 works of art. The art museum's major concentrations are in 19th-century French graphics, Russian and Soviet art, 20th-century American art, and contemporary American printmaking. The collection also includes ancient art and European art of the 15th through 19th centuries, pre-Columbian ceramics, and designs for American stained glass. The Zimmerli incorporates the International Center for Japonisme and presents related art in the Kusakabe-Griffis Japonisme Gallery. A special gallery features the extensive Rutgers Collection of Illustrations for Children's Literature. At the entry level of the modern museum building are special exhibition galleries, the George Riabov Collection of Russian Art, a cafe, and a gift shop; works from the permanent collection are exhibited on the lower level.

The Zimmerli Art Museum, Rutgers University, George and Hamilton Streets, (732) 932-7237, www.zimmerli.rutgers.edu, is open Wed through Sun; check website for current hours. Admission is free.

One of the country's largest collection of American hollies and a bamboo forest that winds alongside a small stream are just two of the highlights at the lovely 180-acre *Rutgers Gardens* on the outskirts of Rutgers University's Cook Campus in North Brunswick. Be sure to include a stroll through Helyard Woods, a 60-acre old-growth forest, and the Donald B. Lacey Display Garden, whose plantings design changes every year.

A much anticipated event is the gardens' Spring Flower Fair, a three-day event held annually in early May. Admission is free, but advance tickets are required. Cook's Market, the gardens' farmers' market, features more than 20 vendors whose products change with the seasons, but shoppers can usually find fresh-baked goods, handmade soaps, local honey, homemade soups, and whatever produce is being harvested.

Rutgers Gardens, 130 Log Cabin Rd., North Brunswick, (848) 932-7000, www.rutgersgardens.rutgers.edu, is open Tues through Sun from 8 a.m. to 5 p.m. Cook's Market is held May to Dec on Fri from 11 a.m. to 3 p.m. Admission is free.

"Life is uncertain. Eat dessert first!" cautions the menu at *Old Man Rafferty's*. To make sure you heed the warning, Rafferty's offers more than four dozen sweets from which to choose. The restaurant, near Rutgers University, also serves moderately priced steaks, sandwiches, salads, and a terrific selection of wines and beers. Old Man Rafferty's is at 106 Albany St., New Brunswick, (732) 846-6153. There's also a Rafferty's at 284 Route 206 in Hillsborough, (908) 904-9731. Both are open daily for lunch and dinner. For information visit www .oldmanraffertys.com.

In East Millstone there is a tract of natural land that is a good deal smaller than the Great Swamp but no less remarkable for having survived in primeval condition right down into our own time. This is the *Hutcheson Memorial Forest Center*, 400 acres of woods and fields maintained by the Department of Ecology, Evolution, and Natural Resources at Rutgers University.

At the core of the Hutcheson tract (it's named after William L. Hutcheson, a past president of the United Brotherhood of Carpenters and Joiners, which was instrumental in securing the forest preservation) is 64-acre *Mettler's Woods*, believed to be the only uncut upland forest in New Jersey. Uncut means that throughout three and a half centuries, while the vast forests of the ever more populous Northeast fell for cordwood, for buildings, and to clear land for agriculture, this tiny tract escaped the ax. This is not to say that the elements haven't taken their toll—fire, wind, and insects interfere in the lives of all primeval forests. But there has never been any timber harvesting or soil cultivation here. The living white oak trees in Mettler's Woods average 235 years in age, while some of the trees that have died within the past 30 years have been up to 350 years old.

Mettler's Woods is surrounded by more than 300 acres of younger forest, consisting of second growth over land that was previously cultivated and logged. This adjacent forest helps researchers understand the difference between untouched climax growth and the far more prevalent reestablished forest; also, it provides a welcome buffer for the primeval woods within.

The Hutcheson Memorial Forest is open to visitors for scheduled tours conducted by Rutgers faculty members on periodic Sundays at 2 p.m. Reservations aren't necessary for individuals and groups smaller than 10, and tours last from 1 to 2 hours. Trips leave from the entrance at 2150 Amwell Rd. (Route 514) about ¾ mile east of East Millstone. There is no charge for individual tours. For more information and the schedule, check https://hmf.rutgers.edu.

Places to Stay in Central New Jersey

Hyatt Regency New Brunswick
2 Albany St., New Brunswick
(732) 873-1234
www.hyatt.com
Expensive

Hyatt Regency Princeton
102 Carnegie Center, Princeton
(800) 233-1234 or (609) 987-1234
www.princetonhyatt.com
Expensive

Inn at Glencairn Princeton
3301 Lawrenceville Rd., Princeton
(609) 497-1737
www.innatglencairn.com
Expensive

Nassau Inn
10 Palmer Sq., Princeton
(609) 921-7500 or (800) 862-7728
www.nassauinn.com
Expensive

The National Hotel
31 Race St., Frenchtown
(908) 996-3200
www.thenationalfrenchtown.com
Moderate–expensive

Olde Mill Inn
225 Route 202, Basking Ridge
(908) 221-1100
www.oldemillinn.com
Moderate–expensive

Widow McCrea House
53 Kingwood Ave., Frenchtown
(908) 996-4999
www.widowmccrea.com
Moderate–expensive

Places to Eat in Central New Jersey

Destination Dogs
101 Paterson St., New Brunswick
(732) 993-1016
This dog house serves up a huge menu of domestic, international, and "pilot your own" creations, and not all are hot dog–based. Among the unusual from the International menu: Andouille Armstrong, with alligator and shrimp sausage, fried shrimp, cabbage, tomato, jalapeño, remoulade, pickle, lemon, and scallions. Open Mon through Wed 11:30 a.m. to midnight, Thurs and Fri 11:30 a.m. to 2 a.m., Sat noon to 2 a.m., and Sun noon to midnight. Inexpensive.

D'floret
18 S. Main St., Lambertville
(609) 397-7400
Local restaurateurs Dennis Foy and Estelle Quinones serve creative farm-to-table fare in their intimate and elegant spot Thurs through Sun. Reservations are a must; no credit cards. Expensive.

Fat Cactus Cantina
350 George St., New Brunswick
(732) 543-1153
A huge menu of authentic Tex-Mex fare in a bustling eatery in the heart of George Street. Some patrons line up for tacos at the indoor taco truck, while others watch guacamole being made tableside. Ongoing entertainment includes mariachi bands, and happy hour at the bar weekdays from 4 to 7 p.m. features $4 tequila shots. Lunch and dinner daily. Inexpensive–moderate.

The Grain House Restaurant
225 Route 202, Basking Ridge
(908) 221-1150
Updated American country inn menu, featuring items such as roast local organic chicken, pan-roasted swordfish, and artisanal cheeses, along with sumptuous desserts. Lunch and dinner daily; Sat and Sun brunch. Expensive.

Hamilton's Grill Room
8 Coryell St., Lambertville
(609) 397-4343
Bring along a bottle of your favorite wine, grab a seat on the outdoor patio (the street is closed to traffic), and select from a menu that reflects seasonal flavors and availability. Dinner nightly; Sat and Sun brunch. Expensive.

Meemah
The Shoppes at Colonial Village, 9 Route 27, Edison
(732) 906-2223
This informal eatery offers both Chinese and Malaysian dishes, with specialties such as roast duck and Malaysian satays. Bring along your own beer, particularly if you order your dishes hot and spicy. Lunch and dinner Tues through Sun. Inexpensive–moderate.

Namli Mediterranean and Turkish Cuisine
88 Central Ave., New Brunswick
(732) 543-0116
Classic Middle Eastern dishes well prepared in a comfortable space; there's a store across the street for BYOB. Lunch and dinner daily. Inexpensive.

Ramen Nagomi
49 Bayard St., New Brunswick
(732) 317-2623
Japanese ramen crafted from organic ingredients, many from Japan, plus rice bowls and a wide variety of appetizers, including pork floss bao and fried gyoza. There's also a branch on Main Street in Freehold. New Brunswick open Mon through Thurs noon to 3 p.m. and 5 to 8:45 p.m., Fri through Sun noon to 9 p.m. Inexpensive.

Stage Left
5 Livingston Ave., New Brunswick
(732) 828-4444
Contemporary American fare with an accent on prime beef and fresh seafood, and an outstanding wine list.

Wood-fired grill. Lunch Fri, dinner nightly. Expensive.

Steakhouse 85 Restaurant
85 Church St., New Brunswick
(732) 247-8585
Beef is king at this upscale classic steak house popular with Rutgers students and faculty. The dry-aged steaks, seared on a 1,200-degree cast-iron grill and then broiled to perfection, pair perfectly with a cocktail or a bottle of wine from the Wine Spectator award-winning list. Open Mon through Sat at 4 p.m. Expensive.

SELECTED REGIONAL INFORMATION CENTERS, CHAMBERS OF COMMERCE & VISITOR CENTERS IN CENTRAL NEW JERSEY

Camden County Regional Chamber of Commerce
295 Route 70W
Cherry Hill 08002
(856) 667-1600
www.camdencountychamber.com

Burlington Mercer Chamber of Commerce
32 Yorktown Rd., PO Box 65
Bordentown 08505
(609) 298-7774
https://burlingtonmercerchamber.org

Princeton Mercer Regional Chamber of Commerce
619 Alexander Rd., Ste. 101
Princeton 08520
(609) 924-1776
www.princetonmercerchamber.org

Trenton Visitors Center
102 Barracks St.
Trenton 08608
(609) 777-1770
www.countyoffice.org

Other Attractions in Central New Jersey

Benjamin Temple House
27 Federal City Rd., Ewing
(609) 883-2455

Beverly National Cemetery
(Civil War and other veterans)
916 Bridgeboro Rd., Beverly
(215) 504-5610

Englishtown Auction
(Open-air flea market)
90 Wilson Ave.,
Englishtown (Manalapan)
(732) 446-9644

Heritage Glass Museum
25 E. High St., Glassboro
(856) 881-7468

Lakehurst Historical Museum
Old St. John's Church, 300 Center St., Lakehurst
(732) 657-8864

Lawrence Township Historic Sites
Lawrence
(609) 844-7000

Longstreet Farm
Holmdel Park, 44 Longstreet Rd., Holmdel
(732) 946-3758

New Jersey State Museum
205 W. State St., Trenton
(609) 292-6464

Red Bank Battlefield
100 Hessian Ave., National Park
(856) 853-5120

Smithville Mansion
803 Smithville Rd., Easthampton
(609) 261-3780

State House Tours
125 W. State St., Trenton
(609) 847-3150

Washington Crossing State Park
355 Washington Crossing–Pennington Rd. (Route 546), Titusville
(609) 737-0623

The Shore

At one time or another, nearly everybody in New Jersey has gone "down the Shore." Little kids have enjoyed the rides at Asbury Park (now, sadly, a memory), and big kids have cruised the boardwalk at Seaside Heights—yes, that Seaside Heights, the setting for MTV's *Jersey Shore*. The well-to-do have gone to Deal and Allenhurst, while the middle class takes its sun at Lavallette or Ortley Beach. Methodists flock to camp meeting at teetotaling Ocean Grove, high rollers hit the blackjack tables at "A.C.," and surfers search for the perfect Jersey wave at—where else?—Surf City (there were never "two girls for every boy" there, regardless of what the song said). And some people are even discovering what savvy summer travelers knew a hundred years ago, by heading for the Victorian guest houses of Cape May as an alternative to four-figure weekends on certain New England islands. For that matter, even a fair number of people who aren't from the Garden State go to the Jersey Shore (and not just Atlantic City) simply because it is one of the finest ocean beaches in the world's temperate zones, period.

So what can there be to learn about the Shore? Plenty, if you want to come in out of the sun for a bit and look behind the slot machines and sausage-and-pepper stands. The Jersey

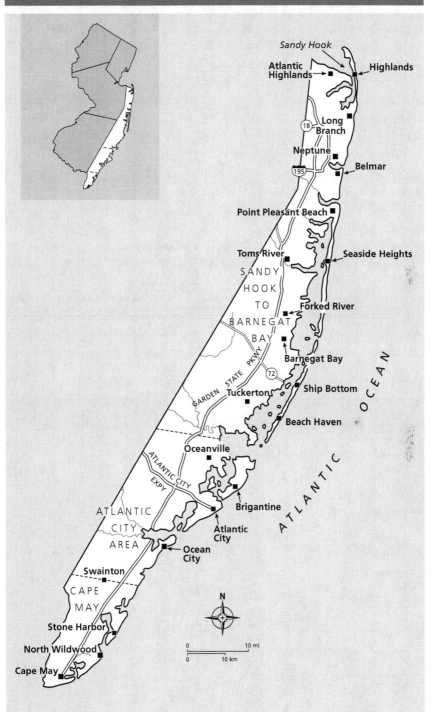

Sandy Hook

Atlantic Highlands ■ — Highlands ■

18

Long Branch ■

Neptune ■

195

Belmar ■

Point Pleasant Beach ■

Toms River ■ — Seaside Heights ■

S A N D Y
H O O K
T O
B A R N E G A T
B A Y

Forked River ■

■

GARDEN STATE PKWY

72

Tuckerton ■ — Barnegat Bay ■

Ship Bottom ■

Beach Haven ■

Oceanville ■

ATLANTIC CITY EXPY

Brigantine ■

ATLANTIC
CITY
AREA

Atlantic City ■

Ocean City ■

Swainton ■

CAPE MAY

Stone Harbor ■

North Wildwood ■

Cape May

A T L A N T I C   O C E A N

N

0   10 mi
0   10 km

Shore has a rich history of settlers, shipwrecks, lighthouses, and naval engagements. There's also the land itself—barrier dunes, salt marshes, and a holly forest. Much of the region would surprise even a lifelong visitor. Like the urban northeastern corner of New Jersey, the Shore is a part of the state that people think they know and few really try to discover.

Note: The orientation in this chapter is from north to south; from Sandy Hook to Barnegat Bay, through the Atlantic City area, and down to Cape May.

Sandy Hook to Barnegat Bay

The northernmost reach of the Jersey Shore proper is the curving finger of land called *Sandy Hook*. Saved from development for nearly two centuries because of its status as a federal military reserve, Sandy Hook is now a unit of the *Gateway National Recreation Area*, other sections of which occupy shoreline stretches of Staten Island and Long Island.

The oldest structure on Sandy Hook is the 1764 *Sandy Hook Lighthouse*, visible 19 miles out at sea. The United States government acquired all of Sandy Hook in 1817, and the first permanent fort construction started in 1859. But construction was suspended eight years later and the fort was never completed.

THE SHORE'S TOP PICKS

Gateway National Recreation Area (Sandy Hook)	Lucy the Elephant
	Somers Mansion
Twin Lights	Ocean City Historical Museum
Ocean Grove	Stone Harbor Bird Sanctuary
Toms River Seaport Society & Maritime Museum	The Wetlands Institute
Popcorn Park Zoo	Cape May County Zoo
Albert Music Hall	Cape May
Edwin B. Forsythe National Wildlife Refuge	Emlen Physick Estate
	Cape May Lighthouse
Tuckerton Seaport & Baymen's Museum	Angel of the Sea
Marine Mammal Stranding Center and Sea Life Museum	

In 1895, shore batteries and attendant facilities were officially named **Fort Hancock**. The fort was deactivated in 1974, and, as surplus government property, it became part of Gateway.

Although a number of the Fort Hancock buildings have been adaptively reused and incorporated into Gateway's interpretive program, most of Sandy Hook is of interest because of the natural environment. The areas along the eastern Atlantic Ocean face of the peninsula are mostly primary and secondary dunes, but you don't have to go very far inland to find dense thickets of bayberry, beach plum, and even random clumps of prickly pear cactus (there's also poison ivy, so be careful). The most unusual aspect of Sandy Hook, to most first-time visitors, is the holly forest. Holly does well in sandy soil, and its leaves are tough enough to withstand salt breezes.

The Sandy Hook Unit of Gateway National Recreation Area, off Route 36, Highlands, (732) 872-5970, www.nps.gov/gate, is open daily 6 a.m. to 8 p.m. There are no entrance fees for the Gateway National Recreation Area. There is, however, a $20 per-car charge for beach parking at Sandy Hook from Memorial Day weekend through Labor Day. A season pass is available for $100 to $200, and America the Beautiful pass holders receive a 50 percent discount; active service members and veterans receive free parking with an America the Beautiful pass. The visitor center and Fort Hancock parking area are free.

Sandy Hook is also home to **Gunnison Beach**, the state's only "naturist" facility, and it's a very popular spot on a fine summer day, when thousands of sunbathers park in lot G and head for the dunes. Clothing is optional, but most folks are there for a full complement of rays. A word of caution: Don't strip until you're officially at Gunnison; you have to walk past a "suit required" beach to get there.

As you approach Sandy Hook from the mainland, it's impossible not to notice the massive stone towers of a double lighthouse that dominate the bluff of the Highlands. These are the **Twin Lights** of **Navesink Lighthouse**

Hidden Ponds

Mention Sandy Hook and most people think of the long stretch of sandy shoreline that defines the narrow peninsula's Atlantic side. But five freshwater ponds lie within the boundaries of the Sandy Hook portion of Gateway National Recreation Area. One was so well concealed by surrounding thickets of beach plum and bayberry that its existence was only revealed when aerial photos of the area were first taken. The ponds were created when freshwater gradually supplanted seawater that had rushed into inland hollows during storms.

Historic Site, decommissioned in 1949 and now maintained as a New Jersey state park.

Twin Lights was once one of the five major lighthouse installations that dotted the dangerous 127-mile-long New Jersey coast. Built in 1862 to replace a pair of stone light towers that had stood on the Highlands since 1828, the north and south towers of Navesink each held beacons to inform mariners of the approach to land.

The south tower held a light of the "first order," indicating simply that landfall was at hand. The north tower was equipped with a "second-order" light, indicating a headland and the approach to a bay—in this case, the lower bay of New York Harbor. As a first-order light, the south-tower installation was always the brighter of the two, and in 1898 it became the brightest in the United States. The Statue of Liberty is traditionally regarded as the first sight of America for passengers on incoming ships, but to any seaman or traveler who approached the coast at night, Twin Lights on the Navesink heralded the New World.

Although a small blinking beacon is still lit in the north tower between dusk and dawn, the south tower is dark. Its giant Fresnel lens, at one time so blindingly powerful that the west-facing windows of the tower had to be paneled over lest the entire countryside be floodlit, is on exhibit today at ground level, in what was formerly the lighthouse's power-generating station. The clockwork mechanism that operated the light is also on display.

thestateshell

In 1995 the knobbed whelk, *Busycon carica*, was designated the official state shell. The large, pear-shaped, yellowish-gray shell can be found along the state's beaches.

A visit to the *Twin Lights Museum* at the Twin Lights Historic Site will reveal more than lighthouse technology. Here also are collections of memorabilia that relate to the Life Saving Service and to the work of Guglielmo Marconi, inventor of wireless telegraphy. It was at Navesink, in 1899, that Marconi gave his first demonstrations of wireless transmission. In September he reported on the progress of Spanish-American War hero Admiral Dewey's triumphal fleet off the Jersey coast; a month later, his wireless wizardry allowed the *New York Herald* to receive instantaneous news of the America's Cup races near Sandy Hook. Before or after visiting the museum, climb the 64 steps to the top of the north tower, 246 feet above sea level.

Twin Lights of Navesink Lighthouse Historic Site, Lighthouse Road (off Route 36), Highlands, (732) 872-1814, www.twinlightslighthouse.org, is open year-round, Wed through Sun from 10 a.m. to 4 p.m. The grounds are open from 9 a.m. until 4:30 p.m. Guided tours ($12 adults, $2 children under 12) are available Wed through Sat from 10 a.m. to 3 p.m. Self-tour admission is free.

Want to visit Manhattan without sitting for hours in traffic and worrying about where to park the car? Hop aboard the **SeaStreak**: It makes trips daily from Atlantic Highlands and Highlands to Pier 11 on Wall Street and East 35th Street in midtown Manhattan. The round-trip fare for adults is $40, with special rates for children 5 to 12; children under 5 are free. For information call (800) 262-8743 or check their schedule at www.seastreak.com.

The Rocky Point section of 794-acre *Hartshorne Woods Park*, (732) 842-4000 or (732) 872-0336, www.monmouthcountyparks.com, has 3 miles of paved paths closed to cars—a perfect spot to bike or hike. There's also fine fishing in the Navesink River and horseback riding. The park's 11 miles of trails are popular with mountain bikers. The entrance is at 1402 Portland Rd. in Highlands. The park is open daily from 7 a.m. to dusk, and admission is free.

With its many nightclubs and cafes, it's astonishing to think that Asbury Park was originally conceived in the 1870s as a temperance resort. The seaside town is enjoying a rebirth after some rather rough years in the 1970s and 1980s: On the *Asbury Park Boardwalk*, www.apboardwalk.com, Convention Hall and the former vaudeville Paramount Theater have been restored and are once again hosting events.

No matter what the town does to gain recognition in days ahead, however, to Bruce Springsteen fans Asbury Park will always be the place that "the Boss" got his start. He began performing at the *Stone Pony* on Ocean Avenue and Second Street, and to this day the club is a premier destination for music lovers in search of the Asbury Sound—and of a glimpse of Springsteen, who shows up here occasionally to jam. Even when he's not in town, though, it's a great place to hear top-rate music.

AUTHORS' FAVORITE ATTRACTIONS AT THE SHORE

Cape May	Ocean Grove
Insectropolis	Popcorn Park Animal Refuge
Lucy the Elephant	Tuckerton Seaport & Baymen's Museum
Marine Mammal Stranding Center and Sea Life Museum	Maui's Dog House

Serious music fans should get a copy of the fourth edition of *Rock and Roll Tour of the Jersey Shore*, by lifelong New Jersey residents Stan Goldstein and Jean Mikle, who for many years ran walking tours of the area. The 200-page book includes information on close to 200 locations of historical rock 'n' roll sites in Monmouth, Ocean, and Middlesex Counties, including many Bruce-related sites. The book retails for $26 and can be ordered at www.backstreets .com, which has been covering the music of the Boss and other Jersey Shore artists for more than 25 years.

After beloved local eatery Mom's Kitchen closed, lovers of solid Italian food were delighted when award-winning chef Salvatore Chiarella opened *Il Posto* in its old space. He offers traditional old-world dishes with a modern twist, and all of the classic favorites are on the menu. The pastas and sauces are homemade, prices are reasonable, and Mondays are half-price spaghetti and meatballs and half-price pizza nights. Il Posto, 1129 5th Ave., Neptune, (732) 775-4823, www.ilpostonj.com, is open for dinner Wed through Mon.

Next door to Asbury Park is an entire town entered on the National Register of Historic Places. *Ocean Grove*, which has one of the largest assemblages of authentic Victorian architecture in the United States, was founded in 1869 for the Ocean Grove Camp Meeting Association by Dr. William B. Osborn. He chose this 1 square mile because it had the highest beach and the best grove of trees around—and no mosquitoes.

When the first camp meeting was held in 1870, the faithful erected tents in which to live. Camp meetings are still held every summer, and today 114 tent structures ring the 6,000-seat Great Auditorium in Auditorium Square. If you're visiting in the summer, be sure to attend one of the Wednesday (7:30 p.m.) or Saturday (noon) organ concerts, played on the magnificent 10,000-pipe organ built in Elmira, New York. Admission is free.

Other summer events include gospel music ministries, an arts and crafts show, and wind ensemble performances. For a complete schedule contact the

The Chain Had to Go

Ocean Grove—"God's square mile at the Jersey Shore"—has always taken its origins as a Methodist camp meeting town seriously: To this day, not one establishment in the community possesses a liquor license. But another tradition connected with Ocean Grove's maintenance of a quiet, sedate atmosphere had to be abandoned a few decades ago, when a New Jersey court ruled that the town could no longer stretch a chain across the only road leading in and out of the place on Sundays. The reason for the chain? Ocean Grove prohibited driving within its precincts on the Sabbath.

TOP ANNUAL EVENTS AT THE SHORE

Note: Schedules may vary; call ahead.

Lighthouse Full Moon Climbs, Cape May Lighthouse; months with full moons; (609) 884-5404; www.capemaymac.org

World Series of Birding, Cape May; May; (908) 396-7380; www.njaudubon .org

New Jersey Seafood Festival, Belmar; May; www.belmar.com

Cape May Music Festival, Cape May; May–June; (609) 884-5404; www .capemaymac.org

Cape May Exit Zero Jazz Festival, North Cape May; May and Sept; (609) 849-9202; www.exitzerojazzfestival.com

Oceanfest, Long Branch; July; (732) 222-7000; www.oceanfestnj.com; www .longbranch.org

Chicken Bone Beach–Jazz on the Beach Concert Series, Atlantic City; July–Aug; (609) 441-9064; www .chickenbonebeach.org

Street Rod Weekend, Ocean City; Aug; (609) 399-1412; www.oceancityvacation .com

Victorian Week, Cape May; Oct; (609) 884-5404; www.capemaymac.org

Chowderfest, Long Beach Island; Oct; (609) 494-7211; www.chowderfest.com

Glasstown Arts District, Millville; Nov; (852) 293-0556; www.levoy.net

Winter Encampment/Wassail Day, Historic Cold Spring Village; Dec; (609) 898-2300; www.hcsv.org

West Cape May Christmas Parade, West Cape May; Dec; (609) 884-1005; www.capemaymac.org

Ocean Grove Camp Meeting Association, 54 Pitman Ave., PO Box 248, Ocean Grove 07756; call the main office at (732) 775-0035 or, in summer, the beach office at (732) 988-5533; or visit www.oceangrove.org.

If your idea of an elegant getaway includes luxurious rooms, ocean views, and European bistro dining, make a reservation at *The Majestic Hotel* at 19 Main Ave., Ocean Grove, (732) 775-6100, www.majesticoceangrove.com. The Victorian hotel, which bills itself as the "Jewel of the Jersey Shore," was built in 1870 and offers 16 spacious rooms, including a three-room penthouse. Many have balconies with sweeping ocean views. The hotel's restaurant, Bia, with subdued lighting and a New York vibe, is temporarily closed but hopes to reopen soon.

"Say good morning to the Atlantic from almost every room" advertises the *Cashelmara Inn*. And indeed, most of the 12 rooms (all with private baths) and 3 suites (with Jacuzzis) at the landmark Victorian mansion have fabulous unobstructed water views. They feature antique furnishings, gas log fireplaces, air-conditioning, and refrigerators, and the rates include a full country breakfast, admission to the inn's Grand Victorian Movie Theater (with popcorn and soda), and beach badges. The inn, at 22 Lakeside Ave., Avon-by-the-Sea, (800) 821-2976 or (732) 776-8727, www.cashelmara.com, is open mid-Apr through mid-Nov. Rates range from $150 to $375.

East meets west at **Klein's Fish Market, Waterside Café & Tiki Bar**, on the Shark River in Belmar. The Klein family has been known throughout the region since 1924, when Ollie Klein Sr. began peddling fish from his truck. Today his family oversees the daily operation of the business. The extensive lunch/dinner menu includes fish-and-chips ($21.95) and a fried shrimp platter ($24.95). Landlubbers can chose from among tacos, chicken, and burgers. The alfresco Waterside Café is a delightful spot to linger over coffee and dessert. Klein's, 708 River Rd., (732) 681-1177, www.kleinsfish.com, is open Wed through Sun for lunch and dinner. Reservations are not accepted.

anunexpected portofcall

On September 8, 1934, the liner *Morro Castle* caught fire off the New Jersey coast on the return leg of a New York to Havana cruise. The blaze took the lives of 134 passengers and crew, and left the powerless ship to the mercy of the waves and wind. The smoldering hulk soon grounded only a few hundred yards off the beach at Asbury Park, where it became a macabre tourist attraction for several months before being towed away and scrapped.

To learn about New Jersey's citizen soldiers and the contributions they've made to the state and the nation, drop in at the **National Guard Militia Museum of New Jersey**, on the campus of the National Guard Training Center on Sea Girt Avenue, Sea Girt, (732) 974-5966, www.njmilitiamuseum.org. The museum exhibits a large selection of artifacts and memorabilia pertaining to the militia and National Guard, including uniforms and weapons. It's open Memorial Day until Halloween, Mon through Fri from 10 a.m. to 3 p.m. Donations are most welcome. There is also a fine library on the premises. A second museum is at the Lawrenceville Armory, 151 Eggert Crossing Rd., Lawrenceville; open Mon through Fri from 9 a.m. to 3 p.m. and Sat. 10 a.m. to 3 p.m.

Casual passersby might drive past **The Crab Shack** in Brick, thinking it's a fish market. It is that, but is also a destination for in-the-know seafood lovers, who flock there for deliciously prepared seafood plates, soups, and sandwiches. The crab cakes and crab soup are homemade, as are the seafood gumbos and, although they're wandering from their home turf a bit, the New England clam chowder. The dinners, all priced under $20, are served with coleslaw and french fries and include fried shrimp (10 large ones per order), fried or broiled flounder, and broiled salmon. The atmosphere is casual and family-friendly. The Crab Shack, 74 Mantoloking Rd., Brick, (732) 477-1115,

Early Resort Development

New Jersey has long been famous for its 120-mile-long ocean shoreline—but the seashore, where Native Americans fished and harvested salt from dried tidal pools, was one of the last places early colonists cared to settle. The barrier beach islands offered few decent harbors, and the mosquitoes were ferocious.

The story of Lavalette, a popular middle-class resort community with a steady year-round population, is typical. Developers started making their pitch in the 1870s, issuing a prospectus that praised the local crabbing and bluefishing. The promoters used a 19th-century version of today's condo timeshare come-on: They'd charter a train to Toms River, 7 miles away on the mainland, hire a sailing yacht, and bring prospects across Barnegat Bay for a picnic on the Lavalette beach. After 1881 the railroad extended across the bay right into Lavalette, and the resort boom began in earnest.

www.the-crab-shack.com, is open Thurs 9:30 a.m. to 5 p.m., Fri and Sat to 5:30 p.m., and Sun to 4 p.m.

There are few more beautiful—and uncrowded—spots to be on an early morning than **Island Beach State Park**, a 3,002-acre paradise of white sandy beach, windswept dunes, wetlands, sea grass, and nature trails that stretches for 10 miles between the ocean and Barnegat Bay. For a wonderful view of Barnegat Light, across Barnegat Inlet at the northern tip of Long Beach Island, drive to the end of the island and hike for 1½ miles to the southern tip of the peninsula.

During the summer, naturalists lead canoe and kayak trips through the tidal marshes to observe nesting ospreys, falcons, and shorebirds. Be sure to reserve a spot well in advance. For a bird's-eye view of the state's largest osprey colony, which thrives on the Sedge Islands—marshy masses of land in Barnegat Bay—park at lot A20 and hike a short distance to the Spizzle Creek Bird Observation Blind. The park is a horticulturist's as well as an ornithologist's dream: More than 300 plants have been identified here, and the grounds include the state's largest expanses of beach heather. Dog lovers and their canine companions are welcome to romp in the surf at any time of the year here—just stay clear of the adjacent people-bathing beaches.

Island Beach State Park, Route 35 (mailing address: PO Box 37, Seaside Park 08752), (732) 793-0506, www.islandbeachnj.org, is open daily year-round, typically from 8 a.m. to dusk; from Memorial Day weekend through Labor Day, the park opens at 7 a.m. on weekends and holidays. The park gets very crowded on summer weekends, and gates close when the parking lot is full. On weekends and holidays from Memorial Day weekend through Labor Day, admission is $10 for New Jersey residents and $20 for nonresidents; off-season, admission is $5 for residents and $10 for nonresidents.

Back on the mainland in Toms River is a museum dedicated to the preservation of New Jersey's maritime heritage, with emphasis on the Barnegat Bay area. A number of boat types were developed and built in the area to allow fishermen access to the area's shallow estuaries and bays. The ***Toms River Seaport Society & Maritime Museum*** displays a number of these craft, including the *Sheldrake*, a 12-foot "sneakbox," in which the late F. Slade Dale cruised from Bay Head to New York and then on to Florida in 1925. (The Barnegat Bay sneakbox, named for its ability to sneak up quietly on waterfowl, was invented by Hazelton Seaman of West Creek; historians credit the sneakbox as possibly the only boat designed in the United States without any old-world ancestors.)

The museum's growing collection includes a lifesaving surf rowboat; a Barnegat Bay garvey; the original sailboat A-Cat SPY, which raced for 76 years between 1924 and 2000; and a Hankins rowing skiff. The two-story museum, headquartered in an 1868 carriage house, also displays numerous artifacts associated with the area's maritime history. One of the highlights of the year is the society's Wooden Boat Festival each July. The Toms River Seaport Society & Maritime Museum, 78 E. Water St., (732) 349-9209, www.tomsriverseaport.org, is open Tues, Thurs, and Sat from 10 a.m. to 2 p.m. Donations are welcome.

If your interests tend to the celestial, visit the ***Robert J. Novins Planetarium*** at Ocean County College. The planetarium, one of the largest in New Jersey, features state-of-the-art laser and sky shows and full-dome movies in its 103-seat theater. The Novins Planetarium, Ocean County College, College Drive, Toms River, is open all year. Call (732) 255-0342 for recorded information or (732) 255-0343 weekdays for general information, or visit www.ocean .edu for details. The box office is open Wed through Sat from noon to 5 p.m., or tickets can be bought online. Admission is $10 for adults and $8 for seniors and children under 12.

It's 7 a.m.—you've been up most of the night watching for shooting stars and are famished. Head on over to the ***Toms River Diner*** on Route 37, (732) 288-2808, www.tomsriverdinernj.com—it's open from 7 a.m. to 9 p.m. daily, and the spinach and feta cheese omelet, served with home fries and toast, will put a dent in the largest appetite. Lunch classics such as chili and meatball parm sandwiches are all moderately priced. Dinner time? All specials are priced under $20 and include soup, salad, potato or pasta, tea or coffee, and dessert.

Who doesn't love a restaurant called ***Shut Up and Eat!***, where pajamaclad waitresses meet you at the door and serve up award-winning breakfasts and lunches, including more than 40 kinds of waffles? The breakfast waffles are all priced at $11.13 and include unusual mélanges such as pumpkin and banana; bacon, apple, and cheddar cheese; and kiwi, strawberry, and whipped cream. Waffles for lunch? Sure! They're all $14.91 and might include avocado, bacon, tomato, and chicken or hot pastrami and Swiss cheese. Pancakes and French toast are also on the menu, along with huge omelets and a large assortment of burgers. The restaurant is at 804 Main St., Toms River, (732) 349-4544, www.shutupandeat-tr.com, and is open Mon through Sat from 6 a.m. to 3:30 p.m. and Sun from 6 a.m. to 3 p.m.

Decidedly not for everyone, but very popular with kids, *Insectropolis*, "The Bugseum of New Jersey," is "dedicated to helping visitors foster a greater appreciation for bugs and their place in the world." Indeed, thousands of beautiful and bizarre insects are on display in a multitude of creative exhibits, and visitors who really want to get up close and personal can even pretend they're termites and crawl through mud tubes. And the gift shop? It's bugtastic! Insectropolis is at 1761 Route 9 in Toms River, (732) 349-7090, www.insectropolis .com, and is open Fri through Sun from 10 a.m. to 3 pm. Admission is $10; children 12 and under are free.

The *Popcorn Park Animal Refuge* in Forked River is the only institution of its kind in the United States. Popcorn Park was founded in 1977 by the Associated Humane Societies for the express purpose of taking in wild animals no longer able to fend for themselves due to age, infirmity, injury, or abuse by humans. Within a few years, however, managers realized that their mission should be extended to domestic and exotic animals in distress, and so it was. Today's Popcorn Park is the home of last resort for all manner of creatures, from abandoned Easter chicks and rabbits to lions, tigers, bears—even an elephant—that were confined and abused by the shady operators of roadside animal shows and fly-by-night "circuses."

All the creatures at Popcorn Park have one thing in common: They very likely would not have made it were it not for the refuge's open-door policy and expert care and for the kindness of those who brought them to this unique facility. Present residents include four Bengal tigers from Texas, a Bactrian camel, wallabies, a civet cat, and several monkeys, as well as a wide variety of birds and farm animals. Popcorn Park offers spacious, clean accommodations for its animals, and tamer species are allowed to wander freely on the grounds as much as possible. The refuge is situated on the eastern fringes of the New Jersey Pine Barrens, and landscaping is deliberately minimal—a natural scrubforest environment prevails.

Popcorn Park Animal Refuge, Humane Way at Lacey Road, (609) 693-1900, www.ahscares.org, is open daily from 11 a.m. to 5 p.m. and on holidays from 11 a.m. to 2 p.m. Admission is $8 for adults and $5 for seniors and

Newarkies and Rah-Rahs

Along the boardwalks of the Jersey Shore in the 1960s, you could tell who was who by the clothes they wore. Among teenagers, there were two basic casts of characters: the Newarkies and the Rah-rahs. The Newarkies mostly came from the cities of North Jersey (hence the name), while the Rah-rahs were suburban kids. Newarkies hit the boardwalk wearing tight black pants, black shoes, and strap T-shirts. Rah-rahs wore white denim cutoffs, anything they could find that was made of madras, and sandals or—on formal occasions—penny loafers with no socks. They also surfed, or pretended they did. Newarkies, as well as we can recall, just hung out.

children 3 to 11; members of the military are free. Admission to the refuge stops at 4:15 p.m.

Forked River is home to another classic Jersey diner—the **Forked River Diner**, at 317 S. Main St. (Route 9), (609) 693-2222. Among the specialties: a pork roll, egg, and cheese sandwich and a monster burger with fries. It's open daily from 5 a.m. to 3 p.m.

More than 45 years ago, a handful of musicians began to gather every Saturday night in the secluded deer camp of Joe and George Albert in the Waretown pinelands to play music. Known as the "Home Place," it became known as the place to go to hear down-home music. The "pickin' pineys" have changed venue several times over the years, but the "Sounds of the Jersey Pines" still ring out every Saturday night, and the pinelands musical heritage lives on.

In 1997 the Pinelands Cultural Society, formed around the original members, completed construction of a 6,000-square-foot building. The air-conditioned, 350-seat **Albert Music Hall** is now the site of year-round concerts featuring country, bluegrass, and folk music. The hall also schedules special Saturday daytime shows, posted on their website, www.alberthall.org.

The Albert Music Hall is at 131 Wells Mill Rd. (Route 532), Waretown. Concerts begin at 6:30 p.m. and end at 9 p.m. Admission is $5 for adults and $1 for children under 12. Musicians are invited to bring their instruments and join in. For more information contact the Pinelands Cultural Society, PO Box 657, Waretown 08758; (609) 971-1593.

Have a yen for some coconut-cluster toasted marshmallows? Milk pecan patties? Double-dipped chocolate mints? **Stutz Candy Company** has been making a wide variety of candies for more than 60 years in their factory in Ship Bottom. The store, at 25th and Long Beach Boulevard, (609) 494-5303, www.stutzcandy.com, is open year-round, Mon through Fri 9 a.m. to 7 p.m.,

Sat 9 a.m. to 6 p.m., and Sun noon to 5 p.m. (Don't miss the cherry vanilla fudge!)

The folks at **ALO** (Alliance for a Living Ocean) are dedicated to promoting clean water and a healthy coastal environment, and they believe that their best weapon is an educated and active public. So they host programs that give everyone a chance to get involved. For information contact the ALO at PO Box 2250, Long Beach Township 08008; (609) 494-7800; www.alolbi.org.

Since Sondra and Stephen Beninati purchased **The Gables** in 2005, they have done extensive and meticulous renovations to the 1892 Beach Haven structure and created an elegant inn and restaurant. All five beautifully appointed guest rooms are furnished with period antiques and have marble bathrooms; four have whirlpool spa tubs, and three have working fireplaces. Rates fluctuate with the seasons and may require a two-night minimum; they begin at $260 a night and include a gourmet breakfast served in the parlor or guest rooms.

A three-course tasting menu is served in the exquisite, candlelit dining room. Opt for a table by the fireplace on a cool night, or on the porch overlooking the Victorian garden on a warm summer's eve. Although the menu changes with the seasons, offerings might include an appetizer of crispy Asian Brussels sprouts, entrées such as roasted Skuna Bay salmon or Long Island duck breast, and, for dessert, the Gables chocolate celebration cake with handmade pistachio ice cream. The cost is $96 per person and reservations are a must. The inn is at 212 Centre St., (609) 492-3553 or (888) LBI-GABLES, www.gableslbi.com.

Indulge your sweet tooth with a treat at the **Country Kettle Fudge Shop**, (609) 492-2800, www.countrykettlefudge.com, in Beach Haven's Bay Village.

Miniature Golf Tournament

Every summer Thursday morning at 9:30 sharp, dozens of the Jersey Shore's fiercest golf competitors gather at Bill Burr's Flamingo Golf, on the Boulevard in Ship Bottom. A tradition "for more than 30 years," according to one volunteer scorekeeper, Burr's weekly miniature golf tournaments draw kids and adults alike. It's a microcosm of the Masters, with a slew of goofy obstacles that put Augusta National's ponds, bunkers, and azaleas to shame.

The Flamingo is serious about its little tournament: The summer's winners to date are always posted on a board near the entrance. The players are no less devoted, talking about their birdies and eagles and critical putts, and even dropping the occasional remark about their prowess on the full-size links . . . which is where you won't find them on Thursday mornings.

The sweet shop has been making hand-whipped fudge for more than 60 years, and it sells 16 flavors, including an incredible Oreo crunch.

If you don't mind singing for your banana split in an outdoor tented venue, ***Showplace Ice Cream Parlor*** has a treat for you. The waitstaff are also professional performers, and serve up show and cabaret tunes along with huge, gooey sundaes. All are named for shows, hence creations such as the Peter Pan—peanut butter ice cream, hot fudge, walnuts, whipped cream, and a cherry. But even in an ice-cream parlor there's room for ham: Customers are invited—even urged—to participate. The parlor, at 202 Centre St. in Beach Haven, (609) 467-5311, www.surflight.org/showplace, is open daily in season. Sun through Thurs shows are at 6, 7, 8, and 9 p.m.; Fri and Sat shows are at 6, 7, 8, 9, and 10 p.m. A refundable advance reservation can be made for $5 per person. The take-out window is open daily.

Be sure to bring along a cooler—or at least an appetite—when you visit ***Mario's Italian Market*** in Surf City. It's been catering to the community for more than 25 years. The aroma alone is worth a visit, but don't stop there: Load up with cheeses (the mozzarella is homemade daily), pastries, cold cuts, fresh-baked breads, homemade soups, freshly made sandwiches, olives, and the market's special stuffed mushrooms and fried ravioli. The shop is at 1905 Long Beach Blvd., (609) 361-2500, www.themariositalianmarket.com, and is open Tues through Sun from 10 a.m. to 6 p.m.

One more lighthouse: This one is ***Barnegat Light***, in ***Barnegat Lighthouse State Park***, at the northern tip of Long Beach Island. "Old Barney," as shore residents call their beacon, was first lit in 1859 to replace an 1834 lighthouse that toppled during a flood. This time the government didn't fool around: Project engineer General George Gordon Meade, later famous as the Union commander at Gettysburg, supervised the construction of a 168-foot tower, with brick walls that are 10 feet thick at the bottom and taper to an 18-inch thickness at the top. The illumination source was a five-ton Fresnel lens rotated smoothly on a bed of bronze rollers by a mechanism that

Red Flag's Up—Ladies off the Beach!

Surf City, on Long Beach Island, was one of the first New Jersey shore communities to feature resort hotels. At the "Mansion of Health," which flourished as early as the 1820s, men and women guests were assigned separate bathing times on the hotel's beachfront. A red flag was the signal for men to use the beach, and a white flag meant it was the ladies' turn. The system was vital for maintaining propriety and decorum—in those days, men swam nude at the Jersey Shore.

Improving the Plovers' Odds

Within sight of the casino towers of Atlantic City, there are low, sandy wilderness islands that hardly anyone ever visits. Some, in fact, are absolutely off-limits—they're managed as part of the Edwin B. Forsythe National Wildlife Refuge as breeding grounds for endangered bird species, most notably the piping plover. Plovers nest on the ground, where their eggs and newly hatched chicks are in danger not only from human intrusion, but from the predations of foxes, raccoons, and other creatures of the barrier beach islands. Refuge personnel erect mesh enclosures over the plovers' nests, designed to allow the parent birds and their chicks access while keeping predators out.

We visited one such island, with a government biologist as our guide, and can report that the plovers have on their side a far better deterrent to unauthorized human visitors than mere warning signs. In the summer the biting greenhead flies are so thick on these islands that our pens began to melt from the volume of repellent we were forced to use.

resembled the innards of a giant grandfather clock. Every four minutes the beacon rotated, and lives and shipping were saved from the sands of Barnegat Beach.

Barnegat Light came to the end of its usefulness even earlier than Twin Lights at Navesink. The great structure was replaced by a lightship anchored offshore in 1927, but its dismantling was prevented by public sentiment and, probably, the fact that nothing short of a full-scale naval bombardment could have taken it down. On January 1, 2009, exactly 150 years to the day it was first lit, the beacon began to shine again due to the efforts of Friends of Barnegat Lighthouse State Park. So it survives as the focal point of a lovely state park that offers some of the Jersey Shore's best swimming, surf casting, and birding, not to mention sightseeing. Anyone who cares to mount the lighthouse's 217 steps, when the building is open, will be rewarded by a panoramic view of Barnegat Bay, the barrier beaches and the distant mainland, and the vast sweep of the Atlantic.

One of New Jersey's last remnants of maritime forest—predominantly black cherry, eastern red cedar, and American holly—is in the park, making it a popular stopover for migrating birds.

Barnegat Lighthouse State Park, 208 Broadway, Barnegat Light, (609) 494-2016, www.nj.gov, is open daily from 8 a.m. to 4 p.m. There is no admission fee. The lighthouse is open weekends, weather permitting, from 10:30 a.m. to 2:30 p.m. from Memorial Day through Labor Day. There is an admission fee of $3 for adults and $1 for children ages 6 through 11; under 5 are free, but must be accompanied by an adult. Those who don't want to make the climb can visit the nearby interpretive center.

At the foot of the flag post at the **Barnegat Light Station**, 601 Bayview Ave., Barnegat Light, (609) 494-2661, is a most unusual granite monument: It's the burial place of Sinbad, a mixed breed dog who served on the Coast Guard ship *Campbell* during World War II. Sinbad, described by *Life* magazine as a "liberty-rum-chow-hound with a bit of bulldog, Doberman pinscher, and what-not. Mostly what-not," became a beloved figure and was awarded six medals for his conduct on board the ship, which was almost sunk by a German U-boat in 1943. After he retired in 1948, Sinbad resided at the light station until his death in 1951.

Atlantic City Area

Route 72 is the only way on and off Long Beach Island, of which Barnegat Lighthouse State Park forms the northern tip. Right after you turn right at the town of Ship Bottom and head back toward the mainland on Route 72, you'll pass the Barnegat Division of the **Edwin B. Forsythe National Wildlife Refuge**. The crowning achievement in the struggle to keep the wetlands of the Jersey Shore from yielding entirely to development, as well as a vital link in the fragile chain of stopover areas in the Atlantic Flyway used by migratory birds, the refuge offers a refreshingly different coastal experience for human visitors, too. Although there are at this time no developed facilities for visitor use at the smaller Barnegat Division of the 48,000-acre refuge, the Brigantine Division, just across Reeds and Absecon Bays from Atlantic City, has a fine 8-mile auto-tour route and two short interpretive nature trails.

If you'd like to take the self-guided auto tour of the Brigantine Division of the refuge, plan on spending about 1½ hours. The tour begins at the division headquarters on Great Creek Road, off Route 9 at Oceanville, and makes a loop back to the starting point. Be sure to pick up a checklist of the refuge's bird species (more than 200 have been identified) at headquarters.

The headquarters of the Brigantine Division of the Edwin B. Forsythe National Wildlife Refuge is open Wed through Sun from 10 a.m. to 2 p.m. It's at 800 Great Creek Rd., Oceanville, (609) 652-1665, www.fws.gov. The refuge, auto route, and nature trails are open daily, all year, from sunrise to sunset. Admission is $4 per noncommercial vehicle and $2 for bicyclists and pedestrians.

The **Jonathan Pitney House**, the 1799 home of the "Father of Atlantic City," Dr. Jonathan Pitney, was added to in 1948 and magnificently restored in 2015. Today it is one of the area's finest lodgings, offering eight period rooms and eight suites in the main inn, carriage house, and a nearby building. All have private baths and air-conditioning and are handsomely appointed with antique furnishings; some have gas fireplaces. Room #3, the Dr. Jonathan Pitney Room, features striking deep-colored Victorian wallpaper, a gas corner fireplace and sitting area, and a bathroom with a claw-foot tub/shower combo. Room #10, the elegant and spacious Atlantic City Room, is in the carriage house and has a fireplace, sitting area, and plump leather chairs.

Guests can opt to enjoy a full breakfast in one of the inn's two dining areas or in one of the areas set aside for those who want a quieter spot. Afternoon tea is served on the porch on nice days or in one the cozy parlors during inclement weather.

The Jonathan Pitney House is at 57 North Shore Rd., Absecon, (609) 748-0536, www.jonathanpitneyhouse.com. Rates begin at $169.

Tuckerton Seaport & Baymen's Museum is a living museum carved out of what has been a working seaport village and shipbuilding center since colonial times. The seaport is dedicated to preserving the rich traditions and heritage of the Jersey Shore region.

The Seaport's 40-acre site includes 17 historic and re-created buildings connected by a boardwalk, a maritime forest and wetlands nature trail, two houseboats, a decoy gallery, a working boatworks building in which restoration of sneakbox designs of the Barnegat Bay occurs, a historic marine railway (under construction as of this writing), decoy-carving workshops, and the re-created Tucker's Island Lighthouse. Daily demonstrators and traditional artists are on hand to bring this shore's maritime heritage to life. The Seaport is also home to the Jersey Shore Folklife Center, which preserves the traditions of the area with a full roster of programs and exhibits.

The ***Jacques Cousteau National Estuarine Research Center***, with its *Life on the Edge* exhibit, located on the upper level of the Seaport's Tuckerton Yacht Club, offers a virtual tour of the 110,000-acre tract in southern New

By the Sea

New Jersey's 127 miles of white sandy beaches offer some of the finest swimming in the East. And like much of the state, they're a study in contrasts, ranging from the crowded, carnival atmosphere at Wildwood to the laid-back, genteel scene along the strand at Cape May. The prize for the most surreal bathing experience has to go to the beach at Atlantic City. The people who bustle along the boardwalk from one high-rise casino to another seem to exist in another dimension from that of the bathers romping on the uncrowded beaches just a few feet away.

Inventing Las Vegas East

The modern era in Atlantic City dates to the opening of the Resorts, Inc., casino on Memorial Day weekend in 1978, a year and a half after New Jersey voters approved a ballot referendum allowing casino gambling. The move was a response to years of declining fortunes at the old oceanside resort city, which had given the world saltwater taffy and Miss America but had fallen on hard times in the postwar era as vacationers found they could fly inexpensively to more distant and exotic retreats.

Jersey that encompass the Pinelands, Great Bay, Barrier Islands, and ocean ecosystems.

Tuckerton Seaport & Baymen's Museum, 120 W. Main St., Tuckerton, (609) 296-8868, www.tuckertonseaport.org, is open year-round Sat through Tues from 10 a.m. to 5 p.m. Tickets can be purchased online in advance, and prices will depend on which activities are selected. Check the website for a listing of events.

More than 60 boutiques and specialty shops, several lodgings, and many eateries are housed in several historic buildings at *Historic Smithville*, a lovely spot with cobblestone and brick paths, a pond with paddleboats and ducks, and a carousel and train on the *Village Greene*, (609) 748-8999, www.historic-smithvillenj.com. Visitors can sample some of South Jersey's finest wines and champagnes at the outlet store for *Tomasello Winery*, (800) 666-9463, and pick up some Betty Boop and Elvis memorabilia at *Celebrity Collectibles*, (609) 652-8110. Among the restaurants is the lakefront, gracious 1787 *Historic Smithville Inn*, (609) 652-7777, serving lunch and dinner; *Costello's Pizza*, (609) 652-0378; and *Fred & Ethel's Lantern Light Restaurant and Tavern*, (609) 652-0544, with daily lunch and dinner specials. *The Colonial Inn*, on the Village Greene, (609) 748-8999, www.colonialinnsmithville.com, features 30 charming rooms at their on-site properties in addition to lodging at the Dr.

averylongwire

The western terminus of the world's first fiber-optic transatlantic cable is in Tuckerton.

Jonathan Pitney House (see above), just 5 miles away. Historic Smithville hosts more than 40 free weekend events, including car shows and a Fourth of July parade; check the website for a complete listing,

The African American Heritage Museum of Southern New Jersey displays, along with its voluminous collection, the dream that founder Ralph E. Hunter Sr. made a reality. He began collecting African-American cultural, artistic, and media images more than 30 years ago, and today those pieces are the centerpiece of the museum's exhibits. Titled *Stereotypes: From Little Black Sambo to Aunt Jemima and Beyond*, they show how mass marketing of negative imagery has affected generations of African Americans. Other exhibits include *Portraits of a People*; *At Home: Furniture & Fixtures of Early African American Life*; and *The Northside: The Way We Were*. The museum also hosts a series of special events and exhibits, including the works of local African-American artists.

The African American Heritage Museum of Southern New Jersey, Noyes Arts Garage, 2200 Fairmouth Ave., Atlantic City, (609) 350-6662, www.aahmsnj .org, is open Wed through Sat from 11 a.m. to 5 p.m. There is a requested donation of $3 for adults and $2 for students; military are admitted free.

You have to go through Atlantic City to get to the Marine Mammal Stranding Center in Brigantine (see directions below), and it's only a one-block detour off the main route to the **White House Sub Shop** at 2301 Arctic Ave., (609) 345-8599. The "Home of Submarines" is hardly undiscovered. Their sign advertises over 15 million sold and the restaurant is a favorite stop for visiting celebrities. The sandwiches are huge and delicious (unless you're positively ravenous, share one or buy a half). The shop is open Mon through Fri 10 a.m. to 7 p.m. and Sat. 10 a.m. to 8 p.m. Be sure to look for the framed pink towel that Frank Sinatra used in his last show at one of the Atlantic City casinos; it's among the huge wall of photos of all of the famous people who have eaten there. If you find yourself on the boardwalk, you can stop in at their second location in the Hard Rock Casino & Hotel.

After you've eaten, follow signs for the State Marina to the Brigantine Bridge into Brigantine. The **Marine Mammal Stranding Center and Sea Life Museum** is on the left, 2 miles past the bridge, at 3625 Brigantine Blvd. Since its founding in 1978, this private, nonprofit center has responded to thousands of calls about stranded whales, dolphins, seals, and sea turtles that washed ashore on New Jersey beaches. The animals are brought to the center for rehabilitation and eventual release.

The museum offers visitors a glimpse into New Jersey's undersea world. Displays and an aquarium focus on local marine life. At the center there are observation and closed-circuit television areas, where visitors can watch marine mammals exercising or receiving treatment. The center also conducts dolphin-watching cruises, where groups can see wildlife in natural surroundings and learn about the local/regional ecosystem.

The Marine Mammal Stranding Center and Sea Life Museum, (609) 266-0538, www.mmsc.org, is open Sat from 10 a.m. to 2 p.m. Donations are greatly appreciated.

One of the Jersey Shore's greatest pieces of folk art—and far and away the largest—stands just south of Atlantic City at Margate City. She's **Lucy the Elephant**, a 90-ton folly, left over from the great age of American looniness.

At one time giant walk-in animals and other outsize curiosities were not at all uncommon on America's roadways. Especially after the automobile caught on, entrepreneurs just naturally assumed that travelers would want to stop for coffee in a shop shaped like a coffeepot or buy a dressed duck for dinner from a vendor in a huge cement duck (we kid you not—just such a monster fowl was saved not long ago by preservationists on Long Island). James V. Lafferty wasn't selling elephants when, in 1881, he built Lucy on the sands of South Beach in what was then South Atlantic City; he was trying to develop a resort. Since he couldn't use free DVD players as a come-on in those days, he decided to construct an elephant that everyone would want to come and see.

Lucy is a six-story wonder. Made out of sheet metal over a wooden frame, she has 20-foot-long legs, a 38-foot-long body, and a covered howdah on her back to serve as an observation deck. Inside were spiral staircases (they ran up Lucy's hind legs) and a restaurant. If having lunch in the belly of an elephant didn't make you want to buy one of Lafferty's house lots, well, you were just against progress.

Lafferty sold Lucy in 1887 to local hoteliers Sophie and John Gertzen. They made her the namesake and an annex of their Elephant Hotel, and even after the hotel closed and Mr. Gertzen passed away, his widow kept the elephant open. Unfortunately, by the time Mrs. Gertzen died in 1963, Lucy was creaky in her bones and shabby in her outward appearance, and officials with no sense of humor had her condemned.

Just in the nick of time, Lucy was saved by—what else?—a Save Lucy Committee. The state declared her a historic site, and a movable site at that. In 1970 she was transported to her present location.

Lucy the Elephant, a National Historic Landmark, stands on the beach at 9200 Atlantic Ave. in Margate City. She is open daily in season; call for off-season hours. A tour of Lucy begins with a 10-minute video on her history, continues with a guided tour through various rooms filled with artifacts and photographs, and ends at the top in Lucy's howdah, which affords a fabulous ocean view. Admission is $6 for adults, $3 for children 2 to 12, and free for kids under 2. For information call (609) 823-6473 or visit www.lucythe elephant.org.

Back on the mainland in Somers Point is the oldest house in all Atlantic County, the **Somers Mansion**. The three-story brick home was built between 1720 and 1726 by Richard Somers, scion of one of the first families to settle at the mouth of the Great Egg Harbor River. The house remained in the hands of

Atlantic City Facts

In Atlantic City . . .

- The year-round population numbers fewer than 38,000, but more than 27 million people visit each year.

- When the first casino opened in 1978, the line of people waiting to get in wrapped all the way around the building.

- Saltwater taffy got its name after a candy store on the boardwalk was flooded during a storm.

- The first boardwalk was built in 1870 to keep sand out of ladies' shoes.

the Somers family until 1937, when it was given to the Atlantic County Historical Society.

Now the property of the State of New Jersey, the Somers Mansion has been carefully refurnished with 18th-century antiques to suggest its character and appearance at the time Richard Somers made it his home. Accessories, acquired over the years by the Atlantic County Historical Society, include paintings, chinaware, quilts, and samplers. The overall effect is significantly different from that encountered in most northeastern colonial restorations, which are often based upon the lives and habitations of people of very modest means; here, on the south shore of New Jersey, we begin to find the northern fringes of the plantation style. Indeed, the 3,000-acre Somers property was called Somerset Plantation—and Somers Point is a lot closer to Virginia than it is to Massachusetts.

The Somers Mansion is at 1000 Shore Rd., (609) 927-2212, www.somersmansionpatriots.org. It's open Sat and Sun from 9 a.m. to 3:30 p.m. Admission is free.

We can't pass Ocean City without visiting a reminder of what happened when lighthouse beacons weren't properly heeded. Here is the **Ocean City Historical Museum** and its roomful of exhibits concerning the wreck of the *Sindia* on December 15, 1901. The *Sindia* was a four-masted bark on the last leg of her voyage from Japan to New York. Pressing northward along the Jersey coast in the teeth of a northeasterly gale, with her officers snug in their quarters and sure that nothing was going to go wrong this close to home, the ship was at the mercy of inexperienced crewmen keeping watch above decks. Seeing a light off to port and assuming it was Sandy Hook, the helmsman rammed *Sindia* onto the bar off Ocean City. There she remains to this day, buried beneath the sand.

The museum's Sindia Room tells the history of this famous wreck, with photographs, videos, charts, and articles—either retrieved from the wreck or washed up on shore—that include many beautiful pieces of Oriental pottery that never made it to the holiday tables of 1901 New York. Other rooms in the museum chronicle the landsman's life of early Ocean County. The domestic atmosphere of the era of Ocean City's 1879 founding is suggested in a series of authentically decorated Victorian rooms, complete with mannequins dressed in period costumes.

The Ocean City Historical Museum, 1735 Simpson Ave., (609) 399-1801, www.ocnjmuseum.org, is open Tues through Sat from 10 a.m. to 4 p.m. Admission is free, but donations are greatly appreciated.

The *Flanders Hotel*, 719 E. 11th St., Ocean City, (609) 399-1000, www .theflandershotel.com, built on the boardwalk in 1923, was nicknamed "The Jewel of the Southern Shore," and today the National Register of Historic Places property is still regarded as one of the landmark hotels of the Jersey Shore. Accommodations range from oceanfront rooms to suites with full kitchens, and the hotel has a spa and fitness center. Emily's Restaurant, which offers indoor and outdoor seating, serves breakfast and lunch daily and dinner in season. Specialties include freshly baked scones, quiche Lorraine, and special all-you-can-eat crab leg dinners certain nights of the week. The hotel and restaurant are open all year.

Shriver's, the oldest continuously operating business on Ocean City's boardwalk, has been making saltwater taffy since 1898. Among their specialty flavors: Creamsicle, sour cherry, coconut, and teaberry. Visitors can watch it being made at the shop on 9th Street and Boardwalk; (609) 399-0100; www .shrivers.com.

If your beachcombing has left you empty-handed, stop at the *Discovery Seashell Museum*, an Ocean City landmark for more than 40 years. The museum, which exhibits and sells more than 10,000 shells and corals from around the world, is at 2721 Asbury Ave., (609) 398-2316, discoveryseashell-museum.business.site, and is open daily from 9 a.m. to 5 p.m. There is no admission fee.

Cape May

Cape May's 21½-acre *Stone Harbor Bird Sanctuary*, a National Natural Landmark, is far, far smaller than the vast tracts protected by the federal government at the Brigantine and Barnegat sites, but it is no less vital to a major group of avian species. Stone Harbor is a heronry, the only one in the United States that is municipally sponsored. It's the nesting place of numerous species of the heron family, including American egret, snowy egret, Louisiana heron, green heron, black-crowned night heron, yellow-crowned night heron, and even the more recently arrived cattle egret. Another arrival, having shown up for the first time in 1958, is the glossy ibis. These dark-bronze birds, with their long, slender, down-turned bills, are the only nesting species at Stone Harbor that are not members of the heron family.

The best time for birders to come to the Stone Harbor Bird Sanctuary is between March and October. The herons, egrets, and ibis build nests and raise their young in spring; later in the season, in the final months prior to their southward migrations, the birds keep to a schedule that takes them almost en masse from their nesting areas in the sanctuary to feeding grounds in the marshes at dawn and back again to the sanctuary at dusk. Often ungainly on their stilt-like legs, herons and their kin are creatures of remarkable grace when they take wing, and to see them in such numbers at first and last light is a rare treat.

There are several paths for visitors, including Heron Overlook, a 120-foot trail with beautiful gardens, and Meadow View, which wanders for 210 feet through wetlands to Paul's Paul, a favorite of the glossy ibis. But the most spectacular, opened in 2009, is Holly Path, which winds for 420 feet past sand dunes, a 300-year-old American holly tree, a demonstration forest, and nesting egrets and herons. Docent-led tours are offered Sat and Sun mornings June through Aug.

Stone Harbor Bird Sanctuary, located between 2nd and 3rd Avenues and 111th and 116th Streets, (609) 368-5102, www.stoneharborbirdsanctuary.com, is open all year. Call or check the website for dates and times of tours.

Another Stone Harbor must-see is *The Wetlands Institute*, an organization dedicated to scientific research and public education concerning intertidal salt marshes and other coastal systems. Begun in 1969 by conservationist Herbert H. Mills, the institute's facilities include a main building, housing exhibits and lecture halls; a gift shop; a library; salt-marsh and aquatic exhibits, with touch tank and touch tables with microscopes; and interactive exhibits for children. There's also a tower that offers a bird's-eye view of the surrounding salt marsh. Outdoors are a salt-marsh trail, a boardwalk, and a 100-foot pier over a tidal creek. The surrounding salt marsh is part of a 6,000-acre publicly owned tract of coastal wetlands. Guided tours, live animal shows, family entertainment, and boat and kayak tours are offered in season. Self-guided tours are offered in the winter.

The Wetlands Institute is located at 1075 Stone Harbor Blvd., (609) 368-1211, www.wetlandsinstitute.org. Call or visit the website for days and hours open, which vary by season. Admission is $8 for adults and $6 for children 3 through 12. A highlight of the year is the mid-Sept Fall Migration Festival, when thousands of birds make their way across the Cape May peninsula in one day. Check the institute website for more information and a schedule of events.

A Cape May Court House site worth visiting is **The Museum of Cape May County**, established in 1927. The history of Cape May County is a bit different from that of the rest of the Jersey Shore. Nearly 300 years ago this was whaling country, and many of the old Cape May families were settlers from New England. (One of the attractions of the museum's library to genealogists, in fact, is its wealth of material that chronicles the *Mayflower* connections of many of the county's early inhabitants.) The museum's exhibits are housed in several buildings, including the 11-room **Cresse Holmes House**, which, like many very old Eastern Seaboard homes, is an amalgamation of structures erected at different times. The oldest section is the 1704 colonial kitchen and loft bedroom; what is now the main section of the house was added in 1830 by John Holmes, an Irish immigrant to Cape May County.

The museum's collections generally relate to the working life of rural Cape May in the 18th and 19th centuries. In the adjacent barn are exhibits of whaling equipment, decoys, and maritime artifacts, including the first-order Fresnel lighthouse lens that formerly stood atop the tower at Cape May Point. In the museum proper are period rooms that illustrate colonial through Victorian living arrangements, a collection of early glassware, and assorted furnishings and chinaware. Most interesting, as long as you don't let your imagination wander, is the collection of surgical instruments in the medical room. These particularly relate to military medicine, and they document field surgical practices from the Revolution to the Spanish-American War—techniques that apparently led many in the military to pray for a quick, fatal hit rather than a wound requiring surgery. Muskets are displayed in an adjacent room, along with swords, uniforms, and other military paraphernalia, covering America's wars from the Revolution to Iraq and Afghanistan. The carriage shed houses items related to transportation, including a vintage horse-drawn market wagon and an early stagecoach.

The Museum of Cape May County, 504 Route 9, Cape May Court House, (609) 465-3535, www.cmcmuseum.org, is open June through Sept, Tues through Sat from 8:30 a.m. to 4 p.m. Off-season the gallery in the administrative building, which houses rolling exhibits of county history, is open Wed and Fri from 10 a.m. to 3 p.m. Donations are much appreciated.

Dogs rule at **Maui's Dog House**—and it's only appropriate in the land of *The Sopranos* that the king of the canines is the "Forget-About-It," a wiener topped with mustard, onions, chili, cheese, and bacon. Don't like that topping? There are 28 others to choose from, including the Drunk Sloppy Shawn, with mustard, ketchup, sautéed onions, and beer-steeped sauerkraut. For the unadventurous, there's plain old mustard and relish. And for cat lovers, there's breaded shrimp, burgers, sausages, and chicken cutlets. But everything goes better with an order of Salty Balls—fresh small potatoes cooked in a brine of salt and spices and served with drawn butter. Forget-about-it is right! Maui's, at 8th and New Jersey Avenues in North Wildwood, (609) 846-0444, www.mauis-doghouse.com, is open daily in season; call or check the website for hours.

Wyland Whaling Wall #43, the work of international environmental muralist Wyland, is at Garfield Avenue and the Boardwalk in Wildwood.

The **Cape May County Park & Zoo** is one of the Jersey Shore's biggest surprises. Perhaps it's because when we think of the shore we think of sea creatures, not landlubbers like giraffes, lions, or camels. Nor do we expect to find an African savanna where sable antelope, kudu, zebra, buffalo, and ostrich roam freely. There are more than 500 species of animals, birds, and reptiles on 128 wooded acres here, including a reptile house with four large alligators. Feeding times are Tues and Fri at 2 p.m.

The Cape May County Park & Zoo, 707 Route 9 North, Cape May Court House, (609) 465-5271, www.capemaycountynj.gov, is open daily in summer from 10 a.m. to 4:45 p.m.; early Nov through mid-March, 10 a.m. to 3:30 p.m. Admission is free, but donations are most welcome.

The town of **Cape May**, at the very tip of Cape May, is the sort of place that doesn't have attractions—it is one. Much of the "city" is a perfect period piece, a throwback to the days when a middle- or upper-middle-class vacation meant a long stay in a big hotel somewhere where the air was supposed to be good for you, and not two weeks in a car or tour bus. Cape May's career as a popular resort began very modestly just after 1800, when the only way to get here was by boat. By 1875 or so, at which time places like Atlantic City and Newport were just getting started, Cape May was a comfortable and thriving resort that could boast of having played host to presidents Pierce, Buchanan, Lincoln, and Grant. Its whaling days might have been over, but its newfound gentility and taste were sure to carry it through the next century as a place to see and be seen.

Well, not quite. Cape May City did fade as the 20th century matured; 40 years ago, few summer vacationers or beach-weekenders ventured south of the neon-lit motels of Wildwood unless they were of a certain age. Then Cape May began to benefit from the desire of more and more travelers to get away from their kind, and also from the revival of interest in Victorian architecture. Cape May had plenty of that particular commodity, despite its notorious combustibility—private homes, hotels, cottages, and guest houses, festooned with gingerbread aplenty, had survived quite nicely into the neon-motel era, needing only paint and patrons. Cape May has gotten to be fashionable once again, even if we haven't seen any presidents rocking on the porches of late. Today the "Nation's Oldest Seashore Resort" is a National Historic Landmark site, with more than 600 authentically restored and preserved Victorian structures.

Perhaps the most impressive of Cape May's Victorian mansions is the beautifully restored *Emlen Physick Estate*, designed by the eminent Philadelphia architect Frank Furness and built in 1879. The Physick Estate belongs to that school of mid- to late-Victorian architecture called the Stick style, in which the structural features of a building were made apparent through the use of exposed exterior timbers. The result was something of a framework effect, elaborated upon by means of steep-gabled, overhanging roof planes, hooded dormers, and a broad veranda, supported by arches almost Gothic in character. A Furness signature, and a staple on finely detailed houses of the related Queen Anne and Shingle styles as well, was the use of massive, heavily ornamented chimneys—quite an ambitious approach for a beach cottage, all in all.

Tours of the first and second floors of the Physick Estate can be arranged through *Cape May MAC*, an umbrella group that is deeply involved in local preservation and cultural affairs. The center offers a number of interesting tour packages and separate events, including whale and dolphin watches, historic district walking and trolley tours, and self-guided auto tours, as well as ongoing music festivals and events, including Christmas in Cape May and the Gardens of Cape May tour. Prices and schedules vary. Over the years, the center has raised more than $2 million for the restoration of the *Cape May Lighthouse* in Cape May Point State Park (www.nj.gov). Built in 1859, the 157½-foot structure has 199 steps. Visitors are welcome daily in summer, and weekends the rest of the year. The admission fee is $12 for adults and $8 for children ages 3 to 12.

Cape May MAC is headquartered at the Physick Estate, 1048 Washington St., Cape May, (609) 884-5404 or (800) 275-4278, www.capemaymac.org.

The innkeepers at the National Register of Historic Places *Mainstay Inn Cape May* describe their rooms and suites as ranging "from ostentatious Victorian splendor to contemporary elegance," and elegance indeed defines this magnificent Italianate villa built in 1872 as a gentlemen's gambling and entertainment club. Architectural highlights include 14-foot ceilings, elaborate chandeliers, a veranda, and a cupola. The inn has six rooms in the main house and six additional rooms across the courtyard in the cottage; there is also a beach apartment for extended stays.

The Mainstay Inn, 635 Columbia Ave., Cape May, (609) 884-8690, www.mainstayinn.com, is open late Mar through early Jan. Rates include breakfast and an elegant afternoon tea. In summer, enjoy a breakfast buffet on the veranda or in the garden.

Each year the elegant 1840 ***Washington Inn & Wine Bar*** in Cape May receives accolades as one of the region's best choices for a night out. There are five dining rooms in the 1840 plantation home, including a summer patio and one with intimate fireside seating. Contemporary American dishes include appetizers such as Maryland crab bisque ($12) and hand-pulled burrata ($16), entrées ranging from cioppino ($34) to filet mignon ($55), and a dessert list topped by chocolate mousse cake with raspberry filling ($12).The wine list is vast and excellent. The restaurant is at 801 Washington St., (609) 884-5697, www.washingtoninn.com, and opens for dinner Thurs through Sat beginning at 5 p.m. Be sure to make a reservation.

If you have time for only one meal at ***The Mad Batter*** in Cape May's Carroll Villa Hotel—a circa 1882 Victorian-style Historic Landmark (www.carroll villa.com)—opt for breakfast starting with a mimosa made with fresh-squeezed orange juice on the porch overlooking historic Jackson Street. If you're flexible, also stop by for lunch and/or dinner, which features a creative assortment of contemporary American and regional dishes, including what is heralded as one of Cape May's best crab cakes. It's open daily at 19 Jackson St., (609) 884–5970, www.madbatter.com.

If you're still hungry for seafood, scuttle down to the ***Lobster House*** on Fisherman's Wharf, 906 Schellenger's Landing Rd., (609) 884-8296, www .thelobsterhouse.com. An institution for over 60 years, the restaurant has five dining rooms as well as a seasonal restaurant aboard the docked 130-foot authentic Grand Banks sailing vessel, the schooner *America*. The menu features treats such as barbecued clams, oysters Rockefeller, and the Lobster House combo. Lunch and dinner are served daily.

In 1850 a Philadelphia chemist named William Weightman built a summer home in the Second Empire style of architecture at the corner of Washington and Franklin Streets in Cape May. In 1884, his son wanted to be closer to the beach, so he bought property on Ocean Avenue, had the building cut in half, and got farmers with horses and logs to move the house. In 1962 the Reverend Carl McIntyre purchased the Weightman buildings to save them from demolition and moved them to their present site on Reading Avenue.

In January 1989, John and Barbara Girton purchased the deteriorating structures and put 103,000 hours of work and more than $3 million into restoring the property. In July 1989 they opened the first of the two buildings of the 57-room, 27-guest-room B&B ***Angel of the Sea***. The restoration was fully completed in a year. In 1990 this gingerbread Victorian placed second in the National Trust for Historic Preservation's Bed and Breakfast Inns contest and has since been consistently selected by two national bed-and-breakfast organizations as one of the top 10 in the country. It is now owned by Theresa and

Ron Stanton, who run it with the help of their three sons. The inn is at 5-7 Trenton Ave., Cape May, (609) 884-3369 or (800) 848-3369, www.angelofthesea .com. Rates begin at $99 a night and include breakfast and afternoon tea and sweets, and wine and cheese every afternoon from 5:30 to 7 p.m.

One of Cape May's favorite stops for locals since it first opened in 1988 is **Tisha's Fine Dining**, 322 Washington Street Mall, (609) 884-9119, www.tishas-finedining.com. The chef prepares American fare with Italian accents, including prime meats with unique sauces and a wonderful mussel dish. Dinner entrées range from $28 for chicken Pasquale to $54 for veal chop marsala. Get there early for an outdoor table overlooking the ocean, and be sure to bring a bottle of wine. Dinner is served nightly beginning at 4:30 p.m.

Each spring millions of horseshoe crabs come up the Delaware Bay to beaches near East Point Lighthouse at the mouth of the Maurice River to lay their eggs. And each year, at the same time, millions of shorebirds migrating north from South America arrive just in time to snack on the eggs, refueling for the long flight still to come. From September to November, Cape May Point becomes the Raptor Capital of North America as an estimated 50,000 migrating hawks pass over.

To learn about these—and other—avian happenings on Cape May Peninsula, visit either of the National Audubon Society's **Cape May Bird Observatory**'s two locations: the Northwood Center, 701 E. Lake Drive, Cape May Point, (609) 884-2736, open Wed through Sun (except holidays) from 9:30 a.m. to 4:30 p.m., or the Center for Research and Education, 600 Route 47N, Cape May Court House, (609) 861-0700, whose self-guided trails are open Mon through Fri from 9 a.m. to 5 p.m.; www.birdcapemay.org.

For information on the Cape May National Wildlife Refuge, see "Delaware Bay Shore" in the Southern New Jersey chapter.

The **Cape May Ferry**, which traverses Delaware Bay between Cape May and the picturesque town of Lewes, Delaware, is the most convenient way to travel from the Jersey Shore to Delmarva Peninsula resorts such as Rehoboth Beach, Delaware, and Ocean City, Maryland. It leaves from North Cape May and operates all year. Write Cape May Terminal, PO Box 827, North Cape May 08204; call (800) 643-3779; or visit www.cmlf.com for a schedule and rates. Advance reservations are required.

Places to Stay at the Shore

The Berkeley Oceanfront Hotel
1401 Ocean Ave., Asbury Park
(732) 776-6700
www.berkeleyhotelnj.com
Moderate–expensive

The Crusader Oceanfront Family Resort
6101 Ocean Ave., Wildwood Crest
(609) 522-6991
www.crusaderresort.com
Moderate

Flanders Hotel
719 E. 11th St. (at the Boardwalk), Ocean City
(609) 399-1000
www.theflandershotel.com
Expensive

Grand Hotel of Cape May
1045 Beach Ave., Cape May
(800) 257-8550 or (609) 884-5611
www.grandhotelcapemay.com
Moderate–expensive

The Hewitt Wellington
200 Monmouth Ave., Spring Lake
(732) 974-1212
www.thehewittwellington.com
Expensive

Hotel Alcott
107–113 Grant St., Cape May
(609) 884-5868
www.hotelalcott.com
Moderate–expensive

The Mason Cottage B&B
623 Columbia Ave., Cape May
(609) 884-3358
www.themasoncottage.com
Moderate–expensive

The Ocean House Bed &Breakfast
102 Sussex Ave., Spring Lake
(732) 449-9090
www.theoceanhouse.net
Expensive

SeaScape Manor
3 Grand Tour, Highlands
(732) 291-8467
www.seascapemanorbb.com
Moderate–expensive

Spring Lake Inn
104 Salem St., Spring Lake
(732) 449-2010
www.springlakeinn.com
Moderate–expensive

Scarborough Inn
720 Ocean Ave., Ocean City
(609) 399-1558
www.scarboroughinn.com
Moderate

Virginia Hotel & Cottages
25 Jackson St., Cape May
(609) 884-5700
www.virginiahotel.com
Moderate–expensive

Places to Eat at the Shore

Anchor Inn
400 Ocean Gate Ave., Ocean Gate
(732) 269-3510
The accent at this popular and casual restaurant/bar is on fresh seafood, but there are several landlubber options, including a highly recommended Delmonico steak. Picky kids will love the homemade pizza. No credit cards. Lunch and dinner Tues through Sun. Inexpensive.

Bareli's by the Sea
Grand Victorian Hotel, 1505 Ocean Ave., Spring Lake
(732) 769-5700
Reserve an outdoor table overlooking the ocean and enjoy creative, contemporary Italian dishes such as rigatoni alla vodka and horseradish grilled salmon. At lunch, try the spicy Italian panini or the tempura-battered soft shell crab. There is a fine selection of local beers. Lunch and dinner daily. Moderate–expensive.

Buckalew's Restaurant and Tavern
101 N. Bay Ave., Beach Haven
(609) 492-1065
One of Long Beach Island's most popular spots features restaurant and tavern menus, with

steak and seafood topping the bill. Outdoor dining; live entertainment; kids' menu. Breakfast, lunch, and dinner daily; takeout available. Sunday lobster or filet mignon special. Inexpensive–expensive.

Graziano's Italian Restaurant

3119 Route 88, Point Pleasant
(732) 899-6336
The Graziano-Muolo family opened this classic eatery in 1966, and the menu has changed little since then. All the traditional Italian favorites are here, including chicken "parm," fettuccini Alfredo, and homemade lasagna. And, of course, pizza. Dinner Tues through Sun. Inexpensive—moderate.

Hemingway's

Grand View Hotel, 800 Bay Ave., Somers Point
(609) 884-5611
Serving modern American fare in a family-friendly environment. Wednesday night prime rib is a favorite, as is the early "Sunset Dining" menu. Try a pork belly burnt ends appetizer in cherry BBQ sauce, or a Taylor ham sandwich at breakfast. Breakfast and lunch Fri through Sun; dinner nightly. Reservations recommended. Inexpensive–moderate.

Il Giardino Sul Mare

2 Hollywood Blvd., Forked River
(609) 971-7699
This award-winning, white-tablecloth Italian restaurant's menu is extensive; its wine list, by the glass or carafe, moderate; and the ambience relaxed. Homemade desserts include Dark Side of the Moon, a fudge cake soaked with coffee liqueur, and cannoli and chocolate mousse cakes. Children's menu available. Lunch and dinner Tues through Sun. Moderate.

Klein's Fish Market, Waterside Café & Tiki Bar and Grill

708 River Rd., Belmar
(732) 681-1177
Overlooking Shark River Basin, the accent at this bustling, multifaceted eatery is on a large selection of flopping fresh fish. It's served raw at the sushi and raw bar, to take home at the market, or in a large variety of preparations including chowders, crab cakes, and grilled and fried dishes. Lunch and dinner Wed through Sun. No reservations. Inexpensive–moderate.

Knife & Fork

3600 Atlantic Ave., Atlantic City
(609) 344-1133
For nearly a century, this splendidly restored throwback to Atlantic City's glory days has been the place for prime aged steaks, thick chops, and fresh seafood. The award-winning wine list features selections from the more-than-7,000-bottle cellar. Lunch on Fri; dinner daily. Expensive.

Mangiare Tu

600 Main St., Bradley Beach
(732) 869-0700
Cozy and casual, with a New York supper club vibe, "The Jersey Shore's Best Kept Secret" specializes in Italian dishes such as veal marsala and zuppa di mussels. On Sunday, there's "Sunday Gravy" rigatoni with a scoop of ricotta, sausage, and meatball. Dinner Thurs through Sun. Reservations recommended. Moderate–expensive.

The Poached Pear

816 Arnold Ave., Point Pleasant Beach
(732) 701-1700
Owner-chef Scott Giordano offers classic bistro dishes with a contemporary twist. The namesake pear appears in dishes including pear pizzetta, with gorgonzola, walnuts, and port wine; also sesame-crusted ahi tuna and rack of lamb persillade. BYOB. Dinner nightly except Mon. Expensive.

SELECTED REGIONAL INFORMATION CENTERS, CHAMBERS OF COMMERCE & VISITOR CENTERS AT THE SHORE

Asbury Park Chamber of Commerce
1201 Springwood Ave.
Asbury Park 07712
(732) 775-7676
www.asburyparkchamber.com

Cape May County Department of Tourism
PO Box 556
Cape May 08204
(609) 884-5508
www.capemaychamber.com

Greater Atlantic City Chamber of Commerce
12 Virginia Ave.
Atlantic City 08401
(609) 345-4524
www.acchamber.com

Monmouth County Department of Economic Development/Tourism
1 E. Main St.
Freehold 07728
(800) 523-2587
www.tourism.visitmonmouth.com

Ocean County Tourism
101 Hooper Ave., PO Box 2191
Toms River 08754
(732) 929-2000 or (800) 722-0291
www.oceancountytourism.com

Ocean Grove Chamber of Commerce
81 Main Ave.
Ocean Grove 07756
(732) 774-1391
www.oceangrovenj.com

Tun Tavern Restaurant and Brewery
2 Convention Blvd., Atlantic City
(609) 347-7800
Atlantic City's first brewpub serves up a wide variety of brewed-on-the-premises beers and ales by the glass or pitcher, and a menu ranging from burgers (a 1-pounder is available) to pasta primavera to steak, shrimp, and seared tuna. Wine bar. Lunch and dinner Wed through Sun. Inexpensive–expensive.

Other Attractions at the Shore

Allgor–Barkalow Homestead Museum
1701 New Bedford Rd., Wall
(732) 681-3806

Atlantic City Boardwalk
Atlantic City

Beach Haven Guided Walking Tours
Downtown Victorian district, Beach Haven
(609) 492-0700

Cape May Stage
405 Lafayette St., Cape May
(609) 770-8311

Cape May Whale Watch and Research Center
1231 Route 109, South Jersey Marina, Cape May
(609) 898-0055

Church of the Presidents
1260 Ocean Ave., Long Branch
(732) 223-0905

The Great Hall
400 Cedar Ave., West Long Branch
(732) 571-3400

Historic Cold Spring Village
735 Seashore Rd., Cape May
(609) 898-2300

Jenkinson's Aquarium
300 N. Ocean Ave., Point
Pleasant Beach
(732) 899-1212

**Jim Whelan Boardwalk
Hall**
2301 Boardwalk, Atlantic
City
(609) 348-7000

River Belle Cruises
47 Broadway, Point
Pleasant Beach
(732) 892-3377

Sea Girt Lighthouse
9 N. Ocean Ave., Sea Girt
(732) 974-0514

**St. Vladimir's Memorial
Russian Orthodox Church**
Rova Farms, 134
Perrineville Rd., Route 571,
Jackson
(732) 928-1248

Southern New Jersey

In a small state like New Jersey, if there is any such thing as terra incognita—a part of the state that is least understood by the people in the other parts—then surely it is southern New Jersey, called South Jersey by New Jerseyans. South Jersey properly includes the Shore, but that's not what we're talking about here. The Shore is a land unto itself, and many think they know it, whether for the right or wrong reasons. But that vast bulge of land west of the littoral, tucked between Philadelphia and Delaware Bay, is what we're after.

South Jersey contains the least densely populated part of the nation's most densely populated state, the Pine Barrens, which even most Jerseyans hadn't heard of until they were threatened by a proposal to build a huge new jetport there in the 1960s. The Pine Barrens are better known and even appreciated now, thanks in part to the environmentalists' crusade that brought much of their remote, scrubby acreage under strict state development guidelines and, in some areas, outright protection. At stake in the Barrens is not only a sense of wilderness so close to civilization but also a wonderfully pure water supply in a state that desperately needs it. The Pine Barrens'

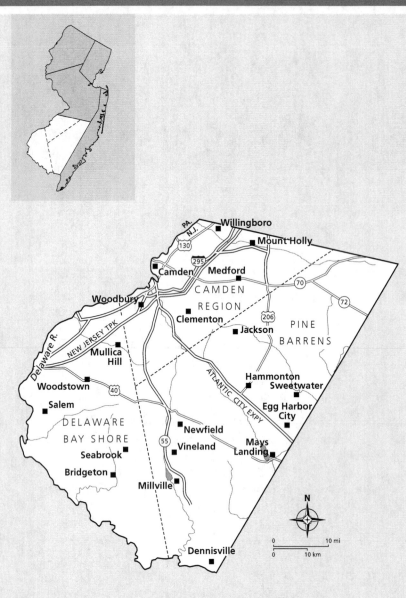

PA.
N.J.
130
295
Willingboro
Mount Holly
Camden
Medford
70
72
CAMDEN
REGION
Woodbury
Clementon
206
PINE
BARRENS
Jackson
NEW JERSEY TPK
Mullica
Hill
Delaware R.
Woodstown
40
Hammonton
Sweetwater
Salem
ATLANTIC CITY EXPY
Egg Harbor
City
DELAWARE
BAY SHORE
Newfield
55
Vineland
Mays
Landing
Seabrook
Bridgeton
Millville

N

0   10 mi
0   10 km

Dennisville

SOUTHERN NEW JERSEY'S TOP PICKS

Batsto	Salem Oak
Renault Resort	Finn's Point National Cemetery
Wheaton Arts and Cultural Center	Cowtown Rodeo
Greenwich	Mullica Hill
Seabrook Educational and Cultural Center	Pomona Hall
A. J. Meerwald	*Waterfront Connection*
Salem Court House	Barclay Farmstead Museum

great water resource is not merely on the surface, in the still rivers and ponds that bring so many canoeists down this way, but in a vast underground aquifer, which could easily be poisoned or depleted by reckless development.

In South Jersey we also find the big truck farms that produce those wonderful tomatoes for which New Jersey is justly famous—why else do you suppose the Campbell Soup Company is in Camden? Along the "other shore" of New Jersey, the coast of Salem and Cumberland Counties along Delaware Bay, are salt marshes and tidal estuaries, quilted with federal and state wildlife-management holdings. Here, at the mouths of meandering rivers like the Maurice and the Cohansey, are towns that seem as if they belong on the eastern shore of Maryland rather than in New Jersey, but the distance from Delaware Bay to the Chesapeake Bay isn't very far at all.

Finally, as the bay narrows to a river and the riverbanks surrender their marshes to wharves and factories, we approach Camden and the great bridges to Philadelphia. Here southwestern New Jersey becomes very much like the northeastern part of the state, a dense cluster of towns and suburbs that would make a respectable metropolitan area anywhere else, but which are ever in the shadow of an urban goliath across the river.

Note: The orientation in this chapter is more or less clockwise, starting in the upper eastern corner of the region in the Pine Barrens, then heading down toward the Delaware Bay Shore, and finally going up the river to the Camden Region.

Pine Barrens

Elsewhere in New Jersey, at Ringwood and at Allaire, we have come upon reminders of the days when iron mining, smelting, and forging were big industries in the state. The greatest of all New Jersey's old iron towns, however, is in the Pine Barrens, deep within the 110,000-acre Wharton State Forest. This is **Batsto**, which, in two centuries, has made the transition from busy industrial village to ghost town to major restoration.

Like the lands that surround Allaire Village, the environs of Batsto yield bog iron that can be collected on or near the surface. In 1766 Burlington attorney and provincial assemblyman Charles Read and a group of associates built a string of four ironworks in the bog-iron country of South Jersey, of which Batsto was to become the most famous. Little could Read have known how famous, and how soon: Within 10 years, under a later owner named John Cox, the furnace at Batsto was producing a steady stream of munitions for the Continental army. So important were the cannon and cannonballs cast at Batsto to the American war effort that the men who worked there were exempt from military service. This was a powerful inducement to owner Cox to keep the fires burning, as he was a Quaker pacifist who was initially disinclined to use his works for military production.

springtime posies

Each April in the Pine Barrens the sand myrtle, a rare, small plant with dark, boxlike leaves and white flowers, blossoms for several weeks.

The British and their Tory allies were very much interested in what was going on at Batsto. Spies regularly reported on shipments of munitions from the

Sounds of Silence

We drove 5 miles east from Batsto, the restored iron-forge community in the heart of the Pine Barrens, along a dead-straight sand track that was a masterpiece of 18th-century surveying. Stopping at a place the map called Washington, we found nothing more than a sand-paved intersection, with a stand of pines at its center, from which other roads went nowhere through the trees. Stagecoaches once stopped here. There were taverns and schools. We got out of the car and looked into the forest, and stood still long enough to surprise a white-tailed deer. The wind gusted; there was a dry whisper of pine needles. We had found the eye of the Jersey storm, here in abandoned Washington, and save for that whisper it was a place of unearthly and un-Jerseylike quiet.

The Hat That Wasn't

Look on a detailed map of the Pine Barrens, and you'll find a place called Ong's Hat. Like many communities in that part of the state today, Ong's Hat is just a lonely crossroads that wouldn't even qualify as a ghost town. But what about that name?

According to the late South Jersey historian Henry Charlton Beck, the Ong in question was one Jacob Ong, who traveled frequently in the Mullica River valley in the early 1700s. He built a little cabin at one of his stopping places and called it a *hoet*, as any Dutch speaker would. The word is related to the English "hut," but it's similar enough to "hat" for the corruption to have crept onto New Jersey maps and stayed there.

works by wagon and by barge along the Mullica River, and on one occasion, in 1778, a British detachment got as close to the forges as Chestnut Neck, near the mouth of the Mullica. Nevertheless the great furnace stayed lit, and it was able to make the transition from military to peacetime production (among Batsto's domestic and commercial products of the era are two firebacks, cast to George Washington's specifications and installed at Mount Vernon).

In 1784, Batsto's great era began when the property was acquired by William Richards, who made Batsto into more than just an ironworks in the forest. It became a self-contained village, with virtually everything its workers needed—store, residences, stables, sawmill, icehouse, and farm. Richards also built the structure that still dominates Batsto today, the stuccoed mansion. Richards retired in 1809, but his son and grandson carried on. The furnace itself was rebuilt in 1829, and in 1846 the first Batsto glass factory was erected.

Although glassmaking at Batsto was profitable enough for a second glass factory to be built in 1848, the great iron furnace was shut down for good that year. The reason was the same as at Allaire: Pennsylvania coal was too cheap for New Jersey charcoal to compete. The furnace was dismantled in 1855. Twelve years later the glassworks went out of business, and in 1874 fire leveled half of Batsto village.

Batsto was purchased by Philadelphia industrialist Joseph Wharton in 1876. When his initial plan to dam the local streams and rivers and sell the water to Camden and Philadelphia failed, he built a sawmill and underground silo, enlarged the mansion and transformed its appearance to reflect the Italianate style of architecture, and cleared vast areas of land to cultivate crops, including cranberries. By the end of the 19th century, Batsto had been transformed into a "gentleman's farm."

Paddling the Barrens

The Pine Barrens offer some of the finest flat-water canoeing opportunities in the Northeast. Two of our favorite rivers are the Batsto, which twists its way through the heart of the Barrens before joining the larger Mullica River, and the Mullica itself, which follows an almost equally circuitous path on its way to tidewater near Green Bank. Each makes for a great two-day adventure, although it's possible to plan one-day trips as well. Along the way you'll feel like you're a thousand miles from civilization, and at night, in spring and summer, the whip-poor-wills keep up their inimitable charming racket. There are numerous sandy banks where you can take a dip, so don't be put off by the dark, brownish color of the water. The soil in the Barrens is highly acidic, and iron and organic contents leach out from it into the rivers and streams.

After Wharton died in 1909, the State of New Jersey had a chance to buy his property for $1 million. State officials said yes, but the voters, feeling frugal, said no. Now the stage was set for the complete dereliction of the Batsto buildings. What nature was accomplishing slowly, the US Air Force proposed to finish quickly in 1954, when plans were announced for a jet-support depot that would have done for the Pine Barrens what the Port Authority's jetport scheme almost did for the Great Swamp. The state opposed the Air Force proposal, as did environmentalists and those who wished to save what was left of Batsto village. This time New Jersey opened its purse: For $3 million, the entire tract was purchased. Thus was Wharton State Forest created. Restoration of the village began in 1958 and has continued ever since.

For camping permits in Wharton State Forest, through which the rivers flow for much of their length, call or visit the administration building in Batsto,

AUTHORS' FAVORITE ATTRACTIONS IN SOUTHERN NEW JERSEY

A. J. Meerwald

American Indian Heritage Museum

Batsto

Finn's Point National Cemetery

Renault Resort

Seabrook Educational and Cultural Center

Wheaton Arts and Cultural Center

Bel Haven Paddle Sports

Sweetwater Riverdeck

Green-Tomato Pie

Here's an unusual recipe, using unripe Jersey tomatoes, that was popular long ago down in the Pine Barrens.

Prepare crust for a 2-crust pie, using your favorite recipe. Line a pie pan with the bottom crust, and roll out the top crust and have it ready.

Dice 6 or 8 green tomatoes, depending on size (there should be enough to fill the pie shell amply). Cut a half lemon into ⅛-inch pieces, rind and all. Put half of the diced tomatoes into the pie shell, dust with flour, add half of the lemon, and sprinkle with 5 heaping tablespoons of sugar. Repeat the procedure, finishing with 6 heaping tablespoons of sugar.

Put the top crust on the pie, sealing well. Bake at 400 degrees for 30 to 40 minutes, or until the crust is golden. If a toothpick inserted into the pie shows the tomatoes are still firm, cover the rim of the pie with foil to prevent burning as baking completes.

(609) 561-0024, or the Atsion Ranger Station, (609) 268-0444. Camping is allowed only at designated sites.

Batsto today offers visitors a look at what life in a 19th-century Pine Barrens village was like. All summer long interpreters can be found in the workers' houses and such key buildings as the mansion and the sawmill. The crafts of weaving and pottery making are also demonstrated. Across the Batsto River milldam from the village are the general store and 1852 post office (open in summer), the gristmill and barns, a visitor center with interpretive exhibits and museum shop, and the Batsto Mansion itself.

Historic Batsto Village, off Route 542 at 31 Batsto Rd. in Hammonton, (609) 561-0024, www.batstovillage.org, is open daily throughout the year. The museum and exhibit gallery are housed in the visitor center, which is open from 9 a.m. to 4 p.m. Admission to the village is free, although there is a vehicle fee of $5 for New Jersey residents and $7 for nonresidents on weekends from Memorial Day weekend through Labor Day. Tours are conducted Wed through Sun at 11 a.m., 1 p.m., 2 p.m., and 3 p.m. Tickets are $3 for adults, $1 for children 6 to 11, and free for children 5 and under. Tickets must be purchased at the visitor center on the day of the tour, and are limited to 10 persons per tour—so get there early. Canoes are available for guided nature trips on the lake. Call ahead for schedules and check the website for a list of events at the village.

Wharton State Forest, encompassing 122,463 acres, is now the state park system's largest single tract of land. It has splendid facilities for hiking, camping, canoeing, horseback riding, hunting, and fishing. Camping is

The Jersey Devil

They didn't just pull the name of New Jersey's hockey team out of thin air.

There is a "Jersey Devil," at least in persistent folklore. Described as having the head of a horse, the wings of a bat, and a dragon-like body, the creature has been the terror of the Pine Barrens for more than 250 years. According to legend, a Mrs. Leeds, of Estellville (though there are variations in the woman's name and town), learned she was pregnant for the 13th time and swore that if she had to have another child, "Let it be the devil." She got her wish, giving birth to a monstrosity that let out a screech, then flew up the chimney and into legend.

Accused over the years of every crime from raiding chicken coops to souring milk to killing whole ponds full of fish with its poisonous breath, the monster at one time carried a reward on his head of $100,000, dead or alive. But no one has ever been able to catch him: The Jersey Devil is still out there, raising hell.

permitted year-round—both at developed areas and at several primitive sites. Nine four- to eight-person cabins on Atsion Lake with indoor toilets, showers, hot and cold water, and bunks are available for public use from Apr through Oct. For information on camping and other facilities, call the forest headquarters at Batsto, (609) 561-0024, or write to Wharton State Forest, 31 Batsto Rd., Hammonton 08037; www.nj.gov.

TOP ANNUAL EVENTS IN SOUTHERN NEW JERSEY

Note: Schedules may vary; call ahead.

Delaware Bay Days, East Point Light, Matt's Landing, Port Norris, Bivalve, and Shellpile; June; (856) 785-2060; www.commercialtwp.com

Jersey Shore Jazz & Blues Festival, Long Branch; Aug; ongoing events throughout the year; (732) 933-1984; www.sjbf.org

Sunset Jazz Series, Wiggins Waterfront Park, Camden; Aug; (856) 757-9400; http://www.camdencounty.com

Chatsworth Cranberry Festival, Chatsworth; Oct; (609) 726-0006; www.cranfest.info

Country Living Fair, Batsto Village; Oct; (609) 561-0024; www.batstovillage.org

Festival of Fine Craft, Wheaton Village, Millville; Oct; (800) 998-4552; www.wheatonarts.org

For a real taste of Pine Barrens seclusion, pick up a self-guided tour at Batsto headquarters and visit two historic landmarks: *Harrisville*, once a thriving paper mill town, was abandoned in 1891 when the mill went out of business and is now a ghost town, complete with workers' homes, the paper mill, and numerous outbuildings. The 1826 *Atsion Mansion* was built as a summer home for a prominent ironmaster who operated the furnace along the Mullica River. The house, without plumbing, electricity, or furniture, is an excellent example of Greek Revival architecture.

What better way to appreciate the wilderness of the Pine Barrens than by taking a backcountry canoe trip along the Upper Toms River as it winds and twists through typical Pine Barrens foliage? There are numerous places to rent canoes and kayaks throughout the area; most will help you arrange your trip—whether for two hours or two weeks—and provide transportation. One, *Mick's Pine Barrens Canoe and Kayak Rental*, 3107 Route 563, Chatsworth, (609) 726-1380 or (800) 281-1380, www.mickscanoerental.com, offers paddles through Wharton State Forest Apr through late Sept, and they can help you make arrangements for overnight camping trips. Pets are welcome.

Estell Manor County Park, 3 miles south of Mays Landing on Route 50, is the site of the ruins of Estellville Glassworks, an early 19th-century glass factory, as well as a World War I munitions plant. The ruins have interpretive signs, and visitors can get an idea of how glass was made from 1825 to 1877, but the main attraction here is the park's incredible diversity of plants and animals. The Fox Nature Center has educational displays and a large collection of taxidermy mounts, insect and plant displays, and information on the history of the local area. The park is open daily from 7:30 a.m. until a half hour after

The Great Paisley Boom

Look on a map of South Jersey's Pine Barrens and you won't see a city named Paisley. But in the late 1880s, real-estate promoters touted the "magic city" of Paisley as a place where colleges would soon jostle against conservatories, where artists and authors would count doctors and composers among their neighbors, and where agriculture and manufacturing alike would boom. There were offices selling Paisley properties in several major cities—in all, 13,000 lots on 1,400 acres were on the market.

Some 3,000 eager buyers took the bait, at prices of around $375 per acre (the promoters had paid roughly a hundredth of that amount), and waited for construction to take off. Trouble was, just about all of them waited. By 1890 there were 12 modest buildings in Paisley—and that was the high point of its development. It's all still Pine Barrens.

sunset. The nature center is open daily from 8 a.m. to 4 p.m. Admission is free. The park is part of the Atlantic County Division of Parks and Recreation, 109 Route 50, Mays Landing, (609) 645-5960 or 625-1897, www.atlantic-county.org.

With an elegantly appointed 55-room hotel, an 18-hole golf course, and a winery that has been in continuous operation for almost 160 years, **Renault Resort** has morphed into a year-round destination. The winery itself has a fascinating history. Louis Renault came to southern New Jersey from Reims, France, in 1864, and the winery—surrounded by acres of vineyards—has been in business ever since. It even operated round-the-clock during Prohibition, when the proprietors made a 44-proof "medicinal tonic" under special government license (Jersey folk always believed in the salubrious effects of a good tonic). Today Renault produces Chablis, Cabernet Sauvignon, Colombard, Riesling, May wine, and even champagne—the winery was, in fact, the largest American maker of champagne before California and New York took over the lead. Their tasting room is open daily.

takeahike

The well-marked 50-mile Batona Trail wanders through the heart of the Pine Barrens, passing near Batsto Village and connecting Wharton State Forest, Lebanon State Forest, and Bass River State Forest. For a camping permit (issued only for designated sites), contact one of the state forest offices.

Adjacent to Renault's French-inspired garden, in the Wine & Beer Garden, diners can select from a menu of classic American dishes including burgers and salads, along with Renault wines and champagnes by the glass or a beer. At the House of Renault, cuisine with a French flair is infused with American

Carranza Monument

Deep in the Pine Barrens, on an unnamed road in desolate Tabernacle Township, a monument adorned with an Aztec eagle and a Spanish inscription marks the spot where a 23-year-old Mexican aviator named Emilio Carranza died on July 13, 1928. Carranza, a Mexican military hero who had made a goodwill flight from Mexico City to Washington and New York, had just left Long Island's Roosevelt Field on what he hoped would be a nonstop return flight when his Ryan Monoplane went down in a thunderstorm. His body was returned to Mexico—and his final, fatal flight was commemorated with what surely must be New Jersey's least-visited monument.

Each year, on the anniversary of his crash, a ceremony is held at the site in his honor. It's organized by the members of American Legion Post 11, which recovered the aviator's body. A word to the wise: There are rumors that the monument is haunted, so it may be best to visit during daylight hours.

farmhouse flavors, and can be enjoyed with a selection of handcrafted cocktails. Or, diners can opt for a more casual ambience in the upscale bar. The restaurant serves breakfast, lunch, and dinner.

The newest addition is Café la Fleur, a Parisian-inspired spot with a farmhouse flair, offering patrons an original menu including "build your own" crepes and wine-infused cupcakes along with artisanal coffees and other beverages. The 18-hole Vineyard National golf course meanders through the original vines first planted by Monsieur Renault.

Renault Resort, 72 North Bremen Ave., Egg Harbor, (609) 965-2111, www.renaultwinery.com, has special brunches, dinners, and events throughout the season.

Another award-winning winery in the area, *Sharrott Winery*, hosts year-round tastings, live entertainment, and special event nights. In addition to tastings, visitors can eat in the Wine Bar, which offers a selection of tasty dishes meant to pair well with wines. Among them are small plates ($11.99 to $19.99) such as truffle parmesan potato wedges, carnitas tacos, and the Winery Cheese Plate served with walnuts, fig jam, and toasted crostini; and scratch-made flatbreads ($12.99 to $14.99) including truffled mushroom, and sausage and peppers. There's also a brunch menu ($10.99 to $14.99) that includes corned beef hash and bananas Foster waffles.

The winery is open Mon and Tues from noon to 6 p.m., Wed through Sat noon to 9 p.m., and Sun 10 a.m. to 5 p.m. Sharrott is at 370 Egg Harbor Road in Hammonton, (609) 567-WINE, www.sharrottwinery.com. Sign up online for their newsletter of upcoming events.

In April of 1930 a group of Vineland growers got together to create the *Vineland Produce Auction*, and today the auction, on 44 acres, is still going strong. It features some of the state's finest produce, including eggplant, kale, squashes, blueberries, and peaches, and is held Mon through Sat during the growing season beginning at 10:45 a.m. Check their website to see what's in season and on sale; even if you're not in the market for bulk fresh fruits and vegetables, the auction is great fun. It's at 1088 N. Main Road in Vineland, (856) 691-0721, www.vinelandproduce.com.

Nearby, the *Delsea Drive-In Theatre*, built in 1949, is the state's only drive-in still in operation. It manages to blend nostalgia with first-run movies, modern technology, and a concession stand that serves up "healthier food choices," but don't fear—along with gluten-free items and low-carb pie, there are onion rings, hot dogs, 1/3-pound cheeseburgers, and popcorn with real butter. Patrons will get to see at least a double feature, and sometimes there may be a triple.

The Delsea Drive-In Theatre is at 2204 S. Delsea Drive, Vineland, (856) 696-0011, www.delseadrive-in.com. General admission for those 4 and over is $12.50 plus tax, and a fee if tickets are bought online (they're also sold at the box office). The theater is open Memorial Day weekend through Labor Day Fri through Sun, and may be open Thurs if there is enough demand. After Labor Day, through Nov, there are shows on Fri and Sat. Patrons are invited to bring lawn chairs and sit in front of their cars.

On June 30, 2008, the historic Sweetwater Casino burned to the ground. The seasonal **Sweetwater Marina & Riverdeck**, on the site of the onetime high-stakes poker casino and restaurant, provides patrons with the same wonderful views of the Mullica River, live entertainment on Sat and Sun, and a pub-style menu. It's at 2780 7th Ave., in Sweetwater, (609) 668-1545, www .sweetwaterriverdeck.com, and is open seasonally Thurs through Sun. There's an ongoing roster of events, including everything from live bands to antique car shows. Check the website for the full listing.

Southern New Jersey seems to be a place that attracts people of vision determined to launch new enterprises. Batsto had Read and his ironworks, Egg Harbor City had Renault and his winery, and just outside Vineland there were whole communities founded by industrious Russian-Jewish immigrants who developed farms and a clothing factory. In Millville a pharmacist named R. T. C. Wheaton set up a glassmaking business; his contributions are remembered at **Wheaton Arts**, a museum and crafts complex that is one of this area's most popular attractions.

The heart of Wheaton Arts is the Museum of American Glass, a modern exhibit building that houses a collection of more than 6,500 examples of artistic and utilitarian glassware, ranging from goblets to paperweights, from Mason jars to the world's largest bottle. The museum traces the development of trends in American household glassware, from the roughly crafted glass of colonial times, through the gorgeous stained-glass creations of Louis Comfort Tiffany, to today's handcrafted and mass-produced articles.

In the re-created 1888 Wheaton Glass Studio, artisans employ traditional skills to fashion vases, pitchers, bottles, and other useful and ornamental articles, all of which are for sale in the Wheaton Village stores. Glassblowing demonstrations are given at 11 a.m., 1:30 p.m., and 3:30 p.m.

Other attractions include the Down Jersey Folklife Center, focusing on the rich and diverse traditions of New Jersey's eight southern counties; an old-time general store, stocked with museum-quality wares that aren't for sale and penny candy that is; a 19th-century Tin Shop, with a working resident tinsmith; the Stained Glass Studio, with artists-in-residence using traditional techniques; an 1876 schoolhouse; demonstrations of pottery making, glass lamp-working, and wood carving; and the Gallery of Fine Craft, which features one-of-a-kind American crafts, with a series of special exhibitions that change regularly throughout the year.

Wheaton Arts, 1501 Glasstown Rd., Millville, (856) 825-6800 or (800) 998-4552, www.wheatonarts.org, is open Tues through Sun, Apr through Dec; closed on holidays. Admission is $12 for adults, $11 for seniors, and $7 for students; children 5 and under are free. There is no fee to shop and stroll. The center hosts events through the year, including the juried Festival of Fine Craft in early Oct.

If you're a Matchbox car collector, you know how rare a No. 41 Ford GT Superfast is. And No. 22 Pontiac Superfast red. They're on exhibit—along with approximately 50,000 other Matchbox vehicles and products—at the **Matchbox Road Museum & Collector Shoppe** on Pearl Street in Newfield; (856) 697-6900. The museum and shop are open by appointment. Donations are welcome.

Delaware Bay Shore

One of the state's finest salt marshes is nestled amid 5,000 acres of forest and reed thickets at **Dennis Creek Wildlife Management Area** in Dennisville. The mile-long Jake's Landing Road, which leads to the area, passes through a densely pined portion of Belleplain State Forest. The tidal creek, which flows into nearby Delaware Bay, is a popular gathering spot for waterfowl such as Canada geese, goldeneyes, and hooded mergansers and is also an excellent spot for crabbing and fishing.

Cape May National Wildlife Refuge is a welcome resting place for migratory birds about to cross the 12-mile-wide mouth of Delaware Bay. The refuge, now comprising more than 8,000 acres, will ultimately protect 16,700 acres of wildlife habitat on Cape May Peninsula. It's strategically located on the Atlantic Flyway, and its 5-mile stretch along the bay is recognized as one of the major shorebird staging areas in North America, providing a critical habitat for hundreds of thousands of migratory birds each year, as well as for other wildlife, including 42 mammal species, 55 reptile and amphibian species, and numerous fish and shellfish.

In addition to May and early June, when the shorebirds arrive (see the sidebar "Red Knots"), one of the most exciting times to visit the refuge is during the annual raptor migration in the fall, when great numbers of 15 raptor species, including peregrine falcons, ospreys, and sharp-shinned hawks, land to rest and refuel.

The refuge has two separate divisions: the Delaware Bay Division in Middle Township, which extends along the Delaware Bay, and the Great Cedar

Red Knots

There aren't too many places to put up for the night along New Jersey's Delaware Bay shore, and aside from a few steamed crab stands, there aren't many places to pull off the road for lunch either. But each May, hungry travelers by the tens of thousands descend upon the Delaware beaches for a much-needed rest and a big, nourishing meal. These are the migratory shorebirds called red knots, and they are heading north from their South American wintering grounds to Canada's subarctic tundra, where they nest and breed.

The birds' New Jersey banquet consists of a superabundance of horseshoe crab eggs, freshly laid in the wet sand. It's been estimated that if it weren't for the migrating shorebirds and their need for a mid-flight protein binge, New Jersey would be paved with horseshoe crabs. And if anything happened to the bay's ecological balance to decimate the population of those primitive creatures, the red knots and other shorebird species would be seriously imperiled.

Swamp Division, which straddles Dennis and Upper Townships. Stop at refuge headquarters to pick up a map and find out the best places for wildlife viewing.

Cape May National Wildlife Refuge Headquarters, 24 Kimbles Beach Rd., Cape May Court House, (609) 463-0994, www.friendsofcapemaynationalwildliferefuge.org, is open weekdays from 8 a.m. to 4:30 p.m. If the headquarters is closed when you arrive, pick up a brochure at the information kiosk. The refuge is open daily from sunrise to sunset. Admission is free.

Heading northwest toward the narrow upper part of Delaware Bay, it's easy to follow the main roads through Bridgeton and miss one of southern New Jersey's best-kept secrets. This is the village of *Greenwich*, nestled a few miles from the mouth of the Cohansey River and looking for all the world as if it has just been transported from coastal New England. Appearances aside, it does differ in one important respect: It was laid out in the 1680s by John Fenwick, a Quaker. The fine, straight street Fenwick had surveyed was called Ye Greate Street, and so it is called today. This is where the best of Greenwich's early buildings are. These include the 1730 brick Nicholas Gibbon House, with an interior hardly altered over 250 years; the 1771 Friends Meeting House; and the Sheppard House, facing the Cohansey River at the foot of Ye Greate Street. The oldest part of this last structure dates from 1683. From this point a ferry was operated across the Cohansey River from 1767 to 1838. On nearby Market Lane there's a monument to a 1774 event that is as suggestive of New England as the local architecture; here a gang of firebrands, disguised to look like Indians (just as their Boston Tea Party counterparts were), burned a consignment of English tea.

Tours of the colonial homes and other historic buildings of Greenwich are given at various times throughout the year. For information contact the Cumberland County Historical Society (headquartered in the Gibbon House), 960 Ye Greate St., PO Box 16, Greenwich 08323; (856) 455-8580.

The **Cohanzick Zoo,** New Jersey's first public zoo, is one of the few in the United States that operates without an admission charge. Free admission, however, hasn't affected the quality or quantity of the exhibits; all the animals you'd expect to see are here—more than 100 in modern, naturalistic exhibits. The zoo, at 45 Mayor Aitken Dr., Bridgeton, (856) 455-3230, www.cohanzick-zoo.com, is open daily from 8 a.m. to 4 p.m. in winter and 9 a.m. to 5 p.m. in summer.

In the spring of 1944, Charles Franklin Seabrook, founder of the largest processor of frozen food in the world, invited a Japanese Relocation Committee to visit South Jersey. He needed workers, and the more than 110,000 Japanese Americans interned in camps because they were deemed "enemy aliens" were

The Ultimate Honor

There are 12 service plazas on the New Jersey Turnpike, each named for a famous native or resident of the Garden State. In alphabetical order:

- Clara Barton (American Red Cross founder)
- Jon Bon Jovi
- Connie Chung
- Grover Cleveland
- James Fenimore Cooper
- Larry Doby (first African American to play in baseball's American League)
- Thomas Edison
- John Fenwick (Quaker founder of first permanent English settlement in New Jersey, at Salem, 1675)
- Alexander Hamilton (founded Paterson)
- Whitney Houston
- Joyce Kilmer
- Vince Lombardi
- Richard Stockton (signer of Declaration of Independence)
- Walt Whitman

eligible for farm work as a result of the War Relocation Authority's seasonal leave policy. Seabrook offered the Japanese Americans jobs, and during the next two years more than 2,500 came from 10 relocation centers nationwide.

The farm, which operated around the clock and packed 100 million pounds of frozen, canned, and dehydrated vegetables a year, also supplemented its workforce with workers from other countries, including Estonia, Romania, Germany, Scotland, Puerto Rico, and the Caribbean. In the 1940s and 1950s, it was the most culturally diverse rural area in the country. In 1994, on the 50th anniversary of the arrival of the Japanese Americans, the **Seabrook Educational and Cultural Center** was opened to preserve Seabrook's rich history.

Exhibits at the center focus on three major areas: the historical role that the Seabrook Farms Company played in the area's settlement and employment, the various ethnic groups who settled and/or worked there, and community activity. Among the displays at the center are a large-scale model of what the village looked like in the 1950s, photographs, and oral histories.

The Seabrook Educational and Cultural Center, Upper Deerfield Township Municipal Building, 1325 Highway 77, Seabrook, (856) 451-8393, www.seabrookeducation.org, is open Mon through Thurs (except on holidays) from 9 a.m. to noon. There is no admission fee.

The **A. J. Meerwald,** a 115-foot, authentically restored Delaware Bay oyster schooner and New Jersey's official tall ship, was built in Dorchester, New Jersey, in 1928 and sets sail from various ports along the Delaware River from mid-Apr through mid-Oct. The public sailings are a part of the Bayshore Discovery Project, whose mission is to help educate the public about the culture, history, and natural resources of the Delaware Estuary. Both daytime and sunset sails are offered aboard the tall ship. The project is headquartered in Bivalve, which is also home to its **Delaware Bay Museum**. The ship sails from here, as well as from other New Jersey ports, and books many special sails throughout the season. For a schedule and/or information, contact the Bayshore Center at Bivalve, 2800 High St., Port Norris (Bivalve) 08349; (856) 785-2060 or (800) 485-3072; www.bayshorecenter.org.

Following what is now no longer the bay but the Delaware River proper, we come to **Salem**, at one time the site of Fort Elfsborg and later, like Greenwich, settled by Quakers (1675) associated with the colonial enterprise of John Fenwick and William Penn. Feisty little Peter Stuyvesant, the Dutch master of New Amsterdam (later New York) and the New Netherland colony, rousted the Swedes from their New Jersey holdings in 1655; little did he know that he was merely the middle fish in a *gulp-gulp-gulp* scenario. The big fish, of course, was dear Britannia.

Many years later Salem City was the site of an event important to the future development of New Jersey. One day in 1820 a man named Robert Gibbon Johnson—a descendant of the Gibbons who built the fine brick house on Ye Greate Street in Greenwich—walked up the steps of **Salem Courthouse**, turned to face a gathered crowd, and ate a tomato. He *ate a tomato*, fresh from his own garden, right before a horror-stricken multitude that fully expected him to crumple dead on the spot. Johnson proved his point: Tomatoes weren't poisonous. The way was clear for New Jersey—with a little help from as-yet-unarrived Neapolitans, who already knew how good *pomodori* were—to take its rightful place as tomato grower of the world, pizza maker, stacker of cans . . . *pace*, Carl Sandburg.

You can still see the courthouse, at 113 Market St., where this landmark event took place. Much altered and added to over the years, it still stands at the corner of Broadway and Market Street, downtown. There is no tomato monument, but since the building represents an amalgam of styles from 1817 to 1908, it does offer more than passing interest in its own right. For information call the Salem County Department of Tourism and Public Information, 94 Market St., at (856) 935-7510 or visit www.visitsalemcountynj.com.

If there is a spiritual center to Salem, and a spot best suited for beginning a walking tour to take in some of its more than 60 colonial and Victorian-era homes, the **Friends Burying Ground**, on West Broadway opposite Oak Street (with its many fine Victorian homes), is surely the place. Here, where many of the earliest settlers of Salem and the lower Delaware Valley lie buried, stands the majestic **Salem Oak**. Estimated to be at least 600 years old, this white oak is the last of the vast forest of trees that covered the site of Salem town when John Fenwick arrived. According to legend, this is the tree beneath which Fenwick sat when he signed his initial treaty with the leaders of the local Delaware Indian tribe. When last measured, the Salem Oak stood 88 feet tall, a dimension easily matched by the spread of its branches. The trunk is 21½ feet in circumference.

The best source of information on the historic houses of Salem, including maps and pamphlets for a self-guided walking tour, is the Salem County Historical Society. Every other spring the society sponsors an open house, taking in most of the town's important sites. For information contact the society at 79-83 Market St., Salem 08079; (856) 935-5004; www.salemcountyhistoricalsociety.com. The society's museum, in the 1721 Alexander Grant House, is open Tues through Sat from noon to 4 p.m. Admission is $5.

At **Finn's Point National Cemetery** there are markers in memory of 2,704 men who died during the Civil War; 2,436 of them were Confederate soldiers who had been interred at a prison camp on nearby Pea Patch Island. Many of them had been captured at the Battle of Gettysburg. There are two monuments here: In 1879 the US government erected a marble memorial to the memory of Union soldiers interred here who died while serving as guards at the camp, and in 1936 a Grecian-type columned cupola was placed over it. In 1910 the government inscribed the names of the Confederate dead on bronze plates and affixed them to the base of an 85-foot obelisk-type structure of reinforced concrete with Pennsylvania white granite facing.

In the northwest corner of the cemetery, 13 white marble headstones mark the burial places of World War II German prisoners of war who died while in custody at Fort Dix. And in another section are markers for 50 veterans who served in World War II, Korea, or Vietnam.

The cemetery was at one point a small part of the Finn's Point Military Reservation, erected by the government in 1896 in anticipation of the Spanish-American War. The name was changed to Fort Mott in 1897 in honor of Major General Gershom Mott, commander of the New Jersey Volunteers during the Civil War. Today, visitors can tour the fortification at **Fort Mott State Park**, as well as the cemetery. Admission is free. For information contact Fort Mott State Park, 454 Fort Mott Rd., Pennsville 08070; (215) 504-5610; www.nj.gov; www.cem.va.gov.

If you don't mind leaving the state for a bit, after visiting Fort Mott State Park, hop aboard the **Three Forts Ferry** for a short ride to two Delaware forts: Fort Delaware on Pea Patch Island, which was used to house those Confederate prisoners during the Civil War (and now home to the largest heron rookery on the East Coast), and Fort DuPont, at the 322-acre Fort DuPont State Park. This fort also dates back to the Civil War, when it housed several hundred prisoners from Rommel's Afrika Korps during World War II.

Lyme Disease

As New Jersey's deer population increases, so does the number of deer ticks, which can cause Lyme disease. To reduce your chances of being bitten, follow these precautions:

- Wear loose-fitting, light-colored clothing that will help you to see the ticks more easily. A long-sleeved shirt and hat also are recommended.

- Stay on trails and keep out of densely foliated areas.

- Leave as little skin exposed as possible.

If you do find a tick on you, don't panic. Pull it off slowly, making sure to remove it entirely. If you suspect you've been bitten, check with your physician.

The Three Forts Ferry, (302) 834-7941 (Fort Delaware), or (856) 935-3218, www.threeforts.com, operates on weekends and holidays from late Apr through early June, Wed through Sun from early June through early Sept, and weekends early Sept through late Sept. No pets other than service animals are allowed on the ferry. No bikes or pets are allowed on Pea Patch Island. Tickets are $12 for adults, $11 for seniors and active military, and $7 for children ages 2 through 12.

Southern New Jersey might seem an incongruous place to find a professional rodeo, but every Saturday night from Memorial Day through September, **Cowtown Rodeo** in Woodstown, the longest-running Saturday night rodeo in the country, hosts some of the finest riding east of the Mississippi by both cowboys and cowgirls. The rodeo is on Route 40 (mailing address: Route 2, Box 23A, Woodstown 08098); (856) 769-3200; www.cowtownrodeo.com. Gates open at 6 p.m., and the show starts at 7:30 p.m.; tickets are $15 for adults and $10 for children 12 and under. The rodeo goes on heat, rain, or shine.

Cowtown Farmers Market, one of the state's largest flea markets, is held every Tues and Sat—rain or shine—throughout the year on the rodeo grounds from 8 a.m. to 4 p.m. Opened in 1926, the market moved to its present location in 1940, and today it attracts almost 700 dealers and up to 40,000 people a day. Among the wares: antiques, collectibles, crafts, and fresh produce. For information call (856) 769-3000 or visit www.cowtownfarmersmarket.com.

It will come as no surprise to learn that Swedesboro was settled by Swedes. They came to the area in the middle of the 17th century to farm, and soon after their arrival they began constructing the state's first Lutheran house of worship. In 1784, after the original log cabin building burned down during the American Revolution, they built what is now **Trinity Episcopal Old Swedes Church** (it became Episcopal in 1786). Today the brick Georgian building is open for tours by appointment. Also on the grounds are the early 1700s Schorn log cabin, moved here from nearby Raccoon Creek, and a wonderful old cemetery.

The grounds of Trinity Episcopal Old Swedes Church, 1208 Kings Hwy. and Church Street, (856) 467-1227, www.trinityswedesboro.org, are open from dawn to dusk. The office is open Mon through Thurs from 8:30 a.m. to 4:30 p.m. Call for information on tours.

The 17th-century village of **Mullica Hill**, on the National Register of Historic Places, is a mecca for lovers of antiques and crafts. Residents have turned their homes, or at least part of them, into shops, and now more than three dozen, many as old as their wares, are on or near Main Street. The **Old Mill Antique Mall**, 1 S. Main St., (856) 478-9810, www.old-mill-antique-mall.com, houses three floors of treasures in a pre-Revolution mill. The **Yellow Garage Antiques Store**, 66 S. Main St., (856) 478-0300, www.yellowgarageantiques

.com, a 6,500-square-foot space originally built as a bus terminal in 1922, is home to 35 antiques dealers and is consistently chosen as one of the best antiques destinations in the area.

Stop in at the **William Heritage Winery**'s tasting room, 480 Mullica Hill Rd., (856) 589-4474, www.heritagewinenj.com, to sample the wine that generations of the Heritage family have been making in Mullica Hill since 1853; open daily 10 a.m. to 6 p.m. The **Amish Market**, 108 Swedesboro Rd., (856) 478-4300, www.amishmarketmullicahill.com, sells a wide range of local delicacies from local vendors including Beiler's Donut & Coffee Shop, Cap'n Chucky's Crab Cake Co., and Country Lane Salads. Their restaurant, which features breakfast, lunch, and dinner buffets, also serves a la carte dishes such as baked oatmeal scrapple, fried chicken, chicken croquettes, and homemade chili. Dessert? Shoofly pie, of course.

For a map or more information on Mullica Hill, contact the Mullica Hill Merchants Association, PO Box 235, Mullica Hill 08062; (856) 881-6800; www .mullicahill.com.

Just 6 miles from Mullica Hill in historic Pitman, **The Inn on Holly**, an informal Victorian B&B, has three handsomely furnished rooms, two lounges, and a wraparound porch. Innkeepers Jake and Yvonne have spared no detail in decorating, and serve a full gourmet breakfast. The town's charming main street is just two blocks away. The inn is at 120 W. Holly Ave., Pitman, (856) 582-2251, www.theinnonholly.com. Call or visit the website for rates.

Clementon Park and Splash World in Clementon combines high-tech thrills with old-fashioned charm to offer a fun day for the whole family. In business since 1907, they have wisely kept enough of their original attractions to bring a smile to Grandma's lips and incorporated enough new rides and activities to keep the kids happy. The Classic Carousel, with antique-style horses, hearkens back to a gentler age, as does the *Clementon Belle* showboat, which circles the lake. But they've also got one of the largest and best log flumes in the country, a 10-story Ferris wheel, and thrill rides including Thunderbolt and Falling Star to keep the scream level up. Kids will enjoy the Safari Train, the Formula 3000, a ride on the C.P. Huntington Railway, and other children-oriented rides.

snakesnackin'

Rattlesnakes were a major threat to early settlers. To protect themselves when they knew they'd be passing through snake country, they'd sometimes drive several hogs in front of them. The hungry swine, protected by coats of bristles and a lining of fat, would scarf up the snakes like popcorn. In the absence of a hog, it is recommended that those who confront an angry rattler back away.

Attractions at Splash World include Ring of Fire, Thunder Drop, Sea Dragon, and a float down Endless River, past waterfalls and rock formations.

Clementon Park and Splash World, 144 Berlin Rd., (856) 783-0263, www .clementonpark.com, is open seasonally. Because it is small, the park can get quite crowded, so be prepared to wait in line at peak times. The daily admission fee is $39.99 for those 48 inches and over, $29.99 for those under 48 inches, and $19.99 for seniors 60 and over. Call or check the website for hours.

In the mood to do some picking? Gloucester County is loaded with U-pick-it farms. To mention just a few: **Mood's Farm Market**, Route 77, Mullica Hill, (856) 478-2500, www.moodsfarmmarket.com, for apples, blackberries, blueberries, raspberries, cherries, grapes, nectarines, pears, plums, blackberry cider, and homemade jams; closed Sundays. **U-Pick**, at the junction of Route 45 and Route 538, Mullica Hill, (856) 478-2864, for peaches, apples, snap beans, okra, black-eyed peas, and eggplants; open daily in season. **Cecil Creek Farm**, 73 Democrat Rd., Mickleton, (856) 599-8925, www.cecil-creek-farm.myshopify .com, grows an extensive collection of organic vegetables, which they sell in their market along with products from nearby farms. Look for artisan cheeses, coffee, fresh-made pasta, and other locally sourced goodies.

What's alleged to be the oldest log cabin in the United States, believed to have been built shortly after the first Swedish settlers arrived in this country and now on the National Register of Historic Places, is the **C. A. Nothnagle Log House** in Gibbstown. Although the actual year of construction is unknown, it is estimated to have been built between 1638 and 1643. The cabin is at 406 Swedesboro Rd.

Camden Region

Like it or not, many of South Jersey's Quakers were dragged into the upheaval of the American Revolution. James Whitall and his wife, Ann, kept a comfortable farm along the Jersey side of the Delaware, just 5 miles south of Philadelphia. Their house, built on land along the river bluffs, may have seemed ideally situated in peacetime, but for many of the same reasons, it became a strategic site once hostilities began. The Continentals, wishing to defend the heights of Red Bank (not to be confused with the city of Red Bank, near the Atlantic coast), appropriated James Whitall's apple orchard for the construction of **Fort Mercer** and commandeered part of the house itself for the officers' quarters. The immediate British threat was not only from the occupied city of Philadelphia, but also from the warships that patrolled the Delaware. The rebels were especially concerned that the naval and land forces not be allowed to unite.

On October 22, 1777, as Rhode Island volunteers were still finishing the earthwork defenses of Fort Mercer, 1,200 British and Hessian troops attacked the rear of the fort. Inside were only 400 Americans, but they had been warned of the attack by Jones Cattell, who ran from Haddonfield to alert the Continental commander, Colonel Christopher Greene. Colonel Greene ordered his troops—many of them free blacks—to wait until the last possible minute to fire. Just as the Hessians reached the base of the earthen ramparts, Greene's men let fly a ferocious volley of grapeshot and musket balls. Four hundred Hessians fell dead or wounded. Again they tried; again they were repulsed. As he lay dying, the Hessian commander, Count Donop, supposedly told his American captors, "I die a victim of my ambition and the avarice of my sovereign."

The pair of unsuccessful Hessian charges upon Fort Mercer lasted barely a half hour, but the engagement between barge-mounted American guns and the British warships in the river carried on into the next day. Ann Whitall had tried to ignore the violence flaring all around her, and she continued her spinning in a room on the second floor of her home. When a British cannonball pierced the upper north area of the attic wall and rolled downstairs to where she was sitting, it is said Ann scolded the British, saying, "If thee would not fight, thee would not hurt." Later when her house was requisitioned to serve as a field hospital, she worked hard to nurse all of the wounded.

Despite the success of Fort Mercer's defenders, General Washington eventually decided that he could not afford to commit enough men to the task of maintaining it. After the position was abandoned, the British overran and looted Whitall's property. The Quaker billed the Continental Congress for compensation, which was never received.

From the return of James and Ann in 1778 until 1897, three generations of Whitalls lived in the stout stone-and-brick house on the heights above the Delaware. The surrounding property was acquired by the United States government in 1872 (hence the name of the municipality—National Park, New Jersey), but it was turned over to Gloucester County authorities in 1905. Since then it has been managed as a park in commemoration of the Battle of Red Bank.

Aside from the preserved and partially reconstructed earthworks of Fort Mercer, the principal attraction of **Red Bank Battlefield** is the restored **Whitall House**. Today the house looks much as it did in the peaceful days before the Revolution, when James Whitall ran his farm from the little first-floor office that faced the river; elsewhere within the 1748 structure (the stone portion is said to have been built by Swedish settlers even earlier) are a formal parlor, a great room with a large hearth, a huge kitchen located in the stone wing, and bedrooms. The furnishings are all in keeping with the period, as are the kitchen gardens and small orchard outside. On a late October day, the wind-fallen apples give off their winy smell, which must have been a welcome change from the stench of black powder and blood.

The Red Bank Battlefield, 100 Hessian Ave., National Park, (856) 853-5120, www.gloucestercountynj.gov, is open all year, except for Christmas and New Year's Day, during daylight hours. The Whitall House is open Apr through Oct, Thurs through Sun from 1 to 4 p.m. Guided tours are on the hour and half hour. Donations are welcome.

In Camden stands the **Walt Whitman House**, where the Good Grey Poet lived from 1884 until his death in 1892. This two-story frame building is the only home Walt Whitman ever owned, and he was able to pay the $1,750 that it cost only because of the unexpectedly large amount of money he earned from sales of the seventh edition of *Leaves of Grass*. Whitman had been boarding with his brother in Camden; when he moved into his own house, he had no furnishings other than a bed, a chair, and his books. Partially paralyzed from a series of strokes, he needed a housekeeper as well as a household. He found both when he engaged a widow, Mrs. Mary Davis, to move in with her own furniture and see to the cooking and cleaning in return for free rent. Whitman himself was by then a poor man, living largely on the generosity of his friends for the last eight years of his life.

Visitors to the house can see the poet's sparse furnishings, many of his books, and an interesting array of memorabilia, including photographs, letters, and documents. The Walt Whitman House, 330 Mickle Blvd. (also known as Martin Luther King Jr. Boulevard), (856) 964-5383, www.thewaltwhitmanassociation.org, is open Wed through Sat from 11 a.m. to noon and from 2 to 3 p.m. Tour times are at 11 a.m. and 2 p.m., by advance reservation only. Admission is free.

If you want to make a pilgrimage to Whitman's grave, head over to **Harleigh Cemetery**, which donated a plot to the poet. He paid for the mausoleum, which he shares with his mother and brother. There's a black granite monument with his likeness on it, and his own elegy:

> I BEQUEATH MYSELF TO THE DIRT TO GROW FROM THE GRASS I LOVE,
> IF YOU WANT ME AGAIN LOOK FOR ME UNDER YOUR BOOT SOLES.

Haiku poet Nick Virgilio is also buried here in a grave overlooking the lake. A lectern is etched with his poem "Lily / out of the water / out of itself."

The Harleigh Cemetery, 1640 Haddon Ave., (856) 963-3500, is open daily from 8:30 a.m. to 4:30 p.m.

Another Camden site worth a visit is **Pomona Hall**, headquarters and museum of the Camden County Historical Society, located at the southeastern edge of town near the Collingswood border. Pomona Hall is a handsome Georgian brick structure, built in 1726 by prominent Quaker Joseph Cooper Jr. and expanded in 1788 by his descendant Marmaduke Cooper. Inside are fine examples of 18th- and 19th-century furnishings and colonial kitchen equipment. The holdings of the society's adjoining museum include Indian artifacts, Civil War memorabilia, representative tools associated with preindustrial crafts, firefighting equipment, and antique toys. A special exhibit chronicles the days, just after the turn of the 20th century, when Camden was the home of the Victor Talking Machine Company. If you've ever heard the voice of Enrico Caruso transcend the decades through the medium of a brittle black disk, you can bet that it was recorded at the Victor studios in Camden.

The Camden County Historical Society is at 1900 Park Blvd., (856) 964-3333, www.cchsnj.org. The museum and Pomona Hall are open for tours Wed and Fri from 10 a.m. to 4 p.m. Appointments are not required for self-guided tours, but are required for guided tours. Call for admission fees.

The state's *Adventure Aquarium*, 1 Riverside Dr., Camden (844) 474-3474, www.adventureaquarium.com, is hardly off the beaten path. With parking for 2,200 cars, it's one of the state's major tourist attractions. Nevertheless, it's easy to miss an extremely pleasurable side trip that departs from the aquarium—the **Waterfront Connection**. This ferry crosses the Delaware River in 20 minutes and deposits passengers at Independence Visitor Center (856-964-5465; www .independencevisitorcenter.com), across from the Liberty Bell in downtown Philadelphia. Several attractions and indoor and outdoor cafes are within walking distance. The ferry operates seasonally; call for information. *Note:* Another ferry, *RiverLink* (856-964-5465; www.delawareriverwaterfront.com), offers service to Penn's Landing in Philadelphia from behind the aquarium as well as several other stops along the waterfront.

passthepopcorn

In 1933 the world's first drive-in movie theater opened its "doors" in Camden, featuring *Wife Beware* with Adolphe Menjou.

Both ferries also makes a stop at "Big J," the country's largest and most decorated battleship, just south of the aquarium. The 887-foot 7-inch *Battleship* New Jersey, built in 1940 at the Philadelphia Navy Yard, served in World War II, Korea, Vietnam, and the Persian Gulf. The Iowa Class ship's motto was "Firepower for Freedom," and firepower it had in spades—its nine 16-inch guns could hit targets 23 miles away. When at war, its crew numbered from 2,500 to 2,900.

Battleship *New Jersey* is open daily in season and weekends during the winter months; check the website or call for hours. Visitors can take self-guided audio tours or guided tours; tickets for the self-guided tours are $25 for adults; $20 for seniors, veterans, and children 5 to 11; $4 for children under 5; and free for active military, WWII vets, and former *New Jersey* crewmembers. Guided tours are $35 for adults and $30 for children. **Note:** Visitors will be going up and down on ladders, stepping through passageways, and sometimes maneuvering in tight spaces, so be sure to wear comfortable walking shoes. A main-deck tour is also offered.

If you can round up a bunch of friends, consider signing up for an overnight encampment aboard Big J, which includes a special tour and a chowline dinner.

For general information and directions to Battleship *New Jersey*, 62 Battleship Place, Camden, call (856) 966-1652 or visit www.battleshipnewjersey.org.

If the kids are getting squirmy, stop at the **Camden Children's Garden**, adjacent to Battleship *New Jersey*. The 4-acre "horticultural playground" encompasses numerous fun exhibits and attractions, including a butterfly house, the tropical exhibit Plaza de Aibonito, and a carousel and train. It's at 3 Riverside Dr., (856) 365-8733, www.camdenchildrensgarden.org. The garden is open seasonally Fri and Sat from 10 a.m. to 3 p.m. and Sun from 10 a.m. to 4 p.m. Admission is $6; tickets for the rides are $2.50 each or 5 for $10.

The National Register of Historic Places' **St. Joseph's Polish Catholic Church**, a Baroque-style masterpiece, was constructed in 1913 and consecrated in 1914. Faced in gray Vermont granite, the church has magnificent stained-glass windows, frescoes, and several fine paintings. Special exhibits in the John Paul II Room and the Szopka Room highlight the church's history and its vibrant community. Three bells in the tower—Mary, John, and Adalbert—were dedicated in 1917.

It is recommended that visitors use the parking lot next to the church, which is located at 110 Liberty St., Camden. Mass is held every Sunday at 10 a.m.; the church is open Mon through Fri from 9 a.m. to 3 p.m.

Amid the urban bustle of Cherry Hill sits **Barclay Farmstead Museum**— a living-history museum dedicated to preserving a way of life that is quickly disappearing in New Jersey. The centerpiece of the 32-acre farm on the north branch of the Cooper River is a three-story brick Federal farmhouse, built in 1816 by a Quaker farmer and completely furnished with period antiques. There are also an operating forge, barn, and blacksmith shop; a corn crib; a Victorian springhouse; and a museum shop. The farmstead, at 209 Barclay Ln., Cherry Hill, (856) 795-6225 or (856) 488-7868, www.www.chnj.gov, is open for tours by appointment, as well as Wed from noon to 4 p.m. Admission is by donation.

Near Barclay Farmstead on Covered Bridge Road is **Scarborough Covered Bridge**, one of two remaining covered bridges in the state and the first to be built in New Jersey in 93 years. It was dedicated on February 14, 1959.

The Cirelli family has been making Leo's Famous Yum Yum since 1936 and describe it thusly: It's "like Italian water ice, but it isn't. It's like sherbet, but it isn't. It's kind of like real Italian gelato, but not really. It is a product that has a taste and a history all its own." Judge for yourself at **Leo's Ice Cream Company**. Flavors include cotton candy, cappuccino, and root beer, and they also have a full roster of ice-cream flavors that include cannoli, amaretto, spumoni, and blueberry cheesecake. Leo's is at 7 Tomlinson Mill Rd., Medford, (856) 797-8771, www.leosicecream.net. It's open Mon through Thurs from 3 to 9 p.m., Fri from 3 to 10 p.m., Sat from noon to 10 p.m., and Sun from noon to 9 p.m.

It's rumored that the Jersey Devil—a phantom beast that has plagued South Jersey since colonial times—has been spotted in the area of the **Jackson Museum**, housed in a 150-plus-year-old schoolhouse. The schoolhouse was formerly on the property of Six Flags Great Adventure. In 1984 Six Flags donated the building to the Jackson Heritage Preservation Society, which paid to have it moved to its present location.

Today the museum exhibits artifacts from the inland, forested section of Ocean County. The museum, open by appointment, is at 95 W. Veterans Hwy., Route 528, Jackson; (732) 928-1200.

Perhaps the most cheerful thing that can be said about Burlington County Prison is that it's now a museum. But from 1811 until 1965 it incarcerated men and women guilty of every crime from debt to murder. Today the **Burlington County Prison Museum** is a National Historic Landmark, and visitors can see the prison yard where those convicted of capital crimes were hung, the workshop where trades such as broom and basket making were taught, the exercise yard with its 20-foot wall, and the cells where prisoners were locked up after being deloused. Graffiti throughout the building depict efforts to keep up hope as well as spirals into despair.

The Burlington County Prison Museum, on Route 541 in Mount Holly, is operated under the auspices of the Burlington County Parks Department, (609) 265-5858, www.prisonmuseum.net. It's open Thurs and Fri from 10 a.m. to 4 p.m. and Sat from noon to 4 p.m. Admission is $5 for adults, $3 for those over 55 and active military, and $2 for students. There is an extra charge of $3 for an audio tour.

Places to Stay in Southern New Jersey

Crowne Plaza Cherry Hill
2349 W. Marlton Pike, Route 70, Cherry Hill
(856) 665-6666
www.crowneplaza.com
Moderate–expensive

Holiday Inn East Windsor
399 Monmouth St., East Windsor (Hightstown)
(609) 448-7000
www.hieastwindsor.com

The Lily Inn
214 High St., Burlington
(609) 526-7900
www.thelilyinn.com

The Victorian Lady
301 W. Main St., Moorestown
(856) 235-4988
Moderate

Places to Eat in Southern New Jersey

Bistro at Cherry Hill
Cherry Hill Mall, 2000 Route 38, Cherry Hill
(856) 662-8621
Hand-tossed and stone-baked pizzas, a classic wedge salad, and the house specialty crab cake are standouts on a menu that includes pastas, wraps, and 8-ounce

burgers—the "Jersey Beach" is topped with pork roll, fried egg, cheese, and Sriracha ketchup. Lunch and dinner Mon through Sat; lunch Sun. Inexpensive–moderate.

Harrison House Diner and Restaurant
98 N. Main St., Mullica Hill
(856) 478-6077
This original 1963 Swingle diner has been contemporized, but the extensive menu, with everything from chipped beef on toast to build-your-own burgers and homemade meat loaf, remains classic diner fare. Don't forget the cappuccino and smoothies. Open 24/7. Inexpensive–moderate.

Kunkel's Seafood and Steakhouse
920 Kings Hwy., Haddon Heights
(856) 547-1225
A stylish ambience, steak house fare, and a popular two-course lunch make this BYOB spot a local favorite. Lunch Wed and Sat, dinner Wed through Sun, Sun brunch. Moderate.

The Little Hen
220 Kings Hwy. East, Haddonfield
(856) 528-2282
Crispy frog legs, duck frites, and chicken breast coq au vin are just a few of the specialties at this intimate BYOB French restaurant. Dinner

Wed through Sun. Moderate–expensive.

Miel Patisserie
1990 Route 70E, Cherry Hill
(856) 424-6435
This branch of a Philadelphia institution serves delightful French pastries and desserts, and homemade sorbets and ice cream. Takeout. Open daily. Inexpensive.

Xinc Café
679 Stokes Rd., Medford
(609) 953-9462
An extensive menu of New American cuisine features creative sandwiches including an avocado chèvre wrap and smoked salmon quesadillas, and entrées such as potato-crusted halibut. Lunch and dinner Tues through Sat; Sun brunch. Inexpensive–moderate.

Other Attractions in Southern New Jersey

Amalthea Cellars
209 Vineyard Rd., Atco
(856) 768-8585

Bridgeton Historic District
217 W. Commerce St., Bridgeton
(856) 455-3230

Garden State Discovery Museum
2040 N. Springdale Rd., Cherry Hill
(856) 424-1233

SELECTED REGIONAL INFORMATION CENTERS, CHAMBERS OF COMMERCE & VISITOR CENTERS IN SOUTHERN NEW JERSEY

Camden County Office of Public Affairs
520 Market St.
Camden 08102
(856) 266-3362
www.camdencounty.com

Delaware River Region Tourism Council
(856) 757-9400
www.visitsouthjersey.com

Pinelands Commission
15 Springfield Rd.
New Lisbon 08064
(609) 894-7300
www.nj.gov/pinelands

Salem County Visitor Center
1 New Market St.
Salem 08079
(856) 935-7510
www.visitsalemcountynj.com

Glasstown Arts District
22 N. High Street, Millville
(856) 293-0556

Esther Rab Holocaust Museum & Godwin Education Center
1301 Springdale Rd.,
Cherry Hill
(856) 751-9500

Indian King Tavern Museum
233 Kings Hwy. East,
Haddonfield
(856) 429-6792

Millville Army Air Field Museum
1 Leddon St., Millville
(856) 327-2347

Potter's Tavern
49–50 W. Broad St.,
Bridgeton
(856) 455-8580

Index